Fairness in the World Economy

Fairness in the World Economy

US Perspectives on International Trade Relations

AMERICO BEVIGLIA ZAMPETTI

United Nations, Geneva

Edward Elgar

Cheltenham, UK • Northampton, MA, USA

Published by
Edward Elgar Publishing Limited
Glensanda House
Montpellier Parade
Cheltenham
Glos GL50 1UA
UK

Edward Elgar Publishing, Inc.
136 West Street
Suite 202
Northampton
Massachusetts 01060
USA

A catalogue record for this book
is available from the British Library

ISBN-13: 978 1 84542 714 6
ISBN-10: 1 84542 714 9

Printed and bound in Great Britain by MPG Books Ltd, Bodmin, Cornwall

Man's highest aspiration [is] the establishment of enduring peace based on justice and fair-dealing for all.

Cordell Hull, Acceptance Speech on the occasion
of the award of the Nobel Peace Prize
Oslo, 10 December 1945

Contents

Acknowledgements   ix

Introduction   1

1   Analytical framework   9
    1.1   Theoretical perspectives on international trade
          policy-making: a brief reminder   9
    1.2   The role of ideas in international relations: a theoretical revival   12
    1.3   The approach of this study   18
2   Fairness: in search of a meaning   26
    2.1   Defining the notion of fairness: insights from political
          philosophy   26
    2.2   The social psychology dimension of fairness   36
    2.3   Fairness concerns in economic theory   38
    2.4   Summary   40
3   Fairness in the US commercial policy discourse before
    the advent of the multilateral trade system   46
    3.1   Fairness in the US socio-economic ethos   46
    3.2   Fairness in the development of US international trade policy
          from its origin to the beginning of the 1930s   50
          3.2.1   The protective tariff   51
          3.2.2   Unfair trade legislation   66
          3.2.3   Reciprocity and equality of treatment through
                  commercial treaties   73
    3.3   Summary   85
4   The fairness idea in the development of the multilateral trade
    regime   98
    4.1   The Reciprocal Trade Agreements Programme   98
    4.2   Fairness concerns in the development of the GATT system   111
    4.3   The results of the negotiations: the GATT and the Havana
          Charter   124
    4.4   A selective look at the evolution of the GATT system   132
          4.4.1   The case of subsidy rules   134
          4.4.2   The case of safeguard rules   142
    4.5   Summary   147

5   Rethinking fairness in the evolution of the international trade
    policy and rule-making discourse   162
    5.1   The GATT and developing countries   163
    5.2   The concept of special and differential treatment   168
    5.3   Bottom-up fairness: the fair trade movement   172
6   Conclusion   181
    6.1   Fairness or equity?   183

Bibliography   191
Index   211

Acknowledgements

The idea for this study was largely prompted by the reading of Thomas Franck's magisterial work on *Fairness in International Law and Institutions* (1995). The section of that book that appeared perhaps less developed, and the one that was of the greatest professional and academic interest to me, was that relating to economic fairness and trade. As the fairness discourse remains crucial to ensuring the legitimacy of the trading system, and as the notion had become in the 1980s and 1990s almost a synonym of protectionism in many circles, it seemed to me useful and academically challenging to go back through history and try to disentangle its core meaning. Since the USA was the main intellectual architect of the postwar trade regime, as well as the country where the notion of fairness has the largest currency, the focus on US trade policy discourse was inescapable. Franck's work provided the intellectual launching pad, for which I am indebted to him.

The writing of this study has benefited greatly from the many discussions I have had over the years with friends and colleagues, too many to name, on issues related to my research. A particular debt of gratitude goes to Professor Bart Kerremans, my doctoral supervisor at Katholieke Universiteit Leuven, who supported my work from the start and trusted that there was more than met the eye in my research project, which could have been shunted aside as academically meaningless, if one were to follow the trend of considering fairness only as a rhetorical gimmick or a protectionist sham (see, for instance, James Bovard, *The Fair Trade Fraud*, 1991). I am also especially grateful to Professor Mavroidis who has been generous in suggestion and counsel. Any errors or omissions remain my own and the views expressed are strictly personal.

A great deal of the initial research for this study was conducted while I was Fulbright Research Scholar at the Harvard University John F. Kennedy School of Government in 1999–2000. The vast resources of the Harvard libraries were of enormous help. Thereafter, my research has been pursued at the Library of the United Nations Office at Geneva, which possesses an extensive collection as well. I am also indebted to Donna Maurer, who provided excellent English language editing.

A final 'thank you' goes to my parents, who always unconditionally supported my endeavours, and to my grandparents, who taught me to love to learn.

Introduction

'Fairness' is a multifaceted notion, comprising several different dimensions. It is used in various areas of law and policy, including intellectual property, consumer protection, antitrust, taxation, public utility, contracts, and international trade.[1] With the progressive maturing of the international system, this notion has acquired relevance at this level as well.[2] In the international context, fairness is particularly important, since only a system that its participants perceive as *fair* can command acceptance and compliance. The main focus of this study is on investigating the development of the notion of fairness in United States (US) trade policy and law and the impact of this notion on international trade discussions and rule-making, and especially on the formation of the multilateral trade regime. The contention is that fairness concerns that have been present in US trade policy debates and treaty practice from the Republic's inception have contributed to shaping these debates and practice over the years, both at home and abroad, and were finally thrust upon the international scene through inclusion in the multilateral trade regime after World War II.

The study focuses on US domestic trade law and policy debate because of the importance that the notion of fairness has been accorded in the USA and because of the USA's role in shaping the multilateral trade regime. In US trade policy discourse, 'fairness' or 'fair trade' has often come to be viewed as either an excuse, by its detractors, or a justifiable reason, by its supporters, for demanding protectionist measures and initiatives.[3] The trade policy objective of pursuing 'free' or 'freer' trade frequently has been couched in terms of demands for 'fair' trade through government intervention to protect domestic industry and to open allegedly closed foreign markets.

The rationale put forward has been that 'fair' trade or a 'level playing field' is a necessary precondition for 'freer' trade. While complaints about unfair trade policies and measures have become entrenched in the USA, they also surface frequently in the debate surrounding trade frictions in many other countries with different traditions and levels of economic development, including in Europe.[4] Hence, despite the fact that there is little uniformity in the way the notion of fairness is understood and used (and often abused), its role in trade policy-making, at both national and international levels, has remained so significant and pervasive over the years that it can be neither underestimated nor ignored. Unfairness allegations remain at the core of the accusations that countries level against each other, and fairness has endured as a central feature of the international trade policy discourse.

Although much protectionist rhetoric[5] meddles with the concept of fairness and its use, even its critics tend to admit that it possesses an added dimension '... of appealing to a notion of natural justice'.[6] In the words of one of its main critics: 'Fair trade is a two-faced creature: One face is friendly to free trade; the other frowns on it, indeed, seeks to devour it, for fair trade mechanisms can be misused to allege unfair trade unfairly and thus undermine free trade'.[7] However, while the notion of fairness is clearly prone to policy capture by protectionist groups, it remains critical for ensuring the public's support for trade liberalization.

Clearly, social pressures are often viewed as an explanation for how policy develops, and interest group activity is certainly a very significant, sometimes decisive, determinant of US trade policy. But equally important appears to be the sets of ideas, values, and ideologies that underpin the various pressures and claims, as well as law-makers and executive agencies' officials' beliefs, which translate and filter such claims into legislation, policy, and implementation.[8] Fairness is certainly one of these ideas. This is not to deny that the notion of fairness is multifaceted and can provide a useful cover for protectionist objectives.[9] For instance, its reciprocity component may be used to support not only legitimate claims by businesses to seek similar or comparable access conditions and commercial opportunities in all markets, but also mercantilist demands for equal outcomes in terms of sales and profits and/or for equalized conditions of production (e.g., in wage levels, as well as health, safety, and environmental standards). However, as with many political and economic ideas, the fact that fairness can be harnessed to support different policy goals and utilized in different and sometimes contradictory ways does not detract from its importance in framing the discourse and influencing policy outcomes.

The notion of fairness contains powerful normative ideas that play an important role in law- and policy-making at both national and international levels. These include an adherence to international commitments and international law, non-discrimination (i.e., most-favoured-nation and national treatment), reciprocity, and the respect of free-market, competitive conditions.[10] This study identifies and investigates the relevant normative ideas that have been used in US trade policy and foreign economic relations, as well as in the domestic regulation of import trade, the so-called trade remedies laws (e.g., antidumping and countervailing duty laws and import relief or safeguard measures), with a view to examining the impact that these ideas have had in forming the trade regime.

By examining the way that such normative ideas have been used over time, especially in the construction of the trade regime, a common theme appears to emerge. Notwithstanding the existing conterminous and often competing protectionist ideas, it seems possible to isolate the main significance of fairness as revolving around the free-market norm and, in particular, the pursuit of competition between economic agents through legitimate market behaviour.[11] The free-market norm obviously requires respect for the law, including international trade law, since no behaviour in the market can be considered legitimate if it breaks or circumvents agreed-upon rules. But the free-market norm also encompasses non-discrimination and reciprocity (in its benign, barrier-reducing form), as both ultimately seek the elimination of market distortions and are, therefore, instrumental to establishing free markets. The strongly held belief in the virtues of free enterprise and the market mechanism that characterizes US polity has provided the basis for this core element. Firms and governments that distort the market's 'natural' functioning are to be condemned. In this sense, fairness is also consonant with the moral imperative to ensure the commutative justice of economic exchanges as existing between the parties to them.[12] This study contends that fairness-related norms are quite widespread in the General Agreement on Tariffs and Trade (GATT) and subsequently in the World Trade Organization (WTO) Agreements, as well as in international practice.[13] In fact, the preservation of the international competitive process is a familiar notion in the GATT/WTO system, which is in line with the objective of protecting 'competitive relationships' and the 'conditions of competition', which is how the basic provisions of the General Agreement have been consistently interpreted.[14]

Fairness may be viewed as lending legitimacy to the competitive process within which (international) economic transactions take place. It integrates a set of principles and rules defining the accepted behavioural parameters for the unfolding of international economic relations between nations, as well as between firms. Hence, fairness concerns apply to both the international economic exchanges of goods and services and the agreed-upon exchanges of 'treatment' concessions between governments (as well as the setting of other behavioural rules) governing such transactions. In this sense, fairness reinforces a rule-based approach to the international trading system, stresses the importance of the equality of opportunities and access, and does not seek to predetermine or influence economic outcomes.

This understanding of the notion of fairness generally consonant with the capitalist tradition of US political life needs to be distinguished from an interpretation that concentrates on its distributive justice elements, which is equally important in ensuring the system's legitimacy.[15] In general, issues linked to resource allocation and redistribution of income appear less grounded in US trade policy discourse, although – at least domestically – redistribution policies, through, for instance, safeguard measures, special regulation for the agricultural sector, and the Trade Adjustment Assistance (TAA) programme, have played an important role.[16]

The recent debate regarding the relative costs and benefits of liberalization and, more broadly, globalization has focused public attention on the sad reality that 'too few share in its benefits [and] too many have no voice in its design and no influence on its course'.[17] Such renewed awareness again stresses the importance of the fairness of international trade. But even in this context, much of US 'fairness-related' attention in the debates surrounding the deep integration and globalization of the world economy has been devoted to ensuring that stark differences in domestic regulatory standards (e.g., in the areas of labour and the environment) prevailing in many trading partners would not translate into 'unfair' production cost disadvantages for domestic producers.[18] On the contrary, the necessity to modify the distribution of income and resources through (inter-)governmental action to ensure a more equitable and inclusive globalization has received relatively little heed. Both fairness as a source of legitimacy for the international competitive process and fairness as distributive justice have given rise to domestic and international law and policy debates, but only the former notion appears to have been heavily influenced by US trade policy discourse and tradition.

The extent to which this understanding of fairness has informed the international debate and has been incorporated in law, or at least has had an impact on rules formulation, provides a measure of the international acceptance of this notion of fairness and its influence in international policy discourse. Despite the particular pressure that the USA can exert in decision-making at the international level, the consensus (or the lack thereof) that fairness-related normative ideas have been able to muster among countries and the adherence to them in international practice indicate the existence of an internationally shared core understanding of what fairness means in international trade relations. Such consensus is also suggestive of the trading system's prospects in terms of its legitimacy, its pull towards voluntary compliance, and further liberalization.

By investigating the meaning of fairness in the multilateral trading system, as well as its role in and impact on creating and developing that system, this study also attempts to reflect on what justice means in international trade relations. The study thus disputes the widespread argument that fairness, like many other 'ethical' concepts, is elusive, subjective, and ultimately meaningless. In this regard, the somewhat facetious quip commonly used that 'fairness, like truth, beauty and contact lenses, lies in the eyes of the beholder'[19] does not reflect the complexity and importance of the issue. The study starts from the premise that 'fairness is not "out there" waiting to be discovered, it is a product of social context and history'.[20] Hence, the methodological approach chosen is that of an 'intellectual history', which seeks to understand the origin of a particular idea, trace its trajectory within (in this case, international trade policy) discourse and evaluate its impact on policy, especially regime formation.

The study is organized as follows. Chapter 1 briefly reviews the role of ideas in international relations and situates the approach selected for the study within the theoretical parameters of social constructivism. Chapter 2 attaches a meaning to and deepens the understanding of the fairness idea by examining its various dimensions in different areas of thought. Chapter 3 examines how fairness (*rectius*, the particular understanding of this idea identified in Chapter 2) has inspired and influenced US political discourse related to international trade issues and how the notion has been translated into domestic law and treaty practice in the period that preceded the creation of the GATT regime. Chapter 4 then considers how this understanding of the notion of fairness has shaped the international debates and negotiations that have led to the creation of the trade regime, and the extent to which fairness-inspired approaches have been accepted and incorporated into international trade law up until the conclusion of the Uruguay Round of trade negotiations and the transformation of the GATT into the WTO. This is done selectively by looking at the cases of the safeguard and subsidies rules. Chapter 5 examines the main competing notion of fairness (based on equity demands) that has emerged in the debate, with its early manifestations already apparent at the time of the regime negotiations, and which mainly has come to be referred to as 'special and differential treatment for developing countries'. The study thus remains within the realm of narrative analysis (in an understanding more than explaining mode) and concentrates on the role that fairness considerations played in the formation of the GATT regime. Through historical research, it elucidates the USA's role as the main intellectual actor in this endeavour. However, the study is ultimately intended to contribute to the ongoing debate about the relationship between globalization and the overlapping notions of justice, equity, and fairness. Additional normative considerations in this regard are advanced in the Conclusion in Chapter 6.

NOTES

1. For an economic investigation of the concept as applied in a domestic regulatory context, see E. Zajac, *Political Economy of Fairness*, The MIT Press, Cambridge, MA, 1995.
2. See, in general, Thomas Franck, *Fairness in International Law and Institutions*, Clarendon Press, Oxford, 1995.
3. 'Until 1980, the proposition that the world was unfair and the USA fair remained an assertion; by 1988 it had become accepted as a fact, beyond question, among most policy-makers and with the general public. More importantly, it had become the cornerstone of US trade policy and a principal excuse for poor US trade performance', see C. Pearson, 'Free Trade, Fair Trade? The Reagan Record', in C. Pearson and J. Riedel, eds., *The Direction of Trade Policy*, Basil Blackwell, Cambridge, MA, 1990, p. 52.

4. See, for instance, L. Brittan, 'How to Make Trade Liberalisation Popular', *The World Economy*, November 1995, pp. 761–7. Quite interestingly, in the draft new EU Constitituion, Art. I-3, setting out the Union's overall objectives and specifically in paragraph 4 the relations with the wider world, states that the Union 'shall contribute to ... free and fair trade'. While no elaboration of the concept is provided, 'the reference to fair trade is more naturally read as an instruction to take account of the interests of developing countries in the international trading system, because the reference is juxtaposed to the "sustainable development of the earth", solidarity and mutual respect among peoples, and the eradication of poverty and protection of human rights and in particular children's rights'. See P. Eeckhout, *External relations of the European Union: Legal and Constitutional Foundations*, Oxford University Press, Oxford, 2004, p. 53.
5. See D. Conti, *Reconciling Free Trade, Fair Trade, and Interdependence: The Rhetoric of Presidential Economic Leadership*, Praeger, Westport, CT, 1998.
6. See P. Low, *Trading Free: The GATT and US Trade Policy*, The Twentieth Century Fund Press, New York, 1993, p. 28.
7. See J. Bhagwati, *The World Trading System at Risk*, Harvester Wheatsheaf, New York, 1991, p. 14; see also J. Bhagwati, *Protectionism*, The MIT Press, Cambridge, MA, 1988, pp. 33–5.
8. See J. Goldstein, 'Ideas, Institutions, and American Trade Policy', *International Organization*, Winter 1988, pp. 179–217.
9. See P. Nicolaides, 'How Fair is Fair Trade?', *Journal of World Trade Law*, no. 4, 1987, pp. 147–62.
10. See K. Abbott, 'Defensive Unfairness: The Normative Structure of Section 301', in J. Bhagwati and R. Hudec, eds., *Fair Trade and Harmonization: Prerequisites for Free Trade*, The MIT Press, Cambridge, MA, 1996, pp. 415–71; R. Hudec, '"Mirror, Mirror on the Wall": The Concept of Fairness in United States Foreign Trade Policy', in D. Fleming, ed., *Canada Japan and International Law*, 1990 Proceedings, Canadian Council of International Law, pp. 88–110; on reciprocity see, in particular, T. Bayard and K. Elliott, *Reciprocity and Retaliation in US Trade Policy*, Institute for International Economics, Washington, DC, 1994.
11. 'The objective of fair trade should be the ultimate elimination of all anti-competitive devices, measures and other impediments. The concept of fair trade can be made operational by using it to identify those government practices that reduce rather than increase competition. Trading firms voice their concerns about competition because they are more distressed by unfavourable discrimination in internal markets than at the border.' See Nicolaides, op. cit., p. 158.
12. See S. Benn, 'Justice', in Paul Edwards, ed., *The Encyclopaedia of Philosophy*, Macmillan, New York, 1972, p. 299.
13. The general objective to achieve greater fairness in the trading system was openly recognised by Ministers at the close of the Uruguay Round when they stated in the Marrakesh Declaration of 1 April 1994 that the establishment of the WTO '... ushers in a new era of global economic cooperation, reflecting the widespread desire to operate in a *fairer* and more open multilateral trading system ...' (emphasis added), in The Results of the Uruguay Round of Multilateral Trade Negotiations. The Legal Texts, WTO, Geneva 1995, p. iv.
14. See, for instance, United States – Taxes on Petroleum and Certain Imported Products, GATT BISD 34th Supp. 136, 1988; EEC–Payments and Subsidies Paid to Processors and Producers of Oilseeds and Related Animal-Feed Proteins, GATT BISD 37th Suppl. 86, 1991.
15. See Frank, *Fairness*, op. cit.
16. For an early discussion, see C. Wilcox, 'Relief for Victims of Tariff Cuts', *The American Economic Review*, December 1950, pp. 884–9. See also E. Kapstein, 'Trade liberalization and the politics of trade adjustment assistance', *International Labour Review*, vol. 137, no. 4, 1998, p. 501; André Sapir, 'Who's Afraid of Globalization? Domestic Adjustment in Europe and America', in Roger Porter et al., *Efficiency, Equity and Legitimacy: The Multilateral Trading System at the Millennium*, Brookings Institution Press, Washington, DC, 2001, pp. 179–204.

17. See the World Commission on the Social Dimension of Globalization, *A Fair Globalization: Creating Opportunities for All*, International Labour Office, Geneva, 2004, p. 2.
18. See J. Bhagwati, 'Trade Liberalisation and "Fair Trade" Demands: Addressing the Environmental and Labour Standards Issues', *The World Economy*, November 1995, pp. 745–59.
19. See D. Das, *International Trade Policy: A Developing-Country Perspective*, Macmillan, London, 1990, p. 125.
20. See Franck, *Fairness*, op. cit., p. 14.

1. Analytical framework

1.1 THEORETICAL PERSPECTIVES ON INTERNATIONAL TRADE POLICY-MAKING: A BRIEF REMINDER

Traditional explanations of international trade policy-making generally have been clustered into system-centred, society-centred and state-centred approaches.[1]

> International, or system-centered approaches explain American foreign policy as a function of the attributes or capabilities of the United States relative to other nation-states. In this view, government officials are perceived as responding to the particular set of opportunities and constraints that America's position in the international system creates at any moment in time. Society-centered approaches view American policy as either reflecting the preferences of the dominant group or class in society, or as resulting from the struggle for influence that takes place among various interest groups or parties. In either case, this approach explains foreign economic policy essentially as a function of domestic politics. Third, state-centered approaches view foreign economic policy as highly constrained by domestic institutional relationships that have persisted over time, and also by the ability of state officials to realize their objectives in light of both international and domestic constraints. This approach emphasizes the institutional structures of the state and the capacities of political and administrative officials who occupy positions within it.[2]

To simplify even further, in the trade policy area, the main division is between exogenous and endogenous explanations for policies. The global economy and power distribution among states are the focus of exogenous theories, while endogenous theories concentrate more on the 'black box' of domestic political and economic developments.[3]

Exogenous, system-centred perspectives take as a point of departure the broader international environment in which trade policy is made. A country's trade policy can be understood primarily as a function of external causes, ranging from global business cycles to a country's position in the nations' hierarchy of political and economic power.[4] Many of the exogenous approaches have strong links with the theory of hegemonic stability, first espoused by Kindleberger in the 1970s. This paradigm is widely, though by no means universally accepted in the international political economy literature. It contends that the global economy's openness depends to a great extent on the presence of a hegemonic power that has both the interests and means to articulate and enforce the rules of interaction among the most important members of the system, including the trade regime.[5] This theory suggests that the dominance of one country, such as Holland in the 17th century and Great Britain in the 19th century, is necessary for the existence of an open world economy and for the decline of the propensity to use protectionism. The US embracing of a more liberal (and perhaps better, less protectionist) trade policy starting in the mid-1930s coincided with its acceptance of hegemonic responsibilities. However, historical and theoretical analyses have produced a consensus that hegemony is neither necessary nor sufficient for creating and developing strong international institutions, and indeed the decline in US power since the 1960s has not led to the system's collapse.[6] Furthermore, such institutions, once created, take on a life of their own and exercise a significant influence on policy and cooperation.

Endogenous theories emphasize the role of domestic political processes and examine the ways in which national interests are determined through a struggle between domestic groups. In the area of trade policy, theories of this kind can be divided mainly into those that focus on the demand for (or the rejection of) protection (due to the interests of the private sector and labour organizations, for instance) and the supply of protection (due to state institutions' willingness to satisfy – or oppose – these demands). The behaviour of policy-makers, both in the legislative and executive branches of government, is often examined using a principal–agent approach, in which the interests of their constituents (principals) are primarily expressed in terms of producers, rather than consumers, interests and hence tend to represent intense rather than diffuse opinions.

Vilfredo Pareto provided an explanation for this phenomenon by noting that individuals will work much harder to achieve a large gain than they will to avert many small losses. 'A protectionist measure provides large benefits to a small number of people, and causes a very great number of consumers a small loss, [which] makes it easier to put a protection into practice.'[7] This simple rule has been the basis for special-interest protectionism ever since the establishment of democratic governments. Constituents are assumed to be interested on direct and local costs and benefits of policies and less so with regard to their broader, national implications. Policy-makers (agents) who fail to satisfy their constituents' demands may face electoral sanctions. Adam Smith stressed this issue when he noted that the monopolies in favour of trade restrictions had become 'like an overgrown army' that 'upon many occasions intimidate the legislature'. Smith considered that these interests were politically unbeatable to the point that 'to expect ... that the freedom of trade should ever be entirely restored in Great Britain is as absurd as to expect that an Oceana or Utopia should ever be established in it'.[8]

E.E. Schattschneider's account of the drafting and passage of the Hawley–Smoot bill remains the classic application of the special-interest approach to US trade politics. Arguing that 'the nature of public policy is the result of "effective demands" upon the Government' by organized interest groups,[9] he found that congressional committees left the initiative to organized interests, and protectionist industries took full advantage of the opportunity to demand tariffs. Opponents of these rent-seeking proposals were scarce and the few who spoke up were either neutralized or ignored. Consumers were not organized and importers were powerless, for 'nationalism makes men willing to bear the burdens imposed by the tariff because it makes private interests seem public'.[10] The only significant antagonists were the intermediate processors of commodities, who would oppose import duties if they raised the cost of production. Their protests were often stifled through '[t]he simple device of giving the manufacturing consumer of raw materials and semi-finished materials a bonus in the form of compensatory duties'.[11] This pattern of 'reciprocal non-interference' not only produced pressure for higher tariffs across the board, but also ensured the protective system's stability.

While those who focus on the demand side tend to stress the role of civil society, including business groups, as leading forces in policy- and rule-making, supply-side theories view parliamentarians, public officials, and negotiators as policy-makers in their own right. These individuals do not merely act upon the private sector's requests, but also pursue other economic, diplomatic, and security objectives. The degree of imperviousness to societal pressures helps to shape policy-makers' preferences and their capacity to implement them. More autonomy *vis-à-vis* business demands for more protection often militate in favour of a more open trade policy.

Supply-side approaches include formal models in which decision-makers are represented by (rational) abstractions, such as those popular among economists. These approaches have addressed questions including apparent governments' irrationality in imposing import restrictions[12] or firm and sector selection for special advantages and protection.[13] However, these studies, and especially those models that consider the state as an undifferentiated entity, often assume rather than explain how and why policy-makers make decisions.[14] Various scholars have also focused on the state's institutional structure as a determinant of policy.[15] A few studies have tried to integrate the 'divided government' dimension of US trade policy-making.[16]

In empirical studies, analysts seek to explain policy-makers' actual behaviour. Most theories of this kind assume that the executive, for economic and political reasons, will support in general internationally open markets and trade liberalization, and focus on the positions adopted by the legislative branch.[17] This paradigm was particularly important in the Cold War era, when the executive branch's political and security interests often steered trade policy choices.[18] Lowi summarized this thesis by stating that the outcome of a policy debate will depend 'upon whose definition of the situation prevailed. If tariff protection is an instrument of foreign policy and general regulation for international purposes, the anti-protectionists win; if the traditional definition of tariff as an aid to 100,000 individual firms prevails, then the protectionists win'.[19]

All these theoretical perspectives share a common focus on interests, often exogenously fixed, with little, if any, attention to ideational factors. As such, they are not hospitable to the study of the fairness notion in trade policy discourse, which has played an important role in shaping the USA's identity as a trading nation, its interests, and its major influence on creating the postwar trade regime.

1.2   THE ROLE OF IDEAS IN INTERNATIONAL RELATIONS: A THEORETICAL REVIVAL

The importance of ideas in political life is clearly evident. As Emerson, the great US poet and philosopher, observed in 1841, 'every revolution was first a thought in one man's mind, ... [e]very reform was once a private opinion ...'. The role of ideas in economic policy-making also has often been recognized; as early as 1936, Keynes poignantly remarked that:

> the ideas of economists and political philosophers, both when they are right and when they are wrong, are more powerful than is commonly understood. Indeed the world is ruled by little else. ... I am sure that the power of vested interests is vastly exaggerated compared with the gradual encroachment of ideas. Not, indeed, immediately, but after a certain interval; for in the field of economic and political philosophy there are not many who are influenced by new theories ..., so that the ideas which civil servants and politicians and even agitators apply to current events are not likely to be the newest. But, soon or late, it is ideas, not vested interests, which are dangerous for good or evil.[20]

However, it is only in more recent years that the role of ideas has gained significant ground in the context of international relations theory. Reacting to the prevailing rationalistic and positivistic approaches[21] to the study of international regimes,[22] which characterize both realism and liberalism, knowledge-based regime theories have emphasized the importance of ideas in policy-making and regime building.

Modern international political economy, including the theoretical perspectives examined in the previous section, is still dominated by rationalist accounts of policy-making, which focus on 'interests' in their explanations of state conduct, while generally neglecting 'ideas'. Hence, the formation of regimes is viewed as resulting from the functional benefits they provide in terms of reducing collective action problems and contracting costs. Yet, the questions of which set of beliefs shapes the definition of 'interest' of any particular state, why and how this happens, and which ideas prevail in the international arena, particularly in the formation of a specific regime, remain unanswered. Knowledge-based theories of regimes have provided important insights in this area.

Among such theories, one strand, sometimes referred to as 'weak cognitivism',[23] argues that the explanation of political action in terms of rational actors maximizing a utility function rooted in material interests cannot adequately account for states' observed behaviour and considers that ideas have an independent causal effect on policy 'even when human beings behave rationally to achieve their end'.[24] The argument rests on an assumption that the state is not merely a captive of private interests. Policy-makers are thought to have strong views on what constitutes correct public policy and believe it is their duty to execute such policies, even in the face of contrary pressure from special interests. This puts ideas alongside interests as explanatory variables of foreign policy. In this approach, the rationalist, 'neo-positivist' perspective is not rejected; ideas are seen as rival or supplementary variables meant to compensate for 'the inability of such [rationalist] analyses to explain particular political outcomes'.[25] The ideational argument suggests that liberal trade ideas are essentially complementary to the pressures brought by pro-trade industries, and thus serve to reinforce – but not to create – an environment in favour of continued openness.[26]

Few analysts have suggested that ideas have a much greater persuasive force and can match or even beat economic interests. Goldstein, in a detailed examination of US trade debates in the 19th and 20th centuries, found evidence to support the contention that 'ideas ... become predictors of the direction of policy at least as powerful as ... simple calculations of interest'.[27] Under this interpretation, protectionist policies do not merely represent the policy-maker's failure to recognize the superior benefits of economic liberalism; instead, they are the manifestation of a competing philosophy of public policy. As Goldstein put it: 'American policy ... cannot be explained exclusively through the study of interests. ... Rather both trade openness and the pattern of industrial exceptions from liberalization reflect institutional structures and the ideational beliefs of elected officials'.[28]

Ideas are defined as 'beliefs held by individuals'[29] that are 'shared' with others. Ideas, then, refer to those 'particular beliefs – shared by a large number of people' that 'have implications for human action'.[30] Goldstein and Keohane put forward a three-tier typology of ideas or beliefs: 'world-views', 'principled beliefs', and 'causal beliefs'.[31] World-views are defined as shared beliefs that

'are entwined with people's conceptions of their identities' and 'defines the
universe of possibilities for action', such as 'the world's major religions', and
'conceptions of sovereignty', as well as 'modern Western world-views'
encompassing 'individual and secular scientific premises'. 'Principled beliefs'
or normative ideas 'specify criteria for distinguishing right from wrong and
just from unjust', such as 'slavery is wrong' and 'people have the right of free
speech'. These principled beliefs serve 'to mediate between world views and
particular policy conclusions' by translating 'fundamental doctrines into
guidance for contemporary human actions'. Finally, 'shared causal beliefs'
relate to 'cause–effect relationships which derive authority from the shared
consensus of recognised elites, whether they be village elders or scientists at
elite institutions'. Scientific knowledge relating, for instance, to 'how to slow
down the greenhouse effect on the earth's atmosphere' is considered to have
an important role in explaining foreign policy decisions and state action.
Jacobsen provided a similar typology distinguishing between 'consensual
shared beliefs', which provide the ends to be pursued and 'economic ideas',
which provide the means for accomplishing the ends.[32] However, it is arguable
whether disaggregating ideas is always useful. An idea that is normative in one
instance may be causal in another.[33]

What is important is that for weak cognitivists, the demand for international
regimes depends on the state's perceptions of international problems which, in
turn, is affected by ideas. The influence of ideas works through 'causal
pathways'.[34] Beliefs may serve as 'road maps,' whereby decision-makers
select from all possible actions those that fit best their normative
understandings. Within their world-views, principled beliefs help define
actors' objectives and preferences, while causal beliefs influence the choice of
instruments. Shared beliefs can also serve as 'focal points' that help define
acceptable solutions to collective action problems, particularly when there is
more than one possible solution, thus facilitating cooperation and regime
formation. Finally, ideas influence the creation of international rules and
become embodied in institutional frameworks, which constrain public policy
for some time, depending on the robustness of the regime they help to create.

In order to be causally effective, ideas require 'political entrepreneurs', who
can first select and then 'market' them. The emergence and ascendance of
ideas respond to a specific demand by policy-makers.[35] Once created, ideas
must be packaged so that they can be sold to both the elites and the public.[36] A
specific role in the generation and circulation of ideas is played by 'epistemic
communities', which are defined as 'network[s] of professionals with
recognised expertise and competence in a particular domain and an
authoritative claim to policy-relevant knowledge within that domain or issue
area'.[37] Members of such communities generally have a shared understanding
of problems and preferred solutions in their issue area, as well as a willingness

to actively speak out and to strive for better public policies. Through their action in the policy process, epistemic communities play an important role in regime formation. Their role is particularly significant in framing the issues for policy debates and subsequently diffusing new ideas through their transnational links. Their influence can also be felt at the level of policy selection and, finally, once a regime has been established by lending it continued support and advocacy.[38]

An even stronger role is attributed to ideas by another theoretical orientation in the study of international relations, which is often referred to as constructivism or 'strong cognitivism'. This school of thought focuses attention on the constitutive role of ideas in generating and constructing interests, determining preferences, defining the problems to which policies are a response, and in designing and building international regimes. The rationalist interpretation of state behaviour in terms of utility maximization is in many instances inadequate, particularly with regard to the study of regimes. Rational choice theorists assume interests and preferences and move to explain regimes as problem-solving devices. In contrast, constructivists consider interests, preferences, and individual choices as deeply influenced, and indeed made possible, by social institutions and practices. Social norms and ideas condition agents to see themselves in particular ways and to seek certain outcomes. The very concept of the state is a social construct made possible by the existing international normative framework.[39] Ideas, in turn, are also seen as elements, sometime constitutive elements, of such social practices that structure the world.

It is then not sufficient to investigate why states cooperate and create regimes. It is also important to understand how cooperation between states is possible. Or, in other words, what are the constitutive, structural preconditions that enable international agents to act? Fundamental rules of the international society, social practices, and ideas have this constitutive function, which allows for the definition of actors and issues and the possibility of choice.

Furthermore, norms[40] and practices do not 'cause' behaviour in the way rationalists assert. As Kratochwil and Ruggie suggested: 'norms may "guide" behaviour, they may "inspire" behaviour, they may "rationalize" or "justify" behaviour, they may express "mutual expectations" about behaviour, or they may be ignored'.[41] They do not externally and objectively influence the behaviour of states. On the contrary, they are intersubjectively constituted. As a result, 'regimes are more than mere incentive-manipulators affecting the utility calculations of rational actors. They comprise understandings shared by the members concerning the right conduct in circumscribed situations'.[42] Hence, regimes can be conceptualized as 'principled and shared understandings of desirable and acceptable forms of social behaviour'.[43] They comprise social knowledge of both a constitutive and regulative character. By defining admissible behaviour and by attaching meaning to individual action, norms, and practices make it possible for states to interact and cooperate.[44] Since norms not only prescribe behaviour but also give it meaning, their effectiveness cannot be assessed simply in terms of compliance, which only relates to their regulative dimension.

The binding power of norms and practices extends beyond the interests of states in solving collective action problems. There is a 'sense of obligation' that leads states to respect international agreements independent of positive or negative sanctions. As Henkin observed: 'it is probably the case that almost all nations observe almost all principles of international law and almost all their obligations almost all of the time'.[45] International norms exhibit an autonomous 'compliance pull', whereby states feel compelled to respect them even when, from a utilitarian perspective, they have an incentive to break them and free-ride.[46] At a general level and with regard to the most fundamental and constitutive rules of the international society, such as sovereignty[47] and the observance of treaties, respecting norms pertains to the realm of necessity, as without them the international society, which states need in order to exist, would collapse.[48] In this sense, 'international law [is] constitutive of the structure of the state system itself – and, one might add, [provides] the legal underpinnings of the capitalist world economy, in terms of both detailed rules and fundamental assumptions'.[49]

The strength of the compliance pull is linked to the extent to which specific rules and regimes are regarded as legitimate. Legitimacy, which can be defined as the quality of prescriptions making states abide by them voluntarily,[50] is dependent on a number of dimensions related to textual clarity and validation through adherence to the 'standards that define how rules are to be made, interpreted, and applied'.[51] But even more importantly, legitimacy derives from 'coherence'. 'Rules to be perceived as coherent must emanate from principles of general application'.[52] Thus, the degree of legitimacy depends in large part on the 'connectedness between rules united by under-lying principles ... manifest[ing] the existence of an underlying rule-skein which connects disparate ad hoc arrangements into a network of rules "govern-ing" a community of states, the members of which perceive the coherent rule system's powerful pull towards voluntary compliance'.[53] It is this link between rules and higher-order principles that leads states to comply, in good measure, with the rules, even when their contingent interests would indicate a different course of action. This respect for the fundamental structure of the international society and its legitimate rules creates a sense of community, which in turn leads to a tendency to disapprove of and often sanction free-riding.[54]

Among the higher-order principles, there are certainly those that derive from a shared sense of justice. These lend a particular compliance pull to the bodies of rules linked to them, such as human rights and environmental rules.

As Hurrell put it: 'rules and norms of this kind do not develop as a result of a distinct interplay of states interests or because of the functional benefits which they provide. Rather they depend on the common moral awareness that works directly, if still in fragile and uneven ways, on the minds and emotions of individuals within states'.[55] Ideas about justice are thus particularly important because they facilitate cooperation and greatly add to the stability and workability of social arrangements. At a general level, as Hayek stated: 'whether we want it or not, the decisive factors which will determine ... evolution will always be highly abstract and often unconsciously held ideas about what is right and proper, and not particular purposes or concrete desires. It is not so much what men consciously aim at, as their opinions about permissible methods, which determine not only what will be done but also whether anyone will have the power to do it'.[56]

Indeed, states, in their cooperative relationships and particularly in institutionalized relationships, rely on discourses[57] in order to arrive at a common understanding of the required behaviour in any given social situation. In an international situation in which the use of force has lost much of its relevance, as in the area of economic relations, and where the identification of national interests is already increasingly difficult due to globalization and interdependence, discourse and persuasion become important instruments of state action coordination. Divergent interpretations and applications of rules are bound to arise in a dynamic, ever-changing, international environment where regimes' rules cannot aspire to cover all possible contingencies. This would make rule-governed cooperation impossible in the absence of communicative action by states aimed at inducing behaviour consistent with shared interpretations and legitimate, patterned expectations of other community members.[58] In their discourses, states argue for a preferred course of action, and they do so in the context of a rule-governed situation, in terms of the legitimacy of their position. Their arguments are more convincing, and their positions more acceptable, the more they are grounded in general principles and shared understandings – or, in other words, the more legitimate they are perceived. Higher-order constitutive principles, such as fairness, reciprocity, equity, and respect for sovereignty and promises lend that legitimacy. The role that ideas play in defining such principles is clear.

However, while it is true that states often make only rhetorical reference to principles to conceal their interests and use coercion and bargaining, it is also true that most of the time they engage in serious discourse in order to justify their actions and do so out of the 'sense of obligation' they perceive. This stresses the important role of moral ideas in international relations, in particular because of the constitutive function these ideas fulfil for the international society, but also in the light of the role they play in shaping the identity of states, their conception of the self as it relates to other actors.[59] The self-understanding of states and their behaviour is an intersubjective and iterative process, which is much influenced by ideas, rules, and institutions. In this sense, it is important to examine the historical and social processes by which rules are created and the sense of obligation engendered.

The unfolding of rule-governed cooperation also reinforces states' willingness to act with a sense of community, to develop a collective identity. The process of cooperation through institutions 'discourages free-riding by increasing diffuse reciprocity and the willingness to bear costs without selective incentives'.[60] Through their socialization into a community, states develop and rely on some form of ethics, defining their members' rights and duties. In summary, ethical concerns and ideas play an important role in the emergence of cooperative behaviour and the creation of regimes, and it is through legal rules that such concerns and ideas are predominantly expressed.

None of these social processes can be fully grasped without reference to the domestic dimension. 'Clearly, the way in which states bargain and cooperate cannot be understood except with reference to the changing nature of the state and the domestic political system'.[61] Ideas, values, and ethical concerns, in the end, bear on and are felt by individual policy-makers in their specific contexts. This is particularly true of conceptions of fairness and equity, which are closely related to distinct histories and specific cultures.[62]

1.3   THE APPROACH OF THIS STUDY

The purpose of this study is to trace the role of the fairness idea in US trade policy discourse and to investigate the impact it had on the creation of the multilateral trade regime. The theoretical framework that appears most hospitable to such an endeavour is Ruggie's social constructivism – his account of how international regimes are formed and his epistemology based on 'narrative' explanation.[63] Constructivism is an approach to social analysis that deals with the role of human consciousness in social life. As noted in the previous section, it asserts that human interaction is shaped by ideational factors, not simply material ones. In the realm of international politics, relevant social facts do not only comprise of such 'physical' elements as material capabilities or border barriers (e.g., customs posts, as well as rivers and mountains), but also ideas. These are mental states that – through human agency – can make things happen. Some forms of agency take shape collectively, what Ruggie, borrowing from Searle, called 'collective intentionality', on the basis of shared or 'intersubjective' beliefs.[64] Ideas, such as legitimacy and fairness, do not directly cause action, but, more importantly, they provide reason for action. Furthermore, shared beliefs help define actors' identities and interests.

The deductive–positivist analytical approach used by most international political economy and international relations experts is often not suited to uncover the meaning of social behaviour and its social significance.[65] Universally valid laws are hard to establish in the world of ideas. Building upon Durkheim and Weber, Ruggie stressed that 'the task of interpreting the meaning and significance that social actors ascribe to social action differentiates the social and natural sciences'.[66] The 'narrative explanatory protocol' is thus necessary to show why events are 'historically *so* and not *otherwise*'.[67] The narrative approach is chosen in this study to delineate an 'intellectual history' of the idea of fairness, its (inter-)subjective meaning from the perspective of the USA and how such understanding has influenced the US's trade policy discourse and its actions in the establishment of the multilateral trade regime.

The importance of ideas in this context, and fairness in particular, cannot be underestimated, as the negotiations to establish an international trade regime produced more than standards and rules of conduct. They also established 'intersubjective frameworks of meaning that included a shared narrative about the conditions that had made [this regime] necessary and what [it was] intended to accomplish, which in turn, generated a grammar, as it were, on the basis of which states agreed to interpret the appropriateness of future acts that they could not possibly foresee'.[68] In the context of such intersubjective frameworks of meaning, regimes are thus composed of both constitutive rules, which 'define the set of practices that make up any particular consciously organised social activity',[69] and specific regulative rules aimed at prescribing desired social behaviour.

The narrative that Ruggie proposed in order to understand the trade regime formation and the particular content it assumed rests on an appreciation of a regime as an institutional manifestation of political authority. In turn, political authority is made up by the fusion of power and what he called 'legitimate social purpose'. There is no need to elaborate on the power that the USA possessed at the end of World War II. What is interesting is to examine its social purpose, as in this context ideas play a key role. Ruggie considered social purpose as defining the relationship between the state and society and prescribing the proper scope of political authority in economic relations. Until World War I, the state–society relationship had evolved around the idea of *laissez-faire* liberalism, but it changed fundamentally in the interwar period, leading to a new compromise, what he termed 'embedded liberalism'.[70] Under *laissez-faire* liberalism, the balance between authority and the market assigns to the state the limited role 'to institute and safeguard the self-regulating market'.[71] Under embedded liberalism, in contrast, governments accept much more direct responsibility for domestic social security and economic stability.

Surely, the US postwar economic planners and trade regime negotiators were not doctrinaire free-traders. To the contrary, they understood the public ambivalence towards *laissez-faire* capitalism and the widespread demand for state intervention to cushion the dislocations that markets produce.[72] The negotiating challenge was to design an open trading system that would preserve the state's ability to pursue domestic stability while, at the same time, prohibiting the mutually destructive protectionist policies that had plagued the interwar period.

The embedded liberalism narrative understands the GATT as an international regime carefully structured to achieve these complex ends. While it was designed to reduce tariffs and other trade barriers, it also incorporated various clauses meant to protect domestic social interests. These included 'trade remedy' rules, safeguards, balance-of-payments exceptions, and renegotiation provisions. Through these and other provisions, the GATT attempted to capture gains from trade, but simultaneously it permitted governments to minimize the dislocations resulting from increased international trade and competition. As such, it 'embedded' a liberal international economic order within a larger commitment to interventionist domestic policies. The underlying compromise was that, in exchange for liberal trade policies, industrialized nations would provide a variety of domestic safety nets, including unemployment compensation and adjustment assistance.[73]

To the extent that regimes express common or at least congruent social purposes (especially, in the case of the trade regime, with regard to the appropriate role of government authority *vis-à-vis* the market), resting on a shared framework of understanding, they possess an authoritative and legitimate basis that is unrelated to the configuration of power. In this sense, the very efficacy of regimes 'has to do with the mutual intelligibility and acceptability of actions within the intersubjective framework of understanding that is embodied in the regime's principles and norms'.[74]

Ruggie's social constructivist approach provides the necessary theoretical framework for this study. However, his 'embedded liberalism compromise' narrative suffers from some limitation, as it is too focused on the impact on the regime construction of *one* idea, liberalism, as understood in one group of countries, the industrialized ones. Fairness is *another* key idea – this study hopes to illustrate – in the establishment of the multilateral trading system. Furthermore, by examining the way this idea has been understood in the main architect of the trade system – the USA – and then contrasting this understanding with that prevailing in developing countries, the study aims to show that the trade regime experiences an important legitimacy shortcoming due to the differences in meaning (and ensuing expectations) that various actors attach to the notion of fairness.

NOTES

1. See, for instance, J. Ikenberry, D. Lake and M. Mastanduno, eds., *The State and American Foreign Policy*, Ithaca Cornell University Press, NY and London, 1988.
2. See, ibid., pp. 2–3.
3. This section draws on C. Van Grasstek, 'The Political Economy of Residual Protection in the Trade Regime of the United States of America', mimeo, 2001.
4. See, respectively, G. Gallaroti, 'Toward a Business-Cycle Model of Tariffs', *International Organization*, vol. 39, no. 1, 1985, pp. 155–87; D. Lake, *Power, Protection, and Free Trade: International Sources of U.S. Commercial Strategy, 1887–1939*, Cornell University Press, Ithacha, NY, 1988.
5. See C. Kindleberger, *The World in Depression, 1929–1939*, University of California Press, Berkeley, CA, 1973; S. Krasner, 'State Power and the Structure of International Trade', *World Politics*, vol. 28, 1976, pp. 317–47; R. Gilpin, *United States Power and the Multinational Corporation: The Political Economy of Foreign Direct Investment*, Basic Books, New York, 1975; id., *The Political Economy of International Relations*, Princeton University Press, Princeton, NJ, 1987; and for a dissenting view J. Gowa, 'An Epitaph for Hegemonic Stability Theory? Rational Hegemons, Excludable Goods, and Small Groups', in J. Odell and T. Willett, eds., *International Trade Policies: Gains from the Exchange Between Economics and Political Science*, The University of Michigan Press, Ann Arbor, MI, 1990, pp. 55–73.
6. See, for instance, R. Keohane, *After Hegemony: Cooperation and Discord in the World Political Economy*, Princeton University Press, Princeton, NJ, 1984; D. Snidal, 'Coordination versus Prisoner's Dilemma: Implications for International Cooperation and Regimes', *American Political Science Review*, December 1985, pp. 923–42; B. Eichengreen, 'Hegemonic Stability Theories of the International Monetary System', in R. Cooper et al., eds., *Can Nations Agree?*, The Brookings Institution, Washington, DC, 1989, pp. 255–98.
7. See V. Pareto, *Manual of Political Economy*, A.M. Kelley, New York, 1971, p. 379.
8. See A. Smith, *The Wealth of Nations*, Random House, New York, 1776 [1937], Book IV, Chapter II.
9. See E.E. Schattschneider, *Politics, Pressure and the Tariff*, Prentice Hall, New York, 1935, p. 4.
10. Id., p. 161.
11. Id., pp. 144–5.
12. See H. Johnson, 'An Economic Theory of Protectionism, Tariff Bargaining, and the Formation of Customs Unions', *Journal of Political Economy*, vol. LXXIII, 1965, pp. 256–83.
13. See W. Mayer, 'Endogenous Tariff Formation', *American Economic Review*, vol. 74, no. 5, 1984, pp. 970–85.
14. In an interesting recent attempt to explain the design of the multilateral trade regime, Bagwell and Staiger construct a theoretical model within which the WTO can be seen as a rational response to strategic inefficiencies in the setting of national commercial policy. The model is that of a non-cooperative equilibrium in commercial policy, which shares the characteristics of a prisoners' dilemma: individually, rational choice of commercial policy by trade authorities in each country generates a non-cooperative trading equilibrium characterized by positive protection in the trading countries. However, there is also a set of cooperative equilibria with reduced protection that is weakly preferred by all trading partners and strongly preferred by at least one as well as a trigger strategy mechanism that will ensure the existence of the cooperative equilibrium in each period if the static game is repeated over an infinite time horizon. The authors' contention is that the principles of the WTO agreements provide the components necessary to replicate the posited cooperative equilibrium in the trading system. See K. Bagwell and R. Steiger, *The Economics of the World Trading System*, The MIT Press, Cambridge, MA, 2003.

15. See, for instance, D. Nelson, 'Domestic Preconditions of US Trade Policy: Liberal Structure and Protectionist Dynamics', *Journal of Public Policy*, vol. 9, no. 1, 1989, pp. 83–108.

16. See, for instance, D. Karol, 'Divided Government and U.S. Trade Policy: Much Ado About Nothing', *International Organization*, vol. 54, no. 4, 2000, pp. 825–44.

17. One theory, introduced in the early 1960s, stressed the dominance of the executive branch in foreign policy. See R. Bauer, I. de Sola Pool and L. Dexter, *American Business and Public Policy: The Politics of Foreign Trade*, Atherton, New York, 1963.

18. See R.N. Cooper, 'The Primacy of Economics: Trade Policy is Foreign Policy', *Foreign Policy*, Winter 1972–3, pp. 18–36.

19. See T.J. Lowi, 'American Business, Public Policy, Case-Studies, and Political Theory', *World Politics*, vol. 16, 1963, pp. 682–3. R. Pastor, *Congress and the Politics of United States Foreign Economic Policy, 1929–1976*, University of California Press, Berkeley, CA, 1980; I.M. Destler, *American Trade Politics*, second edn., Institute for International Economic, Washington, DC, 1992, incorporated similar arguments in their analyses of congressional trade politics.

20. See J.M. Keynes, *The General Theory of Employment, Interest and Money*, Macmillan, London, 1936, pp. 383–4.

21. Positivism, as an epistemology of social sciences, assumes that there are observable regularities in the social world that can be analysed with the same methods used in the study of the natural world. Rationalist approaches hold that state and non-state actors behave in a self-interested, goal-seeking way. Their choices are guided by instrumental rationality, that is, states always act so as to maximize their pre-established utility function. See A. Hasenclever, P. Mayer and V. Rittberger, *Theories of International Regimes*, Cambridge University Press, Cambridge, 1997, pp. 161–2.

22. Classical definitions of international regimes are provided by Stephen Krasner: 'implicit or explicit principles, norms, rules, and decision-making procedures around which actor's expectations converge in a given area of international relations' (see 'Structural Causes and Regime Consequences: Regimes as Intervening Variables', in S. Krasner, ed., *International Regimes*, 1983, Cornell University Press, Ithaca, NY, p. 2) and by R. Keohane: 'institutions with explicit rules, agreed upon by governments, which pertain to particular sets of issues in international relations' (see 'Neoliberal Institutionalism: A Perspective on World Politics', in R. Keohane, ed., *International Institutions and State Power: Essays in International Relations Theory*, Westview Press, Boulder, CO, 1989, p. 4. On international regimes, see in general M. Levy, O. Young and M. Zürn, 'The Study of International Regimes', *European Journal of International Relations*, 1995, vol. 1, pp. 267–330.

23. For such a categorization, see Hasenclever et al., op. cit., p. 136 et seq.

24. See J. Goldstein and R. Keohane, eds., *Ideas and Foreign Policy: Beliefs, Institutions, and Political Change*, Cornell University Press, Ithaca, NY, 1993, p. 5.

25. See J. Goldstein, *Ideas, Interests, and American Trade Policy*, Cornell University Press, Ithaca, NY, 1993, p. 250.

26. Destler and Odell's analysis of anti-protectionist forces in the 1980s offers a good example of this type of claim. They argued that ideologically inspired policy-makers preferred open markets and welcomed the lobbying of pro-trade interests because 'public evidence that protection would hurt other citizens gives liberal-leaning leaders political support they feel they need ... to deny or water down the request' to impose restrictions on imports. See I.M. Destler and J. Odell, *Anti-Protection: Changing Forces in United States Trade Politics*, Policy Analyses in International Economics 21, Institute for International Economics, Washington, DC, 1987, p. 101.

27. See Goldstein, op. cit., p. 3.

28. See, id., p. 137.

29. See Goldstein and Keohane, op. cit., p. 3.

30. See, id., p. 7. See also K. Sikkink, *Ideas and Institutions: Developmentalism in Brazil and Argentina*, Cornell University Press, Ithaca, NY, 1991, who argued that 'it is necessary to grapple with the influence of ideas on the policy-making process, not only the ideas of individual policy makers, but also those ... shared by large groups in society'.

31. See Goldstein and Keohane, op. cit., p. 8 et seq.
32. See J. Jacobsen, 'Much Ado about Ideas: The Cognitive Factor in Economic Policy', *World Politics*, 1995, vol. 47, no. 2, pp. 283–310.
33. See N. Woods, 'Economic Ideas and International Relations: Beyond Rational Neglect', *International Studies Quarterly*, vol. 39, 1995, pp. 162–3.
34. See Goldstein and Keohane, op. cit., pp. 8–24.
35. See J. Ikenberry, 'Creating Yesterday's New World Order: Keynesian "New Thinking" and the Anglo-American Postwar Settlement', in Goldstein and Keohane, op. cit., pp. 57–86.
36. See Goldstein, op. cit., p. 255.
37. See P. Haas, 'Introduction: Epistemic Communities and International Policy Coordination', *International Organization*, vol. 46, no. 1, 1992, pp. 1–35. On the role of epistemic communities in the trading system, see R. Howse, 'From Politics to Technology – And Back Again: The Fate of the Multilateral Trading Regime', *The American Journal of International Law*, vol. 96, January 2002, pp. 94–117.
38. See E. Adler and P. Haas, 'Epistemic Communities, World Order, and the Creation of a Reflective Research Program', *International Organization*, 1992, vol. 46, no. 1, pp. 367–90.
39. R. Price and C. Reus-Smit sum up constructivism as follows: 'Rejecting the rationalist precepts of neorealism and neoliberalism, constructivists advance a sociological perspective on world politics, emphasizing the importance of normative as well as material structures, the role of identity in the constitution of interests and action, and the mutual constitution of agents and structures'. See R. Price and C. Reus-Smit, 'Dangerous Liaisons? Critical International Theory and Constructivism', *European Journal of International Relations*, 1998, vol. 4, no. 3, p. 259. In a much-cited article E. Adler states: 'Constructivism is the view that the manner in which the material world shapes and is shaped by human action and interaction depends on dynamic normative and epistemic interpretations of the material world'. See E. Adler, 'Seizing the Middle Ground: Constructivism in World Politics', *European Journal of International Relations*, 1997, vol. 3, no. 3, p. 322.
40. Norms in regime theory mostly refer to generalized rules of cooperative social behaviour.
41. See F. Kratochwil and J.G. Ruggie, 'International Organization: A State of the Art on an Art of the State', *International Organization*, 1986, vol. 40, pp. 753–75.
42. See Hasenclever et al., op. cit., p. 163. J. Brunnée and S. Toope, 'Persuasion and Enforcement: Explaining Compliance with International Law', *Finnish Yearbook of International Law*, vol. XIII, 2002, pp. 273–95.
43. See Kratochwil and Ruggie, op. cit., p. 764.
44. As Kratochwil put it: 'human action in general is "rule-governed", which means that ... it becomes understandable against the background of norms embodied in conventions and rules which give meaning to action'. See F. Kratochwil, *Rules, Norms and Decisions: On the Conditions of Practical and Legal Reasoning in International Relations and Domestic Affairs*, Cambridge University Press, Cambridge, 1989, p. 11.
45. See L. Henkin, *How Nations Behave: Law and Foreign Policy*, Praeger, New York, 1968, p. 42.
46. See M. Koskenniemi, *From Apology to Utopia: The Structure of the International Legal Argument*, Finnish Lawyers' Pub. Co., Helsinki, 1989, Chapter 1.
47. On the role of ideas in shaping the existing sovereign states system, see D. Philpott, *Revolutions in Sovereignty: How Ideas Shaped Modern International Relations*, Princeton University Press, Princeton, NJ, 2001.
48. The general respect of norms is 'the price of membership in international society and having relations with other nations'. See Henkin, op. cit., p. 32.
49. See A. Hurrell, 'International Society and the Study of Regimes: A Reflective Approach', in V. Rittberger (with the assistance of P. Mayer), ed., *Regime Theory and International Relations*, Clarendon Press, Oxford, 1993, p. 59.
50. At a general level, Franck defines legitimacy as 'a property of a rule or rule-making institution which itself exerts a pull towards compliance on those addressed normatively'. See T. Franck, *The Power of Legitimacy among Nations*, 1990, Oxford University Press, Oxford, p. 16.

51. Id., p. 184.
52. Id., p. 152.
53. Id., p. 181.
54. This is consonant with H. Bull's understanding of the international society: 'A society of states (or international society) exists when a group of states, conscious of certain common interests and common values, form a society in the sense that they conceive themselves to be bound by a common set of rules in their relations with one another and share in the workings of common institutions'. See H. Bull, *The Anarchical Society: A Study of Order in World Politics*, Macmillan, London, 1977, p. 13.
55. See Hurrell, op. cit., pp. 65–6.
56. See F.A. Hayek, *Law, Legislation and Liberty*, vol.1, *Rules and Order*, Routledge, London, 1979, p. 69.
57. A discourse in this context is 'a debate conducted by members of a community aiming at establishing or re-establishing a consensus on common norms of conduct as well as on their interpretation and proper application in concrete situations'. See A. Hasenclever et al., op. cit., p. 176.
58. See Kratochwil, op. cit., and Kratochwil and Ruggie, op. cit. At the same time, it is also important to emphasize that international regimes are not cast in stone but are 'the product of an on-going process of community self-interpretation and self-definition in response to changing context'. See M. Neufield, 'Interpretation and the "Science" of International Relations', *Review of International Studies*, vol. 19, no. 5, 1993, p. 55.
59. 'Identification is a continuum along which actors normally fall between the extremes, motivated by both egoistic and solidaristic loyalties'. See A. Wendt, 'Collective Identity Formation and the International State', *American Political Science Review*, 1994, vol. 88, p. 387.
60. Id., p. 386.
61. See Hurrell, op. cit., p. 69. See also generally P. Evans, H. Jacobson and R. Putnam, *Double-Edged Diplomacy: International Bargaining and Domestic Politics*, 1993, University of California Press, Berkeley and Los Angeles, CA.
62. Id.
63. For an account of this approach, see J.G. Ruggie, *Constructing the World Polity*, Routledge, London and New York, 1998, pp. 1–39. For an application of social constructivism to the WTO regime, see J. Ford, *A Social Theory of the WTO: Trading Cultures*, Palgrave Macmillan, Houndmills, Basingstoke, Hampshire, 2003.
64. See Ruggie, op. cit., pp. 20–21 and 90.
65. For a flavour of the debates on the shortcomings of this approach as applied to the social sciences, see W. Drechsler, 'Natural Versus Social Sciences: On Understanding in Economics', in E. Reinert, ed., *Globalization, Economic Development and Inequality: An Alternative Perspective*, Edward Elgar, Cheltenham, UK and Northampton, MA, USA, 2004, pp. 71–87.
66. See Ruggie, op. cit., p. 30.
67. See M. Weber, *The Methodology of the Social Sciences* (E. Shils and H. Finch, trans.), Free Press, Glencoe, IL, 1949, p. 72 (emphasis in the original).
68. Ruggie, *Constructing the World Polity*, op. cit., p. 21.
69. Id., p. 22.
70. For an analysis of the domestic aspects of embedded liberalism in the USA, see M. Blyth, *Great Transformations. Economic Ideas and Institutional Change in the Twentieth Century*, Cambridge University Press, Cambridge, 2002, pp. 49–96.
71. Ruggie, *Constructing the World Polity*, op. cit., p. 67.
72. The interaction between government and the market was quite clear to policy-makers of the time. President Roosevelt, in his Message on the State of the Union of January 1945, stated: 'It is the responsibility of business enterprise to translate market opportunities into employment and production. It is the responsibility of the Government to hold open the door of opportunity and to assure sustained markets. Then and only then can free enterprise provide jobs'. See S. Roseman, ed., *Papers and Addresses of Franklin D. Roosevelt 1940/45*, Harper and Brothers, New York, vol. 1944/45, p. 480.

73. See id., pp. 62–84; see also J.G. Ruggie, 'At Home Abroad, Abroad at Home: International Liberalization and Domestic Stability in the New World Economy', *Millennium*, vol. 24, 1994, pp. 507–26; J.G. Ruggie, 'Embedded Liberalism Revisited: Institutions and Progress in International Economic Relations', in E. Adler and B. Crawford, eds., *Progress in Postwar Economic Relations*, Columbia University Press, New York, 1991, pp. 202–34.
74. See Ruggie, *Constructing the World Polity*, op. cit., p. 86.

2. Fairness: in search of a meaning

2.1 DEFINING THE NOTION OF FAIRNESS: INSIGHTS FROM POLITICAL PHILOSOPHY

Fairness is a complex idea with a long history. As Woods put it, 'very few ideas are very new',[1] and fairness is certainly not one of them. There is no accepted, uniform, and commonly shared definition of fairness. The notion is strongly associated with such ideas as equality, proportionality, reciprocity, equity, and justice,[2] only to mention other terms that have found currency in the trade policy discourse.[3] These concepts are entangled and their usage across disciplines and policy areas is far from univocal. But fairness, like justice, addresses issues that are fundamental to the social life of individuals as well as to nations.

For the purpose of this study, which only attempts to elucidate the role of this concept in the trade policy discourse and practice, a useful theoretical starting point is found in the 'principle of fairness',[4] or the 'duty of fair play', as developed by Hart and Rawls.[5] The principle has been elaborated in order to justify political and legal obligations, even beyond those based on consensual acts, promises, and contracts. However, there is no reason not to extend its application to cooperative schemes generally. The principle accords with the widespread belief that accepting a benefit creates a liability to contribute to its cost of (re)production. Those who fail to execute this obligation take unfair advantage of others and thus violate a norm of reciprocity or fair play. Rawls's presentation of the principle runs:

> The principle of fair play may be defined as follows. Suppose there is a mutually beneficial and just scheme of social cooperation, and that the advantages it yields can only be obtained if everyone, or nearly everyone, cooperates. Suppose further that cooperation requires a certain sacrifice from each person, or at least involves a certain restriction of his liberty. Suppose finally that the benefits produced by cooperation are, up to a certain point, free: that is, that the scheme of cooperation is unstable in the sense that if any one person knows that all (or nearly all) of the others will continue to do their part, will still be able to share a gain from the scheme even if he does not do his part. Under these conditions a person who has accepted the benefits of the scheme is bound by a duty of fair play to do his part and not to take advantage of the free benefits by not cooperating.[6]

Roughly, the principle of fairness (or fair play) obligates all participants in schemes of social cooperation from which they willingly benefit to do their fair share, and not to free-ride on the burdens shouldered by others.[7] Fairness is thus a morally important property of institutions, schemes, and activities (at all levels, from children's games and sport to international politics and economic relations). This acceptation seems to be in line with the way the notion of fairness is often used in trade policy discourse. It is particularly relevant in the context of a cooperative regime, such as the multilateral trading system.

Fairness relates to (but does not identify with) the propriety of distribution between burdens and benefits. Just outcomes are generally those that flow from fair processes. A 'fair trade' (as a 'fair fight') is one conducted under roughly equal conditions. The definition of such conditions then becomes a key factor. The reciprocity shown in compromise, mutual consent to terms, adherence to common rules, and no recourse to coercion or fraud are crucial to the fairness of many arrangements.

Indeed Rawls considered reciprocity to be the fundamental element shared by fairness and justice.[8] The requirement of fairness and the duty of fair play, as well as the requirement of justice, only arise if the participants in a 'practice', which refers to any form of activity specified by a system of rules, such as markets and systems of property, acknowledge that it satisfies the principle of reciprocity. Namely, none of the participants feels that, by participating in a particular practice, they are being taken advantage of or forced to give in to claims that they do not accept as legitimate. The concept of reciprocity thus involves the idea that bilateral relationships between at least formally equal social partners are not unidirectional, but necessarily involve, at a minimum, some element of *quid pro quo*.[9] This is a manifestation of the mutual recognition of parties to the social scheme ('practice') as free and moral 'persons' (a term that encompasses people as well as nations and firms). If the practice does not fulfil the principle of reciprocity, a basic phenomenon of social interaction, the duty of fair play is violated.[10] Fairness is essentially right dealing or more precisely, reciprocity in institutionalized relationships. If the practice can be mutually (reciprocally) accepted, then it is fair.

From an economic perspective, fairness is then mainly concerned with the process of competition and cannot generally (or at least easily) accommodate competing claims based on, for instance, different needs – as opposed to the relative contributions – of parties to the social cooperation scheme.[11] It certainly does not aim to equalize outcomes. A reciprocity-based duty of fair play implies that the relationship of reciprocity upon which it is grounded results from voluntary agreement that is reversible (what I owe you today, you may owe me tomorrow), and that the reciprocal performances of the parties (and advantages resulting from them) must be in some sense equal in value. These conditions are particularly suited to a society of economic traders, which generally enter into exchanges voluntarily, sometimes as sellers and sometimes as buyers, and where the measure of values is determined in free markets that allow for a broad reckoning of equality.[12] Then, as Rawls put it, fairness '... relates to right dealing between persons who are cooperating or competing against one another, as when one speaks of fair games, fair competition, and fair bargains'.[13] Fairness as 'fair play' thus seems to be concerned in particular with process and how that process contributes to a fair outcome.

A similar distinction is the one between 'substantive' and 'procedural' justice. The latter is concerned with how results are obtained, while the former focuses upon the characteristics of the end results themselves, the (material) justice of the outcome, no matter how it has been achieved. Such distinction has had an important influence on classical contract law, where particular importance is ascribed to the distinction between procedural and substantive fairness: fairness in the process of negotiating and concluding a bargain, a contract, and fairness in the results or the outcome of the bargain.[14] Contract-making is considered akin to participating in a contest or game, and the rules of the game serve to regulate the way the contest is conducted. These rules must be fair, for instance, by applying equally to both parties, being subject to interpretation by a neutral third party, and so on, if the contest is to be perceived as fair. If the contestants play by the rules, the 'best' should win. From this perspective, there is no concern for substantive or 'outcome' fairness. The rules are not designed to equalize the chances of all contestants. According to classical contract theory, the function of the law is confined to ensuring procedural fairness. There are fundamental rules to this effect in most legal systems, including rules protecting the parties from trickery and undue influence, or protecting minors and persons with reduced mental capacity. If procedural fairness is respected and both parties enter into the contract wilfully, then the usual gains from trade ensue. One of the two parties may receive more surplus, but both are better off.

However, even if procedural fairness is respected, a contract can well be perceived as unfair. A clear case of unfairness occurs when the agreed price significantly diverges from the market price.[15] This may happen for many reasons, including because perfect information is generally not available in the market. This leads the law and courts to concern themselves not only with procedural, but, to a limited extent, also with substantive fairness. Beyond contracts, fairness considerations also play an important role in many other areas of the law, both private, such as tort and restitution, and public law, including antitrust, intellectual property, and regulated utility law. Particularly interesting in the context of restitution law is the doctrine of unjust enrichment, which prescribes that a party should not enrich itself at the expense of another.[16]

The notion of fairness as fair play or fair exchange also relates to two traditional categories of justice: commutative and distributive justice. The former addresses the inequality that might result from exchanging goods which, in turn, relates to the concepts of substantive and procedural justice in contract law. The just exchange maintains the parties' equality. Distributive justice instead addresses the basic organization of all things, good and bad, in setting up a society. The distinction between distributive and commutative justice harks back to Aristotle's discussion of justice in the Fifth Book of the *Nicomachean Ethics*. There, Aristotle advanced the general proposition that justice is obtained by treating similarly situated people similarly and dissimilarly situated people dissimilarly. This treatment also governs distributive justice (*dianemetikon dikaion*), namely 'the distribution of honour or money or such other things that are divisible among the members of the community'.[17] Justice in distribution is thus perceived in a broad sense as any proportionate ratio between persons and things; in other words, any proportionate division of benefits or burdens among a group of potential recipients. As such, the notion of distributive justice only requires that each recipient receive a measure according to some criterion. For such distribution there is no absolute or universal principle. Rather, in different societies each citizen receives a share of whatever there is to be divided, according to principles consistent with the political regime of that particular society. Democracies favour the principle that each citizen should receive an equal share, while aristocracies divide goods according to excellence.

The second category of justice, which Aristotle referred to more specifically as corrective (*diorthotikon dikaion*), identifies the justice that rectifies or remedies inequalities that arise in dealings (*synallagmata*) between individuals. Thomas Aquinas, purporting to interpret Aristotle faithfully, subsequently broadened the meaning and introduced the term 'commutative justice'.[18] Exchange or commutative justice provides norms for regulating voluntary transactions between private individuals, and it addresses the inequality that might result from exchanging goods.[19] The principle is that no one should gain at another's expense.[20] Or expressed in a different way, exchange should impose the same burden on each party.[21] Distributive justice is concerned with the way a pie is divided (beyond the parties to individual transactions), while commutative justice is concerned with each party to an exchange preserving its (fair) share.

Commutative justice incorporates the two aspects of procedural and substantive fairness, since it requires fairness in both the process and the outcome of that process between the parties involved in the exchange (equality or at least some reasonable reciprocity in exchange), and, in this sense, it incorporates a distributive element. In comparison, distributive justice proper broadens the view and considers the distribution of benefits and burdens among all members of a society. However, at least for the purpose of ensuring procedural fairness and commutative justice (i.e., fairness in economic exchange), a benchmark is required. Commutative, just contracts are thus those in which commodities are exchanged in a ratio that reflects the fair value of goods – their true value or their just price. In this sense, the moral and non-moral meanings of fair and just tend to converge, as fair connotes straightness, flawlessness, proper proportion, while just, *justus*, bears the sense of true, real.

In the prevailing Aristotlean tradition, for objects that were unique, the true value was to be determined through honest negotiation between seller and buyer, and for commodities, through the consensus of the marketplace established in the absence of fraud or conspiracy.[22] This also accords with the traditional doctrine derived from Roman law, whereby goods are worth as much as they can be sold for.[23] Although Aristotle had not clarified this point, his medieval successors explicitly identified the just price with the market price.[24] In scholastic thought, just price is generally equated with the current market price.[25] According to the canon *Placuit*, a capitulary issued in 884 by Karloman, and later incorporated by Raymond of Pennaforte (1180–1278), parish priests should admonish their flocks not to charge wayfarers more than the price obtainable in the local market (*quam in mercato vendere possint*). Albertus Magnus defined just price as what goods are worth according to the estimation of the market (*secundum aestimationem fori*) at the time of the sale.[26] Thomas Aquinas remained on the same line. He told the story of a merchant who brought wheat to a famine-stricken city, knowing that other merchants were on the way with more wheat. As a matter of justice, should this merchant have sold at the prevailing price or should he have revealed the arrival of more supply, thus causing the price to fall? Aquinas answered that the merchant could remain silent and sell without infringing the rules of justice, although he would be more virtuous if he were to inform the buyers.[27] Aquinas recognized that the just price cannot be determined with precision, but can fluctuate with minor deviations not involving any injustice.[28]

Thomas de Vio, better known as Cardinal Cajetan (1468–1524), an authoritative commentator of the *Summa*, concluded that, according to Thomas, the just price is 'the one, which at a given time, can be gotten from the buyer, assuming common knowledge and in the absence of all fraud and coercion'.[29] A description of the market mechanism, with changes in prices due to supply and demand variations, follows. San Bernardino of Siena (1380–1444) stressed that prices are set either by public authorities in case of necessity and for the common good, or by the estimation currently arrived at in the marketplace. Such price is fair and must be accepted by the producer, whether it gains or loses and whether it is above or below cost.[30] The fairness of the current market price was also emphasized by the School of Salamanca. Francisco de Vitoria and his followers stressed that attention should be paid only to supply and demand, without regard for labour costs, expenses, and incurred risks. Inefficient producers and unlucky speculators should bear the brunt of their incompetence.[31]

The discussion of just price is predicated upon the existence of competitive conditions, but the word 'competition' did not appear in scholastic writing until the end of the sixteenth century. Discussing price formation in an open market, Luis de Molina stated that 'competition (*cuncurrentium*) among buyers – brisker at one time than another – and their greater avidity will cause prices to go up, whereas paucity of purchasers will bring them down'.[32] If the market failed, public authorities had the right and duty to step in through price regulation. Some Scholastic Doctors were critical of the practice since it often proved ineffective. Furthermore, price discrimination was generally considered immoral. San Bernardino stressed that prices should be the same for all and that strangers should not be charged more than local customers.[33] Monopolistic practices, including any agreement to increase or decrease prices above or below the competitive level, were also unanimously regarded as damaging. Such practices were considered to be criminal: engrossers and forestallers were often judged, fined, and punished with exposure on the pillory. According to canon law, monopoly profits were *turpe lucrum* and, like usury, subject to restitution.[34]

To summarize so far, the principle of fairness or the duty of fair play, requiring all participants in schemes of social cooperation from which they willingly benefit to contribute their fair share, and not to free-ride on the burdens shouldered by others, is an important element to achieve fair and commutatively just exchanges. These are exchanges in which a reasonable equality between the parties is ensured so that neither party is enriched at the expense of the other. Such equality is generally preserved at the market price. The problem then becomes whether this kind of justice also entails distributive justice in the society at large or whether further arrangements are required beyond market institutions.

Already Aristotle was concerned with the problem that privately owned goods must be utilized so as to serve the community at large. Lawmakers are to set up the institutional arrangements that will bring about the necessary coincidence between incentive-stimulating private property and communal benefit from the use of property.[35] In the same vein, Adam Smith in *The Wealth of Nations*, asked: 'What are the rules which men naturally follow in exchanging ... goods ... for one another'?[36] Far from being a naïve apologist of the capitalist system,[37] Smith considered that the basic purpose of economic institutions was not to provide maximum profits for capitalists, or to contribute to the state's national power, military or otherwise, but rather to provide a 'plentiful revenue of subsistence for the people'.[38] Capitalist dominance of the political system distorts the economic process and, as such, is morally reprehensible, since it gives priority to producers over consumers and violates the 'self-evident maxim' that 'consumption is the sole end and purpose of all production'.[39] 'The final cause of economic activity, perception of which generates moral guidelines for apprising policy and institutions, is to provide the community with a plentiful supply of consumer goods, whereas profit maximisation is but a secondary, or "efficient" cause'.[40] Conduct based on the profit motive ('the constant and perpetual effort of every man to better his own condition'[41]) is thus acceptable only in as far as it contributes to the realization of the economic activity's ultimate aim, that is, 'plentiful subsistence for the people' through a shift of resources from low-profit to high-profit sectors. The operation of economic institutions is morally justified only when regulated and controlled by strict rules of justice.[42] It is true that the law of supply and demand leads the market price to gravitate around the 'natural' price, which is determined by the amount of wages, profit, and rent that need to be paid for the resources necessary to produce goods. In this sense, the market price realizes the 'proportionate equality', the fair distribution of burden and benefit necessary to ensure justice in exchange.

However, in this context, the government has an important, albeit limited role to play as a provider of public goods, including by 'establishing an exact administration of justice'.[43] The institution of property rights and contract law creates the necessary framework for the market to start operating and to produce desirable consequences, such as the maximization of net product, so as to provide a 'plentiful revenue of subsistence for the people'. This framework is a precondition for the pursuit of private self-interest through the system of division of labour and exchange. Thus, with similarities to modern social-contract theory, Smith considered that rational, self-interested individuals would find it to their mutual advantage to set up the legal framework necessary for the market to function.

However, beyond the legal framework, there are other forms of constraint on self-interest that are necessary to ensure the proper functioning of the market system. Social interaction generates moral principles that, internalized in the conscience of individuals, constrain private, self-interested conduct (i.e., egoism, or what Smith referred to as 'misinterpretation of self-love'[44]). These principles emerged progressively, from perceived conformity to current social practice, as established by consensus in a particular society, to a clearer perception of conformity with an objective and absolute ideal of performance, a moral norm that could be considered the ethical basis of a good society.[45] As moral agents, people first test their behaviour against the social norms prevailing in their society. Then, they move to judge it in the light of a more adequate formulation of moral norms, 'which was apparently discerned and

articulated through reflection on capitalist social experience'.[46] Smith found
this moral root in the role of consumption as the purpose of production. The
goal of economic activity is 'providing a plentiful revenue of subsistence for
the people', not private profit, which is only an efficient cause, a motivating
force. This principle was described as 'so perfectly self-evident that it would
be absurd to attempt to prove it'.[47] But, indeed, it was not so self-evident, and
Smith addressed some of his sharp criticisms towards the 'mercantilist
system', which, in his opinion, had reversed the teleological relationship
between consumption and production. That system was considered to exploit
consumers for the benefit of producers and to protect the 'rich and powerful',
while 'oppressing the poor and the indigent'.[48] Smith attributed the fault for
this state of affairs to the selfishness of the business interest groups that had
been 'the contrivers of this whole mercantile system'.[49]

Viewing consumption as the ultimate end of production might have been
rather straightforward within earlier social arrangements when economic
activity was embedded in the social relations that made up the community as
a whole. However, the emergence of the capitalist market system had
displaced the communal and feudal institutions, such as the manor and guilds.
Social relationships based on status were replaced by relationships governed
by contract. Once the market starts to function and the economy becomes
'disembedded' from its social base, as it was already in Smith's time,
production, distribution, and exchange take place through specialized
institutions, responding to the imperative of supply and demand, and the
notion of personal responsibility for economic behaviour becomes blurred.[50] If
economic activity is governed by the impersonal, self-regulating market
mechanism, where the profit motive is the predominant driving force, the
question becomes how to ensure that such activity is subordinated to moral
principles. In Smith's view, the mercantile system is an example in which such
subordination did not exist, while the competitive market system, inspired by
the primacy of consumption over production, is conducive to it. Indeed,
consumption is not only aimed at biological subsistence, but it also contributes
to higher human and moral values, such as the attainment of leisure and
tranquillity. These, in turn, allow humankind to undertake the study of science
and philosophy.

But more than that, the market-based social system provides a bulwark
for individuals' natural rights. Individuals have a natural right to self-
determination, and the opening up of market opportunity serves to protect
people from arbitrary authority. The market constitutes a 'device for achieving
recognition ... of natural right'.[51] Smith's political ideal was the 'system of
natural liberty', in which every man, as long as he does not violate the laws of
justice, is left perfectly free to pursue his own interests in his own way. The
basic premise of Smith's model of market capitalism is 'the desire of bettering

our own condition', the principle of self-interest, the famous 'invisible hand', which drives individuals to an unrelenting pursuit of private economic advantage and allows them to overcome 'a hundred impertinent obstructions', leading society towards opulence and prosperity.[52] It is this principle that leads businesspeople to respond to market signals and to shift resources towards high-profit sectors, maximizing their product. Self-interest is a virtuous personal quality, a form of what Smith referred to as prudence in *The Moral Sentiments*.[53] 'Steadiness of ... industry and frugality' in pursuit of health, fortune, and rank, as well as 'habits of economy, industry ... are generally supposed to be cultivated from self-interested motives, and at the same time are apprehended to be very praiseworthy qualities'.[54]

In Smith's account, these were morally desirable qualities, not only because they lead to prosperity, but most importantly because an 'impartial spectator' would approve of them. This represents the ultimate check on the moral quality of human behaviour. Building upon the sentiment of solidarity (i.e., 'sympathy', 'fellow-feeling'), each person as a moral agent must be able to transcend his or her own interests and desires that limit his or her capacity to sympathize with others, to a level where disinterested judgement is possible. Thus, the spectator is at once sympathetic and impartial, detached from the differences that set people at odds with one another, yet not so detached from human concerns as to be indifferent towards them. Moral judgement requires an evaluation of what is 'suitable' and 'proportionate' in human conduct.[55] This is 'bound to be rational ... sympathy ... always united with reason'.[56] To the extent that people take up this moral perspective, they live by conscience and tend to develop common standards. This process is not individualistic, as at its essence it requires seeing things as others do. This necessitates a learning process that is achieved within society by heeding the example of those who view the world as impartial spectators. For Smith, morality was a point of view that people develop as members of a society more than as individuals.

Furthermore, the impartial spectator personifies 'a process of interaction which provides the social consensus necessary for ... the stability of society'.[57] The judgement of the impartial spectator puts limits on the unrestrained pursuit of individual self-interest. 'In the race for wealth [an individual] may run as hard as he can, to outstrip his competitors. But if he should jostle, or throw down any of them, the indulgence of the spectators is entirely at an end. It is a violation of *fair play* [emphasis added] which they cannot admit of'.[58] In his system of natural liberty, everyone is free to pursue his self-interest 'as long as he does not violate the laws of justice'.[59] Such laws are basically the requirements of commutative justice. But in his analysis of the market mechanism, Smith went beyond the notion of the just price, establishing the link between justice in exchange and society's welfare. Compliance with commutative justice in private transactions, 'allowing market prices to equate supply and demand and to bring prices into line with costs ... is essential for maximising net product and thus permitting society to "provide a plentiful revenue of subsistence for the people"'.[60] With his understanding of the market system, Smith demonstrated how compliance with commutative justice contributes to the material base of a just society.

Similar to the views of the Scholastic Doctors (e.g., Aquinas), the market is considered a system that ensures commutative justice, so long as monopolistic and fraudulent practices are at bay. However, his theory does not lead to any normative standards with regard to the requirement of distributive justice. The wealth created by the operation of the system is expected 'to extend itself to the lowest ranks of the people'.[61] This distributional effect is expected to happen not through redistribution, but through economic growth that occurs faster than population growth. But inequality is not at issue because it is the property owners that are responsible for capital accumulation and for the use of their resources, where the optimal contribution to net product and society's common good can be realized.

Hence, Smith has achieved the great merit of elucidating the market mechanism's ethical elements. He showed how the play of supply and demand brings market price (the 'going rate of exchange') into line with natural price (the 'fair rate of exchange'), which ensures the equality (which also means independence and freedom from arbitrary authority, characteristic in Smith's view, for instance, of the agricultural labour relationships in pre-commercial Europe) of the contracting parties. The unrestricted market is indeed a manifestation of natural right, since its existence presupposes that each man has the right and the capacity to enter into exchange contracts.[62] Natural price is made up of three component parts: wages, profit, and rent. It is then up to the ensuing marginal analysis to explain how each component is determined, by making recourse to the value of the relevant factor's contribution to production.

> When commodities sell at their natural price, the arithmetic equality essential for commutative justice prevails on both sides of the transaction. Buyers pay a price equal to the natural price or the 'fair rate of exchange' that is determined by the value of the resources required to produce the commodity. Producers receive – indirectly from the consumer, directly from the employer – a reward precisely equal to the value of their respective contributions to production. ... [T]he free play of competitive supply and demand – allowing market participants maximal freedom in the exercise of their natural rights – is indeed the appropriate procedure in a market society for guaranteeing compliance with the moral imperative of commutative justice.[63]

Fairness, or the duty of fair play, is a crucial element in ensuring commutative justice and upholding the market mechanism and, thus – in turn

– in contributing to the realization of distributive justice as understood in the (contribution-based) classical and neoclassical traditions of economics thought. The moral basis of fairness is to be found in the reciprocity norm, which requires a measure of equality or proportionality in exchange and no free-riding. However, ensuring fairness does not necessarily lead to distributively just outcomes. Fairness remains only one (necessary but not sufficient) standard of justice. And this tension has come prominently to the fore in the trade policy discourse of recent years. For the purpose of this study then, and at the cost of a considerable simplification, the core concept of fairness will be identified with the duty of fair play and the rejection of free-riding, as embodied in the operation of the free-market system and its institutions. This represents only one component, albeit an important one, of the broader justice ideal.

2.2   THE SOCIAL PSYCHOLOGY DIMENSION OF FAIRNESS

Similar concerns with outcomes and procedural justice have been investigated in many empirical social psychological studies. The research in this field has been extensive, ranging from organizational studies to law, thus involving the study of many areas of social interaction.[64] When examining how people make judgements about what is fair or unfair, similar notions are used: distributive justice, focusing on outcomes, and procedural justice, concentrating on the processes by which the outcomes are decided.[65] The two dimensions are intertwined and mutually supportive.[66] As Morton Deutsch put it, '"procedural justice," as traditionally conceived, refers to the fairness of the various procedural components of the system that regulates the distributive process'.[67] If the goal of a procedure is to distribute benefits and burdens, at the end of the procedure there are winners and losers. And a sense of injustice is often aroused more by procedures involved in the distributive process than about the distributive values governing it. In exchange relationships, distributive justice deals with how the profits are shared and how the benefits and burdens are divided or allocated between two parties. However, Kumar suggests that procedural justice, which refers to the fairness of a party's procedures for dealing with its vulnerable partners and to the means used to determine the outcomes in the relationship, has stronger effects on relationships, as it is seen by the weaker partner as more accurately reflective of the powerful partner's attitudes.[68]

The systematization of justice judgements observed in a number of studies has led to the identification of three main principles or values underlying perceived justice: proportional equity, equality, and need.[69] Equity, from this perspective,[70] assumes that rewards and costs allocation should depend on contributions or inputs. The equality principle holds that everyone should receive the same allocation, regardless of performance or other contingencies. The need principle calls for allocating rewards and resources based on individual circumstances.

These principles of distribution are in some cases conflicting and are strongly shaped by cultural values, both by precedent and by the specific types of goods or burdens being distributed. In cooperative relations in which economic aspects and competition are primary, equity (in the sense of contribution), rather than equality or need, seems to be the dominant principle of distributive justice.[71] Empirical research on this perspective has been influenced by what in social psychology is referred to as equity theory.[72] The latter posits that people, while trying to maximize their outcomes, also desire that the ratio of perceived inputs to perceived outcomes be constant across individuals. When this is not the case, people experience psychological discomfort and are motivated to restore an 'equitable' balance. At one point, equity theory was suggested as a candidate for a general theory of social behaviour, since its main tenets were argued to be applicable across many areas of human interaction.[73]

However, the belief that equity or the contribution rule is the universally appropriate basis for allocation is a socio-historical product. It reflects the socialized belief emanating from the US industrial capitalist market economy.[74] Equity theory owes much to Aristotle's contention in the *Nichomachean Ethics* that justice is proportional. Both share

> the basic psychological assumption that people believe that, in a just distribution, rewards will be distributed among individuals in proportion to their contributions: people who contribute more to a relationship, to a group, to an organization, or to a society should get proportionally more than those who contribute less. This assumption underlies the meritocratic ideology, derived from the Protestant ethic, which provides the value framework of Western capitalism. The slogan of this ideology, 'to each according to his merit (contribution),' is the basic theme of equity theory.[75]

Equity, or the contribution rule, remains one fundamental standard, among others, when people make judgements of justice. It is particularly consonant with groups and social systems holding an economic orientation, such as in Western societies. Instead, a needs-based principle of distributive justice is more likely to be adopted by groups or social systems that have its members' development and welfare as the primary goal. According to Rawls, the duty to help group members in need or jeopardy is one of the natural duties emanating from membership, provided that one can do so without excessive risk or loss to oneself.[76]

2.3 FAIRNESS CONCERNS IN ECONOMIC THEORY

Fairness, and more broadly, justice-related issues, have also experienced increased attention in economic theory.[77] Indeed, there is a vast literature concerned with the problem of income distribution.[78] There, 'economic justice' relates to the problem of deriving a rule for evaluating the distribution of desired objects in a society.[79] Many theoretical strands have developed. Marginalism provided the analytical framework for the contribution rule. According to this model, each economic agent (and production factor) that makes a contribution to production, receives in exchange a compensation equal to the market value of its contribution. As one of the fathers of marginalist thought put it: 'Free competition tends to give to labor what labor creates, to capitalists what capital creates, and to the entrepreneur what the coordinating function creates'.[80] When P.H. Wicksteed showed in 1894 that the sum of marginal products would, under certain conditions, exactly equal the total product, some economists felt that they had solved the perennial problem of the ethics of distribution. Both the leading US economists and sociologists of that time, J.B. Clark and W.G. Sumner, were particularly enthusiastic about the philosophical salience of the 'marginal productivity theory of distribution'.

However, contribution-based distributive justice exists only if free enterprise and free market competitive forces are allowed to work their way to equilibrium. If unfair, monopolistic practices prevail, then the contribution rule breaks down. Fairness in exchange, commutative justice, needs to be guaranteed. Thus, for instance, when the monopolistic tendency of capitalist firms leads to the restriction of production or the manipulation of prices, a public authority will have to step in and establish an effective antitrust policy in order to ensure fairness in the marketplace and a contribution-based distributive justice. Marginalist analysis and welfare economics have experienced both great success and a similar degree of criticism, which cannot be examined here in any detail. However, what needs to be stressed for the purpose of this study is the impact that both commutative and contribution-based distributive justice have had in economic thought and the role that fairness considerations plays in this context.

There is another strand in economic thought that is also of great importance to the particular understanding of fairness identified in previous sections: fairness as the duty of fair play. This relates to the reflection on the free-rider problem as one of the main sources of market failure in the provision of public goods.[81] Hume already had described this phenomenon in the mid-18th century, noting that efforts to muster the community's cooperation would be thwarted because of the incentive felt by each individual to 'free himself of the trouble and the expense, and ... lay the whole burden onto others'.[82] This would lead to the instability of the institution concerned, which needed to be remedied by public intervention.

However, the (under)provision of public goods is not governed only by self-interest; the behaviour of economic agents is morally embedded. Reciprocity, fair play, and justice count among the fundamental motivations of human action and cooperation.[83] While the consolidated tradition in economics is to view human beings as exclusively self-interested, people often act on considerations of reciprocity. Ultimatum games are a well-known example of a situation in which considerations other than self-interest play a role.[84] A more realistic code of moral behaviour is the principle of reciprocity or 'reciprocal fairness': according to this code, 'you behave the way which you would like the others to behave, but only if they actually meet this expectation'.[85] In other words, people want to be kind to those who have been kind to them (the positive reciprocity aspect) and to hurt those who hurt them (the negative reciprocity aspect).[86] 'Indeed, the power to enhance collective actions and to enforce social norms is probably one of the most important consequences of reciprocity'.[87]

Another growing body of research has been devoted to fairness issues in public policies. This stems from the recognition that the dichotomy that has grown over the years in mainstream economics between the pursuit of economic efficiency and distributive equity considerations is untenable.[88] 'At best, economic efficiency is a necessary but far from sufficient condition for an economically just or fair economy'.[89] Fairness issues have great relevance in public discussion, particularly with regard to issues of economic regulation. Fairness analysis thus tries to shed light on the 'the equity of particular policy proposals, institutional arrangements, or solutions derived from analytic models'.[90]

In this effort, a useful and common instrument is the 'Pareto improvement criterion'. This refers to situations in which everyone affected by a change is expected to benefit, or at least not to be harmed.[91] On the basis of such insights developed by Pareto at the end of the 19th century, the 'New Welfare Economics' of the 1930s and 1940s attempted to provide an objective basis for making welfare propositions about economic policies. For instance, in assessing a trade liberalization measure that could lead to both gains and losses for different groups, such a measure was to be considered a Pareto improvement if, at least potentially, the benefiting group could provide income compensation to the losing group (thus ensuring, one could add, fairness in the distribution of burdens and benefits deriving from a policy measure).[92]

Issues of unfair competition can also be analysed based on the Pareto criterion. Some multi-product firms may reduce the prices of those of its products that face competitive markets by subsidizing their sales through large receipts squeezed from its remaining products that command monopoly prices. The 'cross-subsidization' of low prices in competitive markets by the overpricing of products over which the firms have monopoly power can be considered unfair, since one customer group is benefiting at the expense of another (and it is thus free-riding). This is so unless it can be shown that the latter is also somehow gaining, thus rendering the practice of a Pareto improvement. In this sense, then, situations in which the duty of fair play has been respected and there is no free-riding would represent Pareto improvements.

2.4 SUMMARY

Cognitivist international relations theory stresses the importance of ideas as a determinant beyond purely material factors in the unfolding of world politics. Normative ideas, such as the idea of fairness, are particularly important for their legitimizing and even constitutive functions of international regimes and, more broadly, of the international society. Any attempt at delineating an 'intellectual history' of the idea of fairness (or any other idea) needs to start by tracing back where the idea came from (i.e., the sources of the idea), so as to infer and identify a core meaning. Such meaning is found in fairness as the duty of fair play, requiring that all participants in schemes of social cooperation from which they willingly benefit contribute their fair share, and not free-ride on the burdens shouldered by others. This meaning has solid roots in Western thought and has been recognized as important in both the social psychology and economic literatures. It also appears to be consonant with the use that is made of the fairness notion in international policy discourse and practice. But demonstrating this is the main task of the remainder of the study, where the trajectory of the idea will be examined, with respect to one particularly influential country (actually the real instigator) in creating the postwar trade regime: the USA. In examining this trajectory, it will also be important to observe the evolution of the idea itself in the specific social and historical contexts in which it has been used.

NOTES

1. See Woods, op. cit., p. 168.
2. Although 'justice' is sometimes used as a synonym for law or 'lawfulness', it has a broader sense closer to 'fairness'. See S. Benn, 'Justice', in P. Edwards, ed., *The Encyclopaedia of Philosophy*, op. cit., p. 298.
3. The concept of fairness is increasingly discussed from a normative perspective, although a consensus on its meaning in the trade policy context is still to emerge. See F. Garcia, *Trade, Inequality, and Justice: Toward a Liberal Theory of Just Trade*, Transnational Publishers,

Ardsley, NY, 2003; S. Suranovic, 'A Positive Analysis of Fairness with Applications to International Trade', *The World Economy*, vol. 23, no. 3, March 2000, pp. 283–307; M. Risse, 'Fairness in Trade', KSG Faculty Research Working Paper, February 2005; J. Linarelli, 'Principles of Fairness for International Economic Treaties: Constructivism and Contractualism', mimeo, June 2005; S.K. O'Byrne, 'Economic Justice and Global Trade: An Analysis of the Libertarian Foundations of the Free Trade Paradigm', *The American Journal of Economics and Sociology*, vol. 55, no. 1, Jan. 1996, pp. 1–15; Z. Boda, 'Conflicting Principles of Fair Trade', Business Ethics Papers No. 3, 2001.

4. The principle of fairness or the duty of fair play should not be confused with the two principles of justice, which are at the heart of Rawls's theory of (social) 'justice as fairness', or what Rawls called in his recent writing 'a political conception of justice', namely the Principle of Equal Liberties and the combined Equal Opportunity and Difference Principle, which are intended to govern the basic structure of a just society. The principle of fairness instead serves as a link between the two principles of justice and individual obligations to comply with specific social practices.

5. H.L.A. Hart, 'Are There Any Natural Rights?', *Philosophical Review*, vol. 64, 1955, pp. 175–91; in Hart's words, the thrust of the principle is as follows: 'When a number of persons conduct any joint enterprise according to the rules and restrict their liberty, those who have submitted to these restrictions when required have a right to a similar submission from those who have benefited by their submission', p. 185; J. Rawls, 'Legal Obligation and the Duty of Fair Play', *Law and Philosophy*, S. Hook, ed., New York University Press, New York, 1964, p. 3; for a discussion see A.J. Simmons, *Moral Principles and Political Obligations*, Princeton University Press, Princeton, NJ, 1979. The principle was anticipated in C.D. Broad, 'On the Function of False Hypotheses in Ethics', *International Journal of Ethics*, vol. 26, 1916, pp. 384–90.

6. Id., pp. 9–10; see also J. Rawls, *A Theory of Justice*, Cambridge, MA, Cambridge University Press, 1971, p. 112. In a similar vein, according to Isaiah Berlin: 'The notion of equality and fairness are closely bound up: if as a result of breaking a rule a man derives benefits which he can obtain only so long as other men do not break but keep the rule, then no matter what other needs are being served by such a breach, the result is an offence against a principle best described as that of fairness, which is a form of desire for equality for its own sake', see 'Equality as an Ideal', in F. Olafson, ed., *Justice and Social Policy*, 1961, pp. 128–50.

7. See R.J. Arneson, 'The Principle of Fairness and Free-Rider Problems', *Ethics*, 92, 1982, pp. 616–33.

8. 'Justice and fairness are, indeed, different concepts, but they share a fundamental element in common, which I shall call the concept of reciprocity', J. Rawls, 'Justice as Reciprocity', in S. Gorovitz, ed., *Utilitarianism*, The Bobbs-Merrill Company, Indianapolis and New York, 1971. In particular, justice refers to the concept of reciprocity as applied to a practice in which there is no option regarding whether to engage in it or not, and one must play; fairness to a practice in which there is such an option, and one may decline the invitation, see p. 242. Trade would be a practice to which the concept of reciprocity applies in the form of fairness. On the concept of reciprocity, see also L. Becker, *Reciprocity*, University of Chicago Press, Chicago, IL, 1990.

9. It may frequently be the case that reciprocity does not occur in the same discrete situation, but is provided at another time, in another 'transaction'. R. Keohane has referred to the latter form of reciprocity as 'diffuse reciprocity', see 'Reciprocity in International Relations', *International Organization*, vol. 40, no. 1, 1986, p. 1.

10. 'Every society ... has some notion as to the rightness of meeting reasonable expectations that a favour will be returned, of pulling one's weight in cooperative enterprises, of keeping agreements that provide for mutual benefits, and so on'. See B. Berry, 'Justice as Reciprocity', p. 212, reprinted in B. Berry, *Liberty and Justice*, Clarendon Press, Oxford, 1991; see also A. Gouldner, 'The Norm of Reciprocity', *American Sociological Review*, vol. 25, no. 2, April 1960, pp. 161–78.

11. This is similar to Locke's discussion of the conditions under which property may be rightfully acquired and held. Locke considered that if the acquisition is carried out according to the principles of natural law and natural rights, then property is fairly acquired and no

further scrutiny of the distributive outcome is justified. The requirements of justice are satisfied by the fairness of the competitive process itself. See J. Chapman, 'Justice and Fairness', in C.J. Friedrich and J.W. Chapman, eds., *Justice*, Atherton Press, New York, 1963, p. 151.

12. See L. Fuller, *The Morality of Law*, Yale University Press, New Haven and London, 1964, pp. 19–24.
13. See J. Rawls, 'Justice as Fairness', *The Philosophical Review*, vol. LXVII, 1958, p. 178.
14. See P.S. Atiyah, *An Introduction to the Law of Contract*, 1995, Clarendon Press, Oxford, p. 282 et seq.; S. Smith, 'In Defence of Substantive Fairness', *The Law Quarterly Review*, vol. 112, January 1996, pp. 138–58; C. Willett, *Aspects of Fairness in Contract*, Blackstone Press, London, 1996; A. Kronman, 'Contract Law and Distributive Justice', *Yale Law Journal*, vol. 89, no. 3, January 1980, pp. 472–511. See also M. Golecki, 'Synallagma and Freedom of Contract – The Concept of Reciprocity and Fairness in Contracts from Historical and Law and Economics Perspective', *German Working Papers in Law and Economics*, vol. 2003, Paper 18.
15. 'It can be argued that an unfair contract is simply one in which significantly more (or less) than a fair market price is paid', see Atiyah, op. cit., p. 284. The concept of fair market price or value remains complex. Fair market market value is generally considered the price that the asset (or assets of like type, quality and quantity) would bring by bona fide bargaining between well-informed buyers and sellers at the date of acquisition in a particular market.
16. On this issue, see in general H. Dagan, *Unjust Enrichment*, Cambridge University Press, Cambridge, 1997.
17. See Aristotle, *Nicomachean Ethics*, translated by Martin Ostwald, Macmillan, New York, 1962, Book 5 (ii), 1130b.
18. See J. Finnis, *Natural Law and Natural Rights*, Clarendon Press, Oxford, 1980, p. 177 et seq.
19. See J. Gordley, 'Equality in Exchange', *California Law Review*, vol. 69, Dec. 1981, no. 6, pp. 1587–656.
20. The same principle is present in Roman law, see *Digest of Justinian*, 50.17.206, 'Iure naturae aequum est neminem cum alterius detrimento et iniuria fieri locupletiorem' (By nature it is equitable that no one should be made richer by another's loss or injury).
21. See T. Aquinas, *Summa Theologica*, II–ii, q. 77, a. 1.
22. See R. de Roover, 'The Concept of Just Price: Theory and Economic Policy', *The Journal of Economic History*, vol. XVIII, Dec. 1958, no. 4, pp. 418–34 and D. Herlihy, in discussion of de Roover's article, p. 437.
23. See Accursius, *Glossa ordinaria to Digest*, XXXV, 2, 63: 'Res tantum valet quantum vendi potest, sed communiter'.
24. See de Roover, op. cit. According to Schumpeter, Aristotle actually did mean the market price, see J. Schumpeter, *History of Economic Analysis*, 1954, pp. 60–62.
25. See de Roover, op. cit., and T. Noonan, *The Scholastic Analysis of Usury*, Harvard University Press, Cambridge, 1957, pp. 82–8.
26. See A. Magnus, in *Commentarii in IV sententiarum Petri Lombardi*, Dist.16, Art. 46, in *Opera Omnia*, XXIX, Paris, 1894, p. 638.
27. T. Aquinas, *Summa Theologica*, II, ii, Qu. 77, Art. 3, Ad. 4. See A. Sapori, 'Il giusto prezzo nella dottrina di San Tommaso e nella pratica del suo tempo', in *Studi di storia economica (secoli XIII-XIV-XV)*, Florence: Sansoni, 1955, Vol. I, p. 279.
28. T. Aquinas, *Summa Theologica*, II, ii, Qu. 77, Art. 1, Ad. 1.
29. Quoted in de Roover, op. cit., p. 423.
30. See A. Fanfani, *Le origini dello spirito capitalistico in Italia*, Vita e Pensiero, Milan, 1933, p. 13.
31. The dissenters were mainly John Duns Scotus and his disciples, who maintained that the just price corresponded to cost, including normal profit and compensation for risk. See Schumpeter, op. cit., pp. 98–9.
32. Quoted in de Roover, op. cit., p. 425.
33. See Fanfani, op. cit., p. 110.
34. See Schumpeter, op. cit., pp. 154–5; W. Letwin, 'The English Common Law Concerning Monopolies', *University of Chicago Law Review*, vol. XXI, 1953–4, pp. 355–61;

R. de Roover, 'Monopoly Theory Prior to Adam Smith: A Revision', *Quarterly Journal of Economics*, vol. LXV, no. 3, 1951, p. 501 et seq.

35. Aristotle, *Politics*, with an English translation by H. Rackham, Harvard University Press, Cambridge, MA, II, 5, pp. 121–33.
36. See A. Smith, *The Wealth of Nations*, op. cit., p. 28.
37. See S. Worland, 'Adam Smith: Economic Justice and the Founding Fathers', in R. Skurski, ed., *New Directions in Economic Justice*, University of Notre Dame Press, Notre Dame and London, 1983, p. 1 et seq.
38. See Smith, op. cit. p. 397.
39. See Smith, op. cit., p. 625; see also H. Thomas, 'Adam Smith's Philosophy of Science', *Quarterly Journal of Economics*, Winter 1965, pp. 212–33.
40. See Worland, op. cit., p. 3.
41. Smith, op. cit., p. 324.
42. In A. Smith's conception, political economy is a branch of ethics concerned especially with an 'articulation of rules of justice … specially those practices which concern the provision of … a plentiful supply of material necessities … to the citizenry …', see J.R. Lindgren, *The Social Philosophy of Adam Smith*, Martinus Nijhoff, The Hague, 1973, p. 85.
43. See Smith, op. cit. p. 651 and 669.
44. See A. Smith, *The Theory of Moral Sentiments*, Liberty Classics, Indianapolis, 1759 [1976], p. 266.
45. See L. Billet, 'The Just Economy: The Moral Basis of *The Wealth of Nations*', in *Review of Social Economy*, December 1976, pp. 295–315; E. Gill, 'Justice in Smith: The Right and the Good', *Review of Social Economy*, December 1976, pp. 275–94; Lindgren, ibid.
46. See Worland, op. cit., p. 16.
47. Smith, *The Wealth of Nations*, op. cit., p. 625.
48. Id., p. 608 et seq.
49. Id., p. 626.
50. See K. Polanyi, 'Aristotle Discovers the Economy', in K. Polanyi, C.M. Arensberg and H. Pearson, *Trade and the Market in the Early Empires*, Free Press, Glencoe, IL, 1957, pp. 64–9.
51. See T.J. Lewis, 'Adam Smith: The Labor Market as the Basis of Natural Rights', *Journal of Economic Issues*, vol. 11, 1977, p. 38.
52. See Smith, *The Wealth of Nations*, op. cit., pp. 324 and 508.
53. See A.L. MacFie, *The Individual in Society*, George Allen & Unwin, London, 1967, p. 74 et seq.
54. See Smith, *The Theory of Moral Sentiments*, op. cit. p. 351 and 480.
55. Id., p. 61.
56. See MacFie, *The Individual in Society*, op. cit. pp. 64, 67.
57. See T.D. Campbell, *Adam Smith: The Science of Morals*, Rowman and Littlefield, Totowa, NJ, 1971, p. 137 et seq.
58. Smith, *The Theory of Moral Sentiments*, op. cit. p. 162.
59. Smith, *The Wealth of Nations*, op. cit., p. 651.
60. Worland, op. cit., p. 22.
61. Smith, *The Wealth of Nations*, op. cit., p. 11.
62. See Lewis, op. cit.
63. See Worland, 'Economics and Justice', in R. Cohen, ed., *Justice: Views from the Social Sciences*, Plenum Press, New York and London, 1986, p. 61.
64. See J. Greenberg, 'Organizational Justice: Yesterday, Today and Tomorrow', *Journal of Management*, vol. 16, 1990, pp. 399–432; J. Thibout and L. Walker, *Procedural Justice: A Psychological Analysis*, Lawrence Erlbaum, Hillsdale, NJ, 1975.
65. See, for instance, D. Miller, 'Distributive Justice: What the People Think', *Ethics*, vol. 102, April 1992, pp. 555–93.
66. '[I]t has proven to be the case that participants and observers evaluate procedures as more or less just or fair independent of their outcome, and that this estimation is quite relevant to whether the distribution resulting from a procedure is accepted as just. On the other hand, modern societies lack objective or generally-accepted standards for the just distribution of

life's chances and risks. In many cases, it seems easier to agree on a procedure than on the distribution itself. As a result, material distribution standards are replaced by procedures'. See K.F. Röhl, 'Procedural Justice: Introduction and Overview', in K.F. Röhl and S. Machura, *Procedural Justice*, Dartmouth Publishing, Aldershot, UK, 1997, p. 1.

67.	M. Deutsch, *Distributive Justice: A Social-Psychological Perspective*, Yale University Press, New Haven, 1985, p. 35.

68.	N. Kumar, 'The Power of Trust in Manufacturer–Retailer Relationships', *Harvard Business Review*, November–December 1996, pp. 92–106.

69.	Indeed many different criteria of justice may be delineated, nine according to Lerner, and as many as seventeen following Reis. Even more drastic was Michael Walzer, who maintained that each separate social good has its own criterion of just distribution. See M.J. Lerner, *The Belief in a Just World: A Fundamental Delusion*, Plenum Press, New York, 1980; H.T. Reis, 'The Multidimensionality of Justice', in R. Folger, ed., *The Sense of Injustice: Social Psychological Perspectives*, Plenum Press, New York, 1984, pp. 25–61; M. Walzer, *Spheres of Justice*, Martin Roberston, Oxford, 1983.

70.	To complicate matters this usage of the term 'equity' is different from that accepted in Chapter 5.

71.	Id., pp. 38–40; J. Greenberg, 'Approaching Equity and Avoiding Inequity in Groups and Organisations', in J. Greenberg and R.L. Choen, eds., *Equity and Justice in Social Behaviour*, Academic Press, New York, 1982, pp. 389–435; G.S. Leventhal, 'The Distribution of Rewards and Resources in Groups and Organizations', in E. Walster and L. Berkowitz, eds., *Advances in Experimental Social Psychology*, vol. 9, Academic Press, New York, pp. 91–131, 1976.

72.	See, for instance, G. Homans, *Social Behaviour: Its Elementary Forms*, Harcourt, Brace & World, New York, 1961; J.S. Adams, 'Inequity in Social Exchange', in L. Berkowitz, ed., *Advances in Experimental Social Psychology*, vol. 2, Academic Press, New York, 1965, pp. 267–99; E. Walster, G.W. Walster and E. Berscheid, *Equity: Theory and Research*, Allyn & Bacon, Boston, MA, 1978.

73.	See Walster, Walster and Berscheid, op. cit.

74.	See E.E. Sampson, *Justice and the Critique of Pure Psychology*, New York, Plenum Press, 1983.

75.	See Deutsch, op. cit., p. 9.

76.	'In each single instance the gain to the person who needs help far outweighs the loss of those required to assist him'; see Rawls, *A Theory of Justice*, p. 338.

77.	For a review of the main justice theories from an economic perspective, see J. Konow, 'Which is the Fairest of All? A Positive Analysis of Justice Theories', *Journal of Economic Literature*, vol. XLI, December 2003, pp. 1188–239.

78.	In this context, the issue of income inequality has attracted a lot of attention; see, for instance, A. Sen, *On Income Inequality*, Clarendon Press, Oxford, 1972.

79.	See W.C. Runciman, 'Processes, End-States, and Social Justice', *Philosophical Quarterly*, vol. 28, 1978, pp. 37–45.

80.	See J.B. Clark, *The Distribution of Wealth*, 1902, Macmillan, New York, p. 3.

81.	See, in general, J. Buchanan, *The Demand and Supply of Public Goods*, 1968, Rand McNally & Company, Chicago, IL, especially pp. 77–99.

82.	See D. Hume, *A Treatise of Human Nature*, Dolphin Books, Garden City, NJ, 1739 [1961], p. 478. Hobbes before him had also discussed the instability of cooperative schemes due to the egoistic tendencies of rational agents that know they can benefit from such schemes irrespective of their contributions; see T. Hobbes, *Leviathan*, edited by R. Tuck, Cambridge University Press, Cambridge, 1651 [1991].

83.	See J.M. Rao, 'Culture and Economic Development', *World Culture Report: Creativity and Markets*, UNESCO, Paris, 1998.

84.	In this type of game there are two players: the allocator who can choose what share of a fixed amount of money to allocate to himself and to the other player, who can either accept or refuse, in which case also the allocator gets nothing. In repeated games, the most common is an equal allocation of the sum. In cases when the allocator makes very unequal allocations, it is common for the second player to refuse the pay-off, even if rationally he or

she would be better off with at least something. See W. Guth, R. Schmittberger and
B. Schwarze, 'An Experimental Analysis of Ultimatum Bargaining', *Journal of Economic
Behaviour*, vol. 3, 1982, pp. 367–88.
85. See R. Sudgen 'Reciprocity: The Supply of Public Goods Through Voluntary
Contributions', *Economic Journal*, vol. 94, 1984, pp. 772–87; J. Elster, *The Cement of
Society: A Study of Social Order*, Cambridge University Press, Cambridge, 1989, p. 214.
86. See E. Fehr and J.R. Tyran, 'Institutions and Reciprocal Fairness', *Nordic Journal of
Political Economy*, vol. 23, no. 2, 1996, pp. 133–44; M. Rabin, 'Incorporating Fairness
into Game Theory and Economics', *American Economic Review*, vol. 83, no. 5, 1993,
pp. 1281–302; A.E. Roth, 'Bargaining Experiments', in A.E. Roth and J.H. Kagel, eds.,
Handbook of Experimental Economics, Princeton University Press, Princeton NJ, 1995,
pp. 253–348; R. Frank, *Passions Within Reason: The Strategic Role of Emotions*, Norton,
New York, 1988, pp. 213–16; C. Camerer and R. Thaler, 'Ultimatums, Dictators and
Manners', *Journal of Economic Perspectives*, vol. 9, 1995, pp. 209–19; E. Fehr, S. Gaechter
and G. Kirchsteiger, 'Reciprocity as a Contract Enforcement Device: Experimental
Evidence', *Econometrica*, vol. 65, no. 4, 1997, pp. 833–60; E. Fehr, G. Kirchsteiger and
A. Reidl, 'Gift Exchange and Reciprocity in Competitive Experimental Markets', *European
economic Review*, vol. 42, no. 1, 1998, pp. 1–34; M. Rabin, 'Psychology and Economics',
Journal of Economic Literature, vol. 36, no. 1, 1998, pp. 11–46, a finding confirmed by
questionnaire studies (see, e.g., D. Kahnemann, J.L. Knetsch and R. Thaler, 'Fairness as a
Constraint on Profit Seeking: Entitlements in the Market', *American Economic Review*, vol.
76, no. 4, 1986, pp. 728–41) and by some anthropological works as well (e.g., D. Bromley
and D. Chapagain, 'The Village Against the Centre: Resource Depletion in South Asia',
American Journal of Agricultural Economics, vol. 66, no. 5, 1984, pp. 868–73; C. Boehm,
'Egalitarian Behavior and Reverse Dominance Hierarchy', *Current Anthropology*, vol. 34,
no. 3, 1993, pp. 227–54).
87. See E. Feher and S. Gächter, 'Fairness and Retaliation: The Economics of Reciprocity',
Journal of Economic Perspectives, vol. 14, no. 3, Summer 2000, p. 160; also for a review of
the evidence.
88. 'The general position seems to be that prices in the economy should somehow be set so as
to achieve allocative efficiency, with the policy maker urged to take some *independent*
action to correct any unpalatable effects upon income distribution.' See W. Baumol,
Superfairness, The MIT Press, Cambridge, MA and London, England, 1986, p. 2. See also
A. Okun, *Equality and Efficiency: The Big Tradeoff*, Washington, DC, The Brookings
Institution, 1975; W. Thomson, 'Equity in Exchange Economies', *Journal of Economic
Theory*, vol. 29, 1983, pp. 217–44.
89. See Zajac, op. cit., p. 69.
90. See Baumol, op. cit., p. 7.
91. It is thus different from 'Pareto optimality' (nobody can be made better off unless somebody
is made worse off) since a Pareto improvement does not necessarily lead to a Pareto
optimum, and a move to a Pareto optimum need not be a Pareto improvement since some
people may be harmed in the process.
92. See N. Kaldor, 'Welfare Propositions of Economics and Interpersonal Comparisons of
Utility', *Economic Journal*, vol. 49, September 1939, pp. 549–52. For a critical review, see
J. Chipman and J. Moore, 'The New Welfare Economics, 1939–1974', *International
Economic Review*, October 1978, pp. 547–84.

3. Fairness in US commercial policy discourse before the advent of the multilateral trade system

3.1 FAIRNESS IN THE US SOCIO-ECONOMIC ETHOS

The notion of fairness based on reciprocity in contribution and no free-riding, as identified in Chapter 2, has deep roots in US political tradition, culture, and discourse. Two major traditions of beliefs have dominated US life from its inception: capitalism and democracy.[1] These two sets of beliefs, which integrate what is referred to as the 'American creed' or the 'American ethos', serve as the authoritative values of the nation's political culture.[2]

Particularly with reference to US socio-economic ethos, capitalist values and practices are central. They include: private ownership of the means of production, the pursuit of profit by self-interested entrepreneurs, the right to unlimited gain through economic efforts, competition, a significant measure of *laissez-faire*, and the market-based determination of production and distribution. These values and those related to democracy, such as individual freedom (of speech, press, assembly, and worship) and equality, including the equal right for all to participate in governance activities (both by consenting to the rulers and holding them accountable), share a common origin in protest against the inequities of colonial monarchism, mercantilism, and the remnants of feudalism. Hence, freedom is central to both democracy and capitalism, which presupposes the freedom of competition and exchange between producers and consumers, buyers, and sellers.

This 'liberal tradition', as Hartz described it, is fundamental to US history and experience: '... where the aristocracies, peasantries, and proletariats of Europe are missing, where virtually everyone ... has the mentality of an independent entrepreneur, two impulses are bound to make themselves felt: the impulse towards democracy and the impulse towards capitalism'.[3] In a similar vein, Hofstadter emphasized the importance of capitalist influences on the nation's political tradition:

> However much at odds on specific issues, the major political traditions have shared a belief in the rights of property, the philosophy of economic individualism, the values of competition; they have accepted the economic virtues of capitalist culture

as necessary qualities of man. ... American traditions also show a strong bias in favour of egualitarian democracy, but it has been a democracy in cupidity rather than a democracy in fraternity.[4]

At the same time, the two traditions engender some important value conflicts. Capitalism is primarily concerned with maximizing private profit, values individuals according to their contribution to production, and considers the free market as the most efficient, as well as the fairest system for distributing goods and services. Democracy, on the other hand, aims primarily to maximize freedom and the public good and to ensure a decent livelihood to all individuals; it also upholds the right of the popular majority to override the market mechanism when necessary to pursue the public good. Indeed, the tension between these values was clear to the Founding Fathers, who considered one of their goals 'to secure the public good and private rights ... and at the same time to preserve the spirit and form of the popular government'.[5]

The constituent role of capitalism in US socio-economic ethos has its roots in the centrality of private property and commerce in the construction of the Republic. The Framers of the Constitution sought to create a society based on free commerce in which the marketplace of goods and services was the ultimate economic authority.[6] This was, of course, part of a wider political project meant to create a republican democracy in which individual freedom would be guaranteed. The protection of private property was considered integral to this project, as the right of property ownership was considered to be a bulwark against authoritarianism. From this perspective, a regime of private property is primarily a social achievement. It is a basic social prerequisite to the exercise of human liberty. For if the government could take property away from individuals at a whim, it could intimidate and dominate them, thus, in effect, nullifying all other liberties. On the contrary, the government was thought to be without the authority to deprive people of their natural rights, including that of property. Instead, the protection of property was considered to be one of the government's main goals.[7] This appreciation of the role of property seems to have endured to our times.[8]

The pursuit of personal freedom through economic well-being and property is also manifested in what Diamond called the 'bourgeois virtues' that characterize the 'American person'. The USA's commercial republic unleashes aquisitiveness, which, unlike avarice, emphasizes 'getting', not 'having'. '[A]quisitiveness teaches a form of moderation to the desiring passion from which it derives, because acquiring is not primarily to have and to hold but to get and to earn, and, moreover, to earn justly, at least to the extent that the acquisition must be the fruit of one's own exertions or qualities'.[9] This notion of justice is consonant with Locke's approach, whereby 'justice gives every man a title to the product of his honest industry'.[10]

A person may justly pursue his own self-interest to gain to the maximum, provided he confines the means of that pursuit to 'honest industry' and does not seek to deprive others by unfair means of what their own industry has procured. Justice consists of respecting the private rights, and particularly the property rights, of others. As Goldwin put it: 'perhaps out of our [American] selfishness – that is, out of our sense of injustice (which is easily come by from the natural dislike of acts of unfairness to ourselves) – but in any case in some way there comes a strong sense of morality, of fairness, or aversion to unfairness'.[11]

Appreciating the place of liberty, property, and bourgeois ethics in the US ethos explains the importance that Americans attach to the distributive principle of desert. This principle of distributive justice, loosely defined as reward in proportion to contribution, commands wide support in the Western world, particularly in the USA[12]. Deservingness proportional to contribution, namely that what one should get is determined by what one produces, is closely connected, as an ethical principle, with the commutative justice criterion of fair exchange. Altogether, property achieved by 'honest industry' and distributed based on what one deserves constitutes an important element of the principle of fairness, as defined in Chapter 2. Furthermore, a certain amount of social and economic inequality generally has been considered compatible with the US conception of equality. Differences in property and status often are viewed as evidence not of inequality *per se*, but of individual distinction and achievement. 'Earned' inequalities are seen as the just outcome of fair competition among people of unequal talents and industry. Such emphasis on property, self-interest, and desert is the product of US institutional design. US democracy, Diamond observed, has never denied the unequal existence of human virtues and excellences. On the contrary, the US political order presupposes that an inequality of virtues and abilities is rooted in human nature and that this inequality manifests and flourishes in society's private realm. The protection of different faculties of acquiring property is the first object of government. The prevailing sentiment of US citizens is to accept the relative inequality that the adherence to desert entails. While the principle of equal opportunity is affirmed, most Americans reject equality of economic rewards ('equal outcome') and regard 'deserved' inequalities as natural to democratic life.[13] This is a constant feature of the US political landscape linking the Founders to modern times.[14]

Among the Founding Fathers, even those more inclined towards egalitarian views, such as Jefferson, remained firmly committed to a concept of property rights that promoted and justified unequal material rewards. In his second address as President of the USA, he affirmed his wish that 'equality of rights [be] maintained, and that state of property, equal or unequal, which results to every man from his own industry, or that of his father'.[15] At the same time, the primacy attributed to the pursuit of self-interest and property and the importance of the commercial spirit in the working of a free republic did not signify that there was no role for the government in mitigating economic inequality. For instance, Madison stressed that republicanism was strengthened 'by the silent operation of laws, which, without violating the rights of property, reduce extreme wealth towards a state of mediocrity, and raise extreme indigence towards a state of comfort'.[16] However, the Founders' desire to reduce economic inequality was always mitigated by their concern about preserving the legitimate rights to own property.

'Equal opportunities under fair conditions of competition,' while remaining a defining feature of the US ethos, has somewhat shifted in meaning as economic and social conditions have changed. For Americans of the late 18th and early 19th centuries, equal opportunity was linked to their deep distrust of government. A powerful central government would inevitably become the instrument of the rich and powerful to gain privileges and rob the commoners of their just earnings. The solution was to keep the government small: with less government intervention, the distribution of wealth and property would have become more equal than it was. Direct government action was considered to be 'the fruitful parent of nine-tenths of all the evil, moral and physical, by which mankind has been afflicted since the creation of the world, and by which human nature has been self-degraded, fettered and oppressed'.[17] The *laissez-faire* theories of the early 19th century were reinforced by the social Darwinism of the latter part of the century to stress the importance of competition in the US political culture. As the nation's development and industrialization accelerated after the Civil War, thousands of impoverished families, as well as many millionaires, were being created. William Sumner and other US social Darwinists regarded this situation as the result of natural selection, the survival of the fittest.

However, increasingly, equality of opportunity acquired a wider meaning in the face of industrial conglomerates' monopolistic practices, coupled with the urban working classes' inability to acquire the necessary education and skills required for success. A government-only intent to ensure equal protection under the law was not sufficient. The reform of the late 19th century aimed at breaking up monopolies and countering anticompetitive business practices represented an acknowledgement from both the Republican and the Democratic sides that positive government action was at times necessary to realize the ideal of equal opportunity. Indeed, such measures as the Clayton Antitrust Act were meant to stem abuses and to compel large corporations to adhere to fair competitive practices and the principles of free markets. The government's responsibility in ensuring a fair equality of opportunities was increasingly recognized during the New Deal period and further in the 1960s, when its role in smoothing out the business cycle and tackling social problems consolidated, without supplanting the Americans' basic faith in the fairness of economic individualism, competition, and private property.[18]

3.2 FAIRNESS IN THE DEVELOPMENT OF US INTERNATIONAL TRADE POLICY FROM ITS ORIGIN TO THE BEGINNING OF THE 1930s

The idea of desert-based fairness as fair competition has an important place in both the capitalist and democratic traditions of the USA. Its appeal has remained strong over the years because of its lineage, which harks back to the principle of fair play and commutative justice. However, as with many political ideas, it is often expressed at a level of generality that lends itself to differing and sometimes opposing policy outcomes.

In the trade policy context, the notion of fairness has had a significant influence under the guise of fair trade and reciprocity, as well as equality of treatment and non-discrimination. While it is quite difficult to disentangle these concepts, fairness could be considered the overall normative idea, while reciprocity, equality of treatment, and non-discrimination could be seen as causal ideas or, expressed more simply, operational prescriptions. Such prescriptions have often been translated into legal norms.

So strong has been the appeal of the notion of fairness that arguments, in order to gain broad acceptability, often have had to be cast so as to fit its mould. Indeed, ideas that command a large political and popular approval tend to constrain the available policy choices in a narrower range, as clearly inconsistent approaches are unlikely to be adopted, and if used, at least need to be (sometimes only rhetorically) modified.

Fairness, as well as equality of treatment and reciprocity, have endured virtually all phases of US commercial policy and usually have had to coexist with a strong tendency towards protectionism. Depending on the political situation and the prevailing interests at any particular time, fairness could be used to favour more or less opening of the domestic market. However, even during periods when the protectionist idea had gained the upper hand, the commitment to pursue fairness in foreign economic relations could not be dismissed. In this sense, the two approaches never have been incompatible.

How the notion of fairness has shaped the trade policy discourse, from the origin of the Republic to the 1930s, can be observed with reference to three main and partly connected issues that dominated the trade-related political debate during that period: the protective tariff, the development of so-called 'unfair' trade legislation, and 'equality of treatment' and reciprocity in trade treaties. The first two issues mostly affected imports into the USA, while the latter concerned the bargaining for access to foreign markets. The protective tariffs raised fairness concerns mainly with regard to the distribution of burdens and benefits between different groups in society, such as producers versus consumers, but primarily import-using and export-oriented versus import-competing producers. However, tariff protection as an instrument to retaliate against foreign trade barriers also grew in importance over time. Similar concerns with regard to unacceptable and injurious behaviour by foreign competitors in the US market also explains the introduction of specific legislation to combat 'unfair' trade practices at the beginning of the 20th century. The negotiation of commercial treaties instead was from the start dominated by the objective of fighting foreign barriers and ensuring that access to the domestic market was compensated by equal access in the other contracting party. This concern for reciprocity and equality of treatment has been a continuous element in the international economic relations of the Republic from its inception.

3.2.1 The Protective Tariff

One of the goals and expectations of US independence was the freedom to trade unconstrained by British laws and restrictions.[19] Many early US leaders were familiar with the writings of David Hume and Adam Smith. Liberal ideas had a strong appeal in US society, as they conform with the dominant images that Americans had of themselves.

> American workers aspired to be their own masters, and, far more than their European counterparts, they were owners of their land and tools of their trade. Americans saw their distinctiveness as the result of the absence of constraints of a class society and of their freedom to fulfil their economic potential. Thus developed the myth that an American worker was not only efficient but also free.[20]

John Adams, Thomas Jefferson, and James Madison all believed to a greater or lesser extent in free trade, but also considered that reciprocity was necessary to achieve it. In 1774, Jefferson asserted that 'free trade with all parts of the world' was a 'natural right'.[21] In a letter to Adams, he reiterated in 1785: 'I think all the world would gain by setting commerce at perfect liberty'.[22] Franklin expressed similar ideas: '... freedom of commerce ... is the right of all mankind. ... To enjoy all the advantages of the climate, soil, and situation in which God and nature have placed us, is as clear a right as that of breathing; and can never be justly taken from men but as a punishment for some atrocious crime'.[23] Madison's opinions were close. In writing to Jefferson in 1785, he said: 'Much indeed is it to be wished, as I conceive, that no regulations of trade, that is to say, no restrictions on imports whatever, were necessary. A perfect freedom is the system which would be my choice. But before such a system will be eligible, perhaps, for the United States, they must be out of debt; before it will be attainable, all other nations must concur in it'.[24] Hence, reciprocity was also a concern. In 1785 Jefferson wrote:

> We wish to do it [promote commerce] by throwing open all the doors of commerce and knocking off all its shackles. But as this cannot be done for others, unless they will do it for us, and there is no probability that Europe will do this, I suppose we may be obliged to adopt a system which may shackle them in our ports, as they do to us in theirs.[25]

Along similar lines, in 1786, Adams stated: 'The United States must repel monopolies by monopolies and answer prohibitions by prohibitions'.[26] The use of trade instruments, particularly the tariff, to fight foreign unfair trade practices was established at the outset of the Republic.

Actually, even before the birth of the Union, the colonies moved to penalize British interests by disrupting commerce in an attempt to punish the Motherland, which, in their view, was exploiting them unfairly.

> The 'first complete piece of national commercial legislation' in [America] was the resolution of the first Continental Congress of 20 October 1774, creating what was called the 'continental association'. According to this resolution, the importation of all goods from Great Britain or Ireland, of various products from British West Indies, and tea from East India, was to cease. A later resolution sought to stop all exportation to the places just named. These resolutions were adopted by nearly all colonies and so vigorously enforced that both imports from and exports to British territory fell to the vanishing point.[27]

While colonists benefited from 18th century Atlantic commerce with Britain, they also felt the aggravation of higher taxes and commercial regulations (such as the British Navigation Acts) meant to sustain the empire and the mercantile system. Thus merchants and colonial leaders, such as Benjamin Franklin, were led to seek the establishment of a new nation that would, *inter alia*, protect US commerce and promote US industry and agriculture.

During the years of the Confederation, the need for revenue and the desire to protect local industries were contentious issues among the 13 states. Under the Articles of Confederation, they retained the power to levy taxes and regulate commerce, and they did so by imposing both import and export tariffs *vis-à-vis* their sister states, in order to raise revenue and protect local manufacturers. Between 1776 and 1789, without the authority to effectively levy taxes, the new government was devoid of actual economic and political power. This arrangement proved to be very ineffectual, both with regard to internal economic development and with respect to negotiations of commercial treaties with third parties. It led to the conviction that commerce ought to be regulated by Congress.[28] Thus the Constitution of 1787 entrusted Congress with the responsibility to regulate commerce and levy taxes (Art. I:8), forbade the states to discriminate against the commerce and citizens of sister states (Art. I:10 and IV:2), and assigned to the executive branch the power to conduct diplomatic relations and negotiate treaties subject to Congress's approval (Art. II:2). This arrangement created a two-pronged commercial policy: Congress was to fix tariffs and regulate commerce and the Executive was to negotiate with foreign countries. The government's role in trade policy-making was then firmly established. However, the extent of this role has remained a bone of contention ever since, with the small-government, Jeffersonian vision clashing with the more interventionist, Hamiltonian approach.

The first tariff of the USA, contained in the Tariff Act of 1789, imposed a moderate, single-schedule tariff, applying the same rate of duty of about 8 per cent *ad valorem* to all countries. Earlier, Madison had proposed a plan of duties for revenues only, but a plan largely based on the existing Pennsylvania system of protection was preferred to his approach.[29] This plan was meant to be 'protective in intention and spirit' by raising revenues, promoting infant industries, and ensuring reciprocity.[30] The War of Independence had stimulated the development of several industries, particularly in the northern states, which immediately became strong and vocal advocates of protection. However, the problem of how the benefits and burdens deriving from international trade were to be apportioned already had emerged. Against the plea for high tariffs, Representative Tucker, from South Carolina, argued: 'The reason for which I am opposed to high duties on enumerated articles is, because it tends to the oppression of certain description of citizens and particular states, in order to promote the advantages of other states and other citizens'.[31] The arguments for protection were later developed in the *Reports on Manufactures* prepared by Alexander Hamilton in his capacity as Secretary of the Treasury, in reply to Washington's call for limited protection. He made a thorough examination of the need for protection in order to respond to unfair practices of foreign nations and to encourage the development of infant industries and manufactures necessary for national defence.[32] He analysed the various means available to promote 'useful manufactures', focusing on duties and 'bounties' (i.e., subsidies), generally finding the latter preferable to the former. However, the US Congress chose the opposite course, declining to enact his proposed system of bounties. While he supported free trade in theory, Hamilton noted that manufacturing nations, such as Britain, sought to preserve a 'monopoly of the domestic market to its own manufactures.' Thus, in order to ensure 'reciprocity of advantages', the USA needed to pursue a 'similar policy'.[33]

This low-tariff policy lasted until the Napoleonic wars, when US neutral rights were generally disregarded. This led President Jefferson to use sanctions, including trade bans and embargoes, and his successor, President Madison, to embark on the ill-fated war against Britain in 1812. After the war,

British merchants used dumping in the US market to dispose of inventories accumulated during the war years; a policy that was openly acknowledged. For instance, in a speech before Parliament in 1816, Lord Brougham stressed that 'it was well worthwhile to incur a loss upon the first exportation in order by the glut to stifle in the cradle those rising manufactures in the United States which the war had forced into existence contrary to the usual course of things'.[34] This entrenched the demands of protection for fledging US manufacturers. A more nationalistic Congress, led by House Speaker Henry Clay, enacted a substantially higher tariff. The nationalistic trade policy that ensued, known as the 'American System', lasted until World War II, with tariffs averaging more than 25 per cent *ad valorem* in all but six years and 40 per cent or higher in sixty of those years.[35] 'Internal improvements', such as the federally sponsored construction of canals and turnpikes, were to be financed from the proceeds of the tariff.[36] 'In the nineteenth-century America substantial tariffs were not simply trade barriers imposed to advance the narrow interests of favored manufacturers. They served a larger national purpose, one intended to secure American independence from foreign interference and to promote national prosperity'.[37] In his 1823 annual message, President Monroe urged continued protection in the name of national defence and economic independence: 'I recommend a review of the tariff for the purpose of affording such additional protection to those articles which we are prepared to manufacture, or which are more immediately connected with the defence and independence of the country'.[38]

However, the idea of fairness was still exerting influence. In his 1829 message, President Jackson stated that: 'The general rules to be applied in graduating the duties upon articles of foreign growth or manufacture is that which will place our own in fair competition with those of other countries'.[39] In these years, the issue of wage differentials also emerged, as wages in the USA were reckoned to be higher than abroad. Protection was considered necessary to preserve such wages.[40] Hence, domestic fairness concerns between different groups of producers were also hotly debated. A redistributive measure such as the tariff could not but elicit strong fairness issues. In commenting on the passage of the 1824 tariff bill, democratic Senator Hayne stated:

> Considering this scheme of promoting certain employments at the expense of others as unequal, oppressive, and unjust, viewing prohibition as the means and the destruction of all foreign commerce the end of this policy, I take this occasion to declare that we shall feel ourselves justified in embracing the very first opportunity of repealing all such laws as may be passed for the promotion of these objects.[41]

In the period leading up to the civil war, political controversies over trade policy continued to emphasize the issue of fairness between different groups of the US polity.[42] In his message to Congress in 1832, President Jackson said:

> Large interests have grown up under the implied pledge of our national legislation, which it would seem a violation of public faith to suddenly abandon. Nothing could justify it but the public safety, which is the supreme law. But those who have invested their capital in manufacturing establishments cannot expect that the people will continue permanently to pay high taxes for their benefit (in the form of high prices supported by tariffs) when the money is not required for any legitimate purpose in the administration of government'.[43]

The south opposed the tariff as detrimental to the export of cotton and argued that protective duties imposed a tax on consumers, harming workers and the poor to the benefit of particular interests; burdened agriculture; and promoted smuggling. Furthermore, in the south, the tariff was seen as a redistributive instrument used by the north to fund expensive internal improvements.

Jackson was mindful of the risks of sectional divisions and tried to reduce some duties, but Congress did not follow him, and the Tariff of 1832 basically confirmed the high duties introduced with the so-called 'Tariff of Abominations' of 1828, leading South Carolina to threaten secession. As the need for revenue had subsided, and confronted with an actual peril for national unity, Congress agreed to a compromise brokered by Clay in 1833. The deal limited tariffs in most cases to revenue purposes, thus prevailing over Northern support for protective duties. Under the influence of 'tariff-for-revenue-only' Democrats, duties declined from an average of about 60 per cent in 1830 to less than 20 per cent in 1860.[44] The domestic fairness concern that animated the Democratic position in these years was clearly expressed by Secretary of the Treasury Walker, who in his report to Congress in 1845 stated that when considering tariffs, the government should adhere to a number of principles, including: 'That the duty should be so imposed as to operate as equally as possible throughout the Union, discriminating neither for or against any class or region'.[45] However, the Republican emphasis on the defence of the US worker through the protective tariff was part of a broader ideology, which had as its basis 'a belief in the dignity and rights of labor. In their critique of southern slave labor, the Republicans extolled the superiority of the capitalist system, which enabled the average laboring men to prosper.'[46] Tariffs would protect against unfair foreign labour competition; they would protect free labour from foreign slavery. As such, the Republican preference for high tariffs cannot be dismissed as a simple protectionist device catering to domestic industrial interests; it also had fairness-related ramifications.

From the Civil War until the depression of the 1930s, Congress was dominated by protectionist lawmakers, and every Republican presidential candidate ran on a platform supporting the protective system. This meant an upward trend in tariff rates, which continued with very few exceptions for the rest of the 19th century.[47] Already in 1864, Congress had increased duties to an average rate of 47 per cent *ad valorem*.[48] With some changes in specific rates and a short-lived 10 per cent reduction in 1872, the 1864 Tariff Act remained the basis of US tariff policy until 1883. During this period, Democrats with a strong support base in the rural south continued to argue in favour of promoting exports and limiting tariffs, which they saw as exploiting consumers for the benefit of rich monopolists. However, during the period between the Civil War and the New Deal, many protectionist battles were won with the help of individual Democrats.

In 1884, the Democrat Grover Cleveland, governor of New York, won the presidency and tried to pursue the reduction of tariffs sought by his party. He defined 'our present tariff laws, the vicious, inequitable, and illogical source of unnecessary taxation, [which] ought to be at once revised and amended'.[49] While he favoured tariffs for revenue, he did not oppose duties, which could protect domestic producers through an equalization of conditions of production. As such, tariffs 'render it possible for those of our people who are manufacturers to make these taxed articles and sell them for a price equal to that demanded for the imported goods that have paid customs duty'.[50] What Cleveland fought was 'excessive' tariffs, which allowed colluding manufacturers to keep prices high; what he advocated was a fair distribution of the tariff burden. In this regard, Republicans attacked him as a friend of the British monopolists, who were eager to exploit the US market, and as an enemy of US workers, who could see their wages reduced because of foreign competition. Cleveland's plan to lower the tariff, and to substitute it with an income tax during his second mandate (1893–97), did not succeed, as he lacked a Democratic majority in Congress, and an economic crisis in 1893 weakened his position.

In the 1888 election, Cleveland had been defeated by the Republican Henry Harrison, who favoured high tariffs. During his administration the policy of nurturing infant industries became 'a policy of fostering the embryo, rather than protecting the infant'.[51] However, the pressure to reduce tariffs continued, albeit without much success. The Democrats emphasized that the high protective tariff amounted to the perversion of government powers in pursuit of 'the policy of unjust and unequal taxation of the many for the benefit of the few'.[52] The tariff was essentially a policy of discrimination. The 1890 McKinley Act, while significantly increasing duties, also enacted the principle of reciprocity.[53] Thus tariffs could be used to pressure foreign nations into allowing US imports. The tariff treatment for a number of items was made contingent upon the foreign treatment of like or similar products from the USA. A less favourable, but not necessarily discriminatory treatment by a foreign country, was met with a reimposition or an increase in duty. This represented a departure from the consolidated, US non-discriminatory tariff policy embodied in the single-column schedule. Reciprocity gave the President authority to punish countries that did not give US exporters fair access to their markets. However, reciprocity should come without injury to domestic workers and producers of import-competing goods. This was a key fairness principle that has played an enduring role in US trade policy.

In 1892 Cleveland was elected for a second term. The Wilson–Gorman Act of 1894 was a moderate step in the direction of tariff reduction. Reciprocity was abandoned, as the Democrats considered that 'the McKinley reciprocity policy was "in intention and effect" not for reciprocity but for retaliation, that it provoked ill feeling in countries discriminated against'.[54] In 1896, the Republicans regained a majority in the House of Representatives and elected McKinley to the White House. Shortly after, the 1897 tariff, the Dingley Act, reversed the policy of tariff reduction and introduced significant tariff increases. It also reinstated reciprocity as a policy objective. The Act served as the basis of US tariff policy until 1909.

At the beginning of the 20th century, protection remained entrenched. In 1901, Theodore Roosevelt, in his first annual presidential message, stressed that: 'every application of our tariff policy to meet our shifting national needs must be conditioned upon the cardinal fact that the duties must never be reduced below the point that will cover the difference between the labor cost here and abroad. The well-being of the wage-worker is a prime consideration of our entire policy of economic legislation'.[55] This approach was restated in the 1908 Republican platform, which dubbed it the 'true principle' of protection. 'In all protective legislation the true principle of protection is best maintained by the imposition of such duties as will equal the difference between the cost of production at home and abroad, together with a reasonable profit to American industries'.[56] Such an approach ensured that US goods would be generally cheaper than foreign goods, thus essentially defeating the notion of comparative advantage. As Taussig noted, anything can be made within any country if the producer is assured a price high enough to cover all the costs of production together with a reasonable allowance for profits.[57] The true principle thus 'seems to say – no favors, no undue protection; nothing but equalization of conditions. Yet little acumen is needed to see that, carried out consistently, it means simple prohibition and complete stoppage of trade'.[58]

While standing firm behind protection, the business community also started to become concerned about discrimination against US products abroad. The National Association of Manufacturers (NAM), founded in 1895, urged the adoption of a dual schedule tariff, already largely used in Europe, with maximum and minimum rates, which would give the Executive leverage and discretion to negotiate reciprocal access to foreign markets.[59] The Payne–Aldrich Tariff of 1909, while introducing some reduction in duties as demanded by President Taft, also allowed the Executive more flexible powers to increase duties in case of discrimination by foreign countries. The Act introduced a system of minimum and maximum rates, setting the limits within which the President was authorized to retaliate. The President was allowed to increase the minimum duty by 25 per cent on imports from countries that were 'unduly discriminatory' to US exports. Discrimination was broadly defined as either high foreign tariffs or export bounties. The Act also created a Tariff Board to advise the President on this new authority.

A pronounced split over the tariff questions developed in the Republican Party during Taft's administration. On one side was the conservative element, the so-called 'standpatters', who wanted a high tariff and opposed the kind of reforms that Roosevelt had initiated. On the other side were the so-called 'insurgents', later known as progressives, who denounced the high rates of the Payne–Aldrich tariff, sought to regulate tariffs with more attention to the interest of the consumer, and criticized the administration for refusing to continue the reforms begun by Roosevelt, who openly sided with the progressives. In January 1911, the Republican senator LaFollette organized the National Republican Progressive League to take political action for the principles of the progressive element in the Republican Party. Standpatters and progressive Republicans engaged in a bitter battle for control of the Republican national convention of June 1912. Defeated in their efforts, the progressives, led by Roosevelt, organized the Progressive Party and nominated Roosevelt for president. The Republican convention renominated Taft.

On that occasion, the traditional position of the Republican Party was once more emphasized. The notion of fairness as between domestic industry and workers and foreign competitors was again present. The Republican platform stated:

> The Republican tariff policy has been of the greatest benefit to the country, developing, our resources, diversifying our industries, and protecting our working men against competition with cheap labor abroad, thus establishing for our wage-earners the American standard of living. We hold that the import duties should be high enough, while yielding a sufficient revenue, to protect adequately American industries and wages. Some of the existing import duties are too high, and should be reduced. Readjustments should be made from time to time to conform to changing conditions and to reduce excessive rates, but without injury to any American industry.[60]

The no injury principle remained key.

In 1912 a Democrat, Woodrow Wilson, won the presidential election and the Democratic Party also gained control of both houses of Congress. Issues of fairness, albeit from a different perspective, were present in the Democratic platform, which stated: 'The high Republican tariff is the principal cause of the unequal distribution of wealth. It is a system of taxation which makes the rich richer and the poor poorer'.[61] Democrats stressed that farmers and industrial workers were hurt by the protective tariff, which 'raises the cost of necessaries of life to them, but does not protect their product or wages'.[62] An important issue in the debate surrounding high tariffs was that it provided domestic firms with an opportunity to price monopolistically at home, while at the same time it protected them from the reimportation of goods they sold competitively in world markets. Many Democrats thus saw the tariff as the handmaiden of domestic monopolies. Cordell Hull, who was to become the key figure in US trade policy of the 1930s and 1940s, recalled in his memoirs that in his first speech as Democratic Representative in 1907 he 'made a vigorous attack on the high tariff and the monopolies and trusts that had grown up behind it. No kind of effort to curb and suppress trust violators [can] succeed unless such effort strikes at the main source of their constant creation – the protective tariff'.[63] Wilson decided to lower tariffs, as he considered that 'the object of tariff duties must be effective competition, the whetting of American wits by contest with the wits of the rest of the world'.[64] The Democratic Congress followed the President and passed the Underwood–Simmons Act of 1913, which halved the average duties.[65] This was the only significant deviation from the long-term upward trend in tariffs since the Civil War. However, while replacing the notion of the equalization of production costs with that of the 'competitive tariff', the Democratic reform still fully accepted the need for protection. The competitive tariff should protect only 'legitimate industries'. It was not clarified at which level an industry was overly protected and thus became illegitimate, and the method to calculate the competitive tariff was quite close to the Republican equalization of production costs.[66] The main difference between the two parties resided in the preferred level at which to set tariff rates.[67]

The provisions for maximum and minimum duties and the Tariff Board were eliminated. The Act also continued the emphasis on the principle of reciprocity. However, World War I disrupted commerce, providing a different but effective form of protection to US producers, while not permitting them to tackle foreign discrimination. Furthermore, the Wilson Administration sought to promote the League of Nations and a multilateral approach to reduce trade barriers. As the conflict ended, US business grew even more concerned about cheap European imports and barriers to US exports overseas.

These fears played into the hands of Republicans, who had regained the presidency with Warren Harding. Agricultural commodity prices fell drastically in 1920 and 1921 because of overproduction resulting from the recovery of European agricultural output after the cessation of the hostilities,

and Congress raised duties on agricultural products through emergency tariff
legislation. Congress also passed the 1921 Antidumping Act. In 1922,
the Republican Congress introduced a thorough tariff revision with the
Fordney–McCumber Act, which incorporated the higher emergency duties
introduced the previous year for a number of agricultural commodities, as well
as new protection for the 'war babies', industries characterized by war-
stimulated production of goods that had previously been imported. Currency
depreciation in Europe fuelled the fear that foreign producers could engage in
exchange rate dumping. Having obtained emergency protection for
agricultural commodities, farmer representatives were unable to effectively
stem the increase in duties in other sectors. 'Logrolling' held sway in
Congress.[68] 'The outcome was a tariff with rates higher than any in the long
series of protective measures'.[69] Average tariffs went up from about 9 per cent
under the Underwood Act to 14 per cent.

The Act was based on the principle of the equalization of foreign and
domestic costs of production. This principle had been included already in the
Republican Party's platforms of 1904 and 1908. But before that, the platform
of 1892 also had stated that 'on all imports coming into competition with the
products of American labor, there should be levied duties equal to the
difference between wages abroad and at home'. Similarly, the Democratic
Party's platforms of 1884 and 1888 contained essentially the same idea of
equalizing foreign and domestic wages.[70] This principle was finally enacted in
Section 315 of the Fordney–McCumber Act, which allowed the President to
increase or lower the duty prescribed in the Act by 50 per cent whenever he
determined that this was necessary to equalize costs between the USA and the
principal competing foreign country. Such modification in duty could be
effected after the independent Tariff Commission, created in 1916, had
investigated the issue. However, the provision proved very difficult to
administer because of the inherent difficulties associated with computing
production costs.[71]

After 1890 and increasingly up to the 1920s, the difference between
Republican and Democrats over the protective tariff had diminished so
that:

> the differences that exist between the two great parties are not the issue of
> protection against free trade, but the true issue is that one desires to write a
> protective tariff that leans towards prohibition of imports and the other a revenue
> tariff that favors fair competition. Although we occasionally find a free-trader
> within the ranks of the Democratic party, the great rank and file of the party do not
> favor the doctrine of free trade.[72]

The protection of domestic industries and workers was accepted by both
parties, albeit the level and extent of such protection remained hotly debated,

in good measure because of the unfair distribution of burdens and benefits that the tariff engendered, which was the core of the fairness concern in the domestic context.[73]

A further revision and increase in US duties was enacted after a tense and protracted period of hearings and debate in Congress between January 1929 and June 1930 with the Tariff Act of 1930, better known as the Hawley–Smoot Tariff.[74] The Hawley–Smoot Tariff grew out of the campaign promises of Herbert Hoover during the 1928 presidential election. Hoover, the Republican candidate, had pledged to help farmers by raising tariffs on imports of farm products. Although the 1920s were generally a period of prosperity in the USA, this was not true for agriculture; average farm incomes actually declined between 1920 and 1929. The Act was the last exercise in unhindered congressional tariff-making. The House concluded its work relatively quickly and passed a bill on 28 May by a vote of 264 to 147. The bill faced a considerably more difficult time in the Senate. A block of Progressive Republicans, representing midwestern and western states, held the balance of power in the Senate. Some of these Senators had supported the third-party candidacy of Wisconsin Senator Robert LaFollette during the 1924 presidential election, and they were much less protectionist than the Republican Party as a whole. It proved impossible to put together a majority in the Senate to pass the bill, and the special session ended in November 1929 without a bill being passed.

By the time Congress reconvened the following spring, the Great Depression was well under way. Economists date the onset of the Great Depression to the cyclical peak of August 1929, although the stock market crash of October 1929 is more generally regarded as its inception. By the spring of 1930, it was already clear that the downturn would be severe. The impact of the Depression helped to secure the final few votes necessary to put together a slim majority in the Senate in favour of the bill. Final passage in the Senate took place on 13 June 1930 by a vote of 44 to 42 and in the House the following day with a larger majority of 245 to 177. The vote was cast largely along party lines. Republicans in the House voted 230 to 27 in favour of final passage. Ten of the 27 Republicans voting 'no' were Progressives from Wisconsin and Minnesota. Democrats voted 150 to 15 against final approval. Ten of the 15 Democrats voting for final passage were from Louisiana or Florida and represented citrus or sugar interests that received significant new protection under the bill.

President Hoover had expressed reservations about the bill's wide-ranging nature and had privately expressed fears that the bill might provoke retaliation from the USA's trading partners. He received a petition signed by more than one thousand economists, urging him to veto the bill. Ultimately, he signed the Hawley–Smoot bill into law on 17 June 1930. 'The Tariff Act of

1930 ... brought no change in the United States tariff policy. It simply reaffirmed and reinforced the high protective principle of the Tariff Act of 1922 by raising duties even higher'.[75]

For the first time in a tariff act, the protection of labour interests was explicitly mentioned in the title, which read: 'An Act to provide revenue, to regulate commerce with foreign countries, to encourage the industries of the United States, to protect American labor, and for other purposes'. In this regard, Representative Hawley claimed during the discussion of the bill that the average rate of wages abroad was 40 per cent lower than in the USA.[76] The Act also maintained the provision on equalization of costs of production included in the 1922 tariff. Section 336(a) of the Act, entitled 'Equalization of the Costs of Production', provided that the Tariff Commission shall, on request of the President or of either or both Houses of Congress, on its own motion, or on application of an interested party, 'investigate the differences in the costs of production of any domestic article and of any like or similar foreign article'. The Act specified that this rule be applied in order to give effect to the Congress-mandated policy aiming at the promotion of domestic industries and the protection of US labour. If the Commission found that the duty fixed by statute did not equalize such differences in production costs, it was required to report to the President and to specify what increases or decreases of duty, within a maximum of 50 per cent, were necessary to effect such equalization. The President was given the uncontrolled authority to approve or not the changes proposed by the Commission. In line with the practice under Section 315 of the 1922 act, President Hoover used such authority to raise tariffs on many products and to reduce tariffs on only a few. However, Hoover had justified his signing of the Hawley–Smoot Act on the grounds that the authority granted him under Section 336 should make it possible 'to secure prompt and scientific adjustment' of any 'serious inequities and inequalities' contained in the Act. He added: 'I do not assume that the rate structure in this or any other tariff bill is perfect. ... I believe that the flexible provisions can within reasonable time remedy inequalities; that this provision is a progressive advance and gives great hope of taking the tariff away from politics, lobbying and logrolling'.[77]

The protectionist theory put forward by the sponsors of the Hawley–Smoot bill could be summarized as follows:

> domestic producers are entitled to a 'preferential' position in the American market; because of lower costs abroad – principally labor costs – a tariff is necessary to insure this; competition between American producers prevents tariffs from raising prices; the test to apply in determining the need for higher rates is the increase in imports; tariffs help rather than injure our foreign trade; everyone enjoys the benefit of the tariff; our position as a creditor nation is not to be given any consideration in the determination of our tariff policy.[78]

Albeit in the context of such a dominating protectionist approach, fairness concerns regarding the distribution of benefits and burdens from trade policy decisions (particularly higher or lower tariffs) remained important. An interesting example is the notion entertained by many western and southern Congressmen that a 'just' tariff was one that gave 'tariff equality' to agriculture. The line of thinking was as follows: 'as the staple agricultural crops are all on an export basis, the only way in which the benefits of the bounty system known as protection can be extended to the farmer is by granting a bounty on his exports'.[79] While the proposal was not accepted, it played a significant role in the tariff debates.

The main line of opposition to the Hawley–Smoot bill stressed that duties were higher than needed to 'equalize costs of production' or that they conferred unfair benefits to domestic monopolies, special interests, or specific geographical groups. The conviction that high duties enabled domestic monopolies, which, freed from foreign competition, could exploit the US consumer, was diametrically opposed to the view of the bill's proponents, who assumed effective competition in the USA and monopolies abroad.[80] An appreciation of the importance of comparative advantage in trade relations was almost absent. Similarly downplayed in the debates were some traditional protectionist arguments, such as infant industry and national security. However, a number of Eastern protectionists opposed a high tariff on food-stuffs and raw materials because they raised the costs of living and production. Republican Representative La Guardia, for instance, while advocating the tariff to protect US labour, opposed high tariffs on cement, sugar, and butter and denounced an increase in the potato duty on the grounds that it 'is not a protection for American industry, it is nothing but downright larceny'.[81]

The economic consequences of this climax in US protectionist policy are well known, albeit their extent and gravity remain a matter of debate.[82] Beyond that, this policy raised important fairness-related issues. If the proponents saw it as a way to re-establish an equality of conditions in international trade in the primary interest of domestic producers, opponents viewed it as a negation of a fair distribution of benefits and burdens in international trade. A contemporary commentator considered that 'the object of the legislation is "to encourage the industries of the United States" and "to protect American labor" by equalizing the costs of production at home and abroad, and in so doing to expropriate money from importers and consumers of goods, both foreign and domestic, and bestow it upon domestic producers'.[83] The opposition of many in Congress, including Republicans who opposed the bill, was not grounded in a stance against protection *per se*, but was simply predicated on the belief that producers would not gain and the benefits had not been fairly distributed.

Furthermore, the Act caused a large number of protests from trading partners, which also led to the introduction of retaliatory duties against US exports.[84] Upward tariff revisions selectively aimed against US exports followed Hawley–Smoot in Australia, Canada, Cuba, France, Italy, Mexico, New Zealand, Spain, and other countries. As Cordell Hull recalled in his memoirs: 'when I came into the State Department I found in the files no fewer than thirty-four formal and emphatic diplomatic protests presented by as many nations, following the passage of the Hawley–Smoot high tariff Act. Nor had their protests been confined to words ... they retaliated in kind'.[85] The Act encouraged the expansion of the British preferential system in the 1932 Ottawa Agreements, and it gave impetus to discriminatory, bilateral, trade-balancing practices everywhere.

In summary, during the 19th and early 20th centuries, US trade policy approach remained firmly protectionist. During this period, the protective tariff was a major issue of national political debate and controversy. Protection against import competition was generally justified on infant industry and national defence grounds and to defend the well-being of US workers. In this context, the fairness idea played an important role, supporting the view that national economic development should be shielded from unfair foreign practices, such as the dumping of British goods after the Napoleonic wars and the importation of foreign goods produced by pauper labour in Europe and Asia. By ignoring the differences in factor productivity across countries, the protective tariff was thought to ensure the equalization of conditions of competition. Foreign producers and workers were thus prevented, as the argument went, from taking unfair advantage of US producers and workers and from taking over the US market, which would lead (after driving out US producers) to higher prices. Protection instead would guarantee higher wages and levels of employment for US workers. In the long run, consumers also would gain, it was argued, as the country's industrial development would eventually result in lower prices. Competition among domestic producers would ensure reasonable consumer prices. However, what the protective tariff actually did in this phase was to eliminate comparative advantages, thus often affecting the international distribution of benefits and burdens. Penalty duties were also used as a way to combat foreign discriminatory practices, but without much success.

Strong fairness concerns were also voiced against the protective tariffs, which were seen as unfairly favouring some producer groups and regions over others (particularly those with specific export interests, which could not use cheap foreign inputs), supporting domestic monopolies, and operating against the national interest of guaranteeing a domestic competitive market and ultimately hurting workers and consumers.

The use of the protective tariff also needs to be considered in connection with the US policy stance *vis-à-vis* quantitative restrictions. These devices were used extensively during World War I as emergency measures, but were only partially dismantled after the end of the hostilities. They remained rather widespread, particularly in central and eastern Europe during the 1920s and became very common in the following decade. France was the first country to reintroduce quantitative restrictions on a large scale during the 1930s,[86] and by 1932, 11 European countries had fully-fledged import quota systems.[87] If not their original intent, quantitative restrictions proved to be effective instruments for protecting domestic industries. The USA hardly used such instruments at all, while being hurt, already during the 1920s, by prohibitions and restrictions imposed by third countries, for instance with regard to its automobile exports. But, more importantly for the present discussion, the USA objected in principle to quantitative restrictions, as these were considered an 'improper form of trade control'. 'The United States view was that if domestic industries were to be protected from foreign competition, then this protection should take the form of tariffs. The reason for this ... preference ... can be accounted for in part ... as a reflection of the United States devotion to the free-enterprise economic system'.[88] Quantitative restrictions are indeed inimical to the market-based price mechanism. They sever the link between domestic and world markets and do not allow price adjustments via changes in trade volumes. Furthermore, they are discriminatory, as they lead to distortions in trade patterns, which unfairly favour some foreign suppliers and domestic importers over others.[89] This would be the case, even if an equitable-share approach in the allocation of import licences were used, based on the 'normal volume of trade' commensurate to a previous 'representative period', since the choice of such a period would always be open to contention.[90]

The objective of abolishing quantitative restrictions was repeated in many declarations of the postwar economic conferences: the Brussels Financial Conference of 1920, the Portorose Conference of 1921, and the Genoa Conference of 1922.[91] An agreement reached at the 1923 Geneva Conference on the Simplification of Customs Formalities committed its signatories to reduce quantitative restrictions 'as soon as circumstances permit ... to the smallest number', but did not set a definite time for their removal.[92] Furthermore, in 1927 and 1928, two Conferences on the Abolition of Import and Export Restrictions drafted a Convention to that effect.[93] The Convention provided for the abolition of all import and export prohibitions and restrictions within a period of six months, subject to two types of exceptions. First, various prohibitions and restrictions related to national defence, public health, public morality, and the like were considered acceptable. Second, and more controversially, the Convention allowed the imposition of prohibitions and restrictions necessary to meet 'extraordinary and abnormal circumstances and to protect the vital economic and financial interests of the State'. The USA, together with other countries, favoured a tightening of this safeguard provision, and at the 1927 conference it was agreed that exempted prohibitions and restrictions were to be listed in an annex to the Convention. Another Conference the following year dealt specifically with this issue. At the Conference, a number of countries also made the connection between quantitative restrictions and high tariffs. Freedom of trade could not be achieved only by reducing quotas. But the USA refused to discuss tariffs, in line with its approach that tariffs were a matter of strict domestic concern, and thus no reference to them was included in the Convention. Not enough states ratified the Convention and by 1934, the USA withdrew, together with the other seven countries that had given effect to it. Albeit in the context of a very high, non-negotiable tariff, the rejection of quantitative restrictions, together with the adoption of the unconditional form of the MFN pledge (which is discussed in Section 3.2.3), defined the parameters of US non-discrimination policy, which were later to become constitutive elements of the GATT edifice. This policy, together with the principle of no injury to domestic producers as a result of tariff reductions, had in the fairness idea an important normative underpinning.

3.2.2   Unfair Trade Legislation

The protective tariffs performed the function of shielding domestic producer from import competition from the inception of the Republic. This role began to diminish only in the mid-1930s, when a general movement towards tariff reduction finally set in. Together with the infant industry and the national defence arguments, the fight against 'unfair foreign competition' has been among the prominent issues of US trade policy since Hamilton's Report on Manufactures. And by the mid-1930s, the main prongs of US unfair trade legislation had already been established.

Hamilton warned about foreign country dumping aimed at underselling competitors in other countries so as to 'frustrate the first efforts to introduce [a business] … into another by temporary sacrifices, recompensed, perhaps by extraordinary indemnifications of the government of such country …'.[94] With regard to export bounties specifically, Hamilton lamented that foreign countries used them in order to 'enable their own workers to undersell and supplant all competitors in countries to which … commodities are sent'.[95] Hence, as the international economy became more complex and governments' interventions in foreign trade more pervasive, the US Congress felt that it was necessary to defend the degree of protection afforded by the tariff. Foreign export 'bounties' were viewed as means of neutralizing US duties. Hence, countervailing duties were introduced in the tariff legislation as a way to offset the amount of the subsidy and, therefore, to restore the tariff's effectiveness.

Congress enacted the first countervailing duty provision in 1890.[96] The provision aimed to protect US sugar producers, which were exposed to competition from European firms being subsidized by their respective governments.[97] Indeed, the practice of granting bounties to foster domestic production in addition to protective duties had spread rapidly throughout Europe in the late 1870s and 1880s. The Tariff Act of 1897 generalized the countervailing duty provision to all subsidized imports that were otherwise dutiable. In section 5 of the 1897 Act, Congress provided: 'That whenever any country ..., shall pay ..., directly or indirectly, any bounty ... upon the exportation of any article ..., and such article ... is dutiable under the provision of this act ..., there shall be levied ... an additional duty equal to the amount of the net amount of such bounty ...'.[98] These provisions remained essentially unchanged until 1979, when the US countervailing duty law was changed to conform to the agreement reached in the Tokyo Round of Multilateral Trade Negotiations.

Summarizing the provision's rationale, Representative Skinner stated: 'We do not say to them, you shall or shall not impose this tax or this bounty, but we do say that when we find your export bounty or other device enables you to come here and undersell our own people, we will meet you at the shore with a countervailing duty'.[99] However, there was no statutory need to prove any injury to domestic producers. It was the negation of tariff protection (and the nullification of the benefit it allegedly produced) by means of the bounty that was considered unacceptable. Hence, the subsidized imports of goods that did not receive tariff protection could not be countervailed. Countervailing provisions were also included in the Tariff Acts of 1909 and 1913. The Tariff Act of 1913 provided that when 'any country, dependency, colony, province, or other political subdivision of government' granted any bounty on the exportation of any article and that article was imported into the USA, it was to be subjected to an additional duty equal to the net amount of the bounty. Several early countervailing duties were targeted at tax subsidies on sugar exports. The law provided for countervailing duties only when the bounty or grant was made by a governmental organization. However, as Culbertson noted: 'the most insidious and undesirable preferential treatment accorded to exporters', including preferential railroad and steamship rates, were granted by 'private cartels or associations' and other organizations, which were used 'as a cloak for Government activities'.[100]

In an important change in 1922, Congress expanded the scope of the countervailing provisions to offset subsidies granted to the 'manufacture and production of goods'.[101] From then on, US legislation covered both export and domestic production subsidies. Following the same approach, the Tariff Act of 1930 (which continued until 1995 to govern cases involving dutiable imports from nations that had not acceded to the GATT 1979 Subsidies Code) provided that, if another country had paid a 'bounty or a grant upon the manufacture or production or export' of any dutiable product, then upon importation of that product into the USA, the Secretary of the Treasury was to assess and collect a countervailing duty equal to the bounty or grant.[102] Unlike the dumping laws, for many years there was no inquiry into the effect of the subsidy on US industries prior to issuing a countervailing duty order. The injury test was not introduced until the 1974 Trade Act.

The enactment of the first countervailing provision coincided with that of the first antitrust statute, the Sherman Antitrust Act,[103] thus starting an interesting, albeit sometimes difficult, relationship between the body of 'unfair trade' laws and antitrust laws. The Sherman Act, the basic charter of US antitrust doctrine, the 'Magna Carta of free enterprise', as the US Supreme Court later described it,[104] demonstrates the importance Congress attached to protecting undistorted competition. It prohibits, under severe penalties, every contract or combination that restrains interstate or foreign commerce and every monopolization of or attempt to monopolize such commerce. Thus, it broadly proscribes practices, including predation, that unduly restrain competition, in particular, focusing on coordinated anticompetitive activities among firms. However, the Supreme Court's interpretation limited the application of the Act in the area of domestic commerce. In section 73 of the Wilson Tariff Act of 1894, Congress attempted to extend the scope of the Sherman Act to imports by making unlawful every conspiracy or combination that was engaged in importing and intended to restrain trade or to increase the US price of imported articles. The provision did not prove very effective. Until 1923 the law was invoked only once, against an association of US bankers and importers and the Brazilian state of São Paulo, to limit Brazilian exports and thereby rig the price of coffee in the US market.[105]

In 1914, the Clayton Antitrust Act expanded the prohibition of anticompetitive and predatory behaviour to include price discrimination. Similar preoccupations motivated the passage of the 1916 Antidumping Act. Beginning in 1913, President Wilson and the Democratic Congress staged a vigorous opposition to the power of domestic and international cartels and trusts. In the 1912 election, Wilson campaigned on a message of free trade and fair competition: 'The men who created the monopoly ... have taken advantage of the protective tariff [to] shut out competition and to make sure that the prices are in their own control'.[106] During Wilson's first term, the Underwood Tariff Act was passed, reducing tariffs in order that 'no concern shall [have] a monopoly ... gained other than through the fact that it is able to furnish better goods at lower prices than others'.[107]

Across the Atlantic, World War I forced European manufacturers to turn their resources towards domestic defence, freeing US industries from their foreign competition and serving 'as protection more effective than any tariff legislation could possibly be'.[108] Various US government officials and legislators feared that after the war European industries – especially German –

would resort to selling their goods at artificially low prices, out of necessity if not by choice, to recover a portion of the US market. Democratic Representative Saunders warned that European manufacturers would have to 'have business, profitable business if possible, but if not profitable, then business on any terms that will bring subsistence to the families of thousands of labourers' who had worked in the war efforts.[109] Secretary of Commerce Redfield predicted as a result of 'the outreach of American industries, ney their very existence in our own land in some cases, will be resisted to the full and every stratagem of industrial war will be exerted against them. Expecting this, we shall prepare for it. If it shall pass beyond fair competition and exert or seek to exert monopolistic power over any part of our commerce, we ought to prevent it.'[110] He suggested that Congress enact antidumping legislation supplemental to the Clayton Act's domestic prohibition against price discrimination, because, while 'unfair competition' was forbidden by law in domestic trade, '… the door, however, is still open to "unfair competition" from abroad which may seriously affect American industries for the worse. It is not normal competition of which I speak, but abnormal'. The Secretary concluded that he would 'prefer … to deal with it by a method other than tariffs, classing it rather as an offense similar to the unfair domestic competition we now forbid'.[111]

Such legislation would condemn the sale of foreign articles in the USA at a price 'materially below' their price in the country of production.[112] Democratic representative Kitchin outlined the goal of the proposed antidumping legislation: 'we believe that the same unfair competition law which now applies to the domestic trader should apply to the foreign import trader'.[113] The Antidumping Act of 1916 was enacted as a small part (Sections 800–801) of the Revenue Act passed that year, after a very limited debate in Congress.[114] The existing legislative history reveals that both Republicans and Democrats spoke out in favour of protecting US industry against dumping. The Democrats characterized the legislation as being consistent with their longstanding free trade policy, framing it in pro-competition terms.[115] The Republicans capitalized on the bipartisan fear of import competition and considered the antidumping bill protectionist.[116]

Indeed, the language ultimately chosen for the Antidumping Act of 1916 is an interesting blend of words connoting protection of both US industry and competition. The House Committee report stated that the Act would place importers of foreign goods 'in the same position as our manufacturers with reference to unfair competition'.[117] This comment reflects the Democratic Party's ideal of protecting healthy competition. Interestingly, however, the language that was finally included in the Antidumping Act was not borrowed from the Clayton Act, which is the primary US antitrust law directed at unfair price discrimination. The 1916 Act included phrases that are nearly identical to the language of the Sherman Antitrust Act (i.e., prohibition against 'restraint of trade' and 'monopolization'), but it also contained general prohibitions against any form of dumping committed with the intent of 'injuring' an industry in the USA. As finally adopted, the Antidumping Act allowed civil actions and criminal proceedings to be brought against importers who 'commonly and systematically' have imported or sold foreign-produced goods in the USA at prices that are 'substantially less' than the prices at which the same products are sold in the country of their production or in other foreign countries where such goods are commonly exported, provided that such action is committed with the intent of 'destroying or injuring an industry in the United States, or of preventing the establishment of an industry in the United States, or of restraining or monopolizing any part of trade and commerce in such articles in the United States'.

The 1916 Act was soon considered ineffective as a dumping deterrent. In 1919, the Tariff Commission reported that, by requiring to show intent, the Act made it 'difficult, if not impossible' to enforce its purpose.[118] However, the Tariff Commission also surveyed the incidence of foreign unfair competition in the US market in 1916. Through a very large set of interviews with US enterprises, the Tariff Commission sought 'personal knowledge of unfair competition through the selling in the United States of articles of foreign origin at less than the fair market value when sold for home consumption in the country of origin'.[119] Of the complaints about foreign competition, by far the largest share was classified by the Commission as 'severe competition', but not unfair competition.[120] Nonetheless, Congress remained preoccupied with foreign dumping and responded by passing the Antidumping Act of 1921 (as part of the Emergency Tariff Act of 1921), which vested in the Secretary of the Treasury the authority to impose duties on dumped goods without regard to the dumper's intent.[121] Unlike the 1916 Act, criminal penalties for dumping and a private right of action for treble damages were not provided in the 1921 Act (nor in its successor, the Trade Agreements Act of 1979). The Act provided a purely administrative remedy for dumping violations and relied on enforcement solely by the US Government and not by the (injured) private parties, as is typical of an antitrust statute.

The Treasury Secretary (whose department included the customs service) was empowered to determine when a US producer was – or was likely to be – injured (or prevented from being established) by imports of a product at a price below its fair value in the exporting country or in other export markets. In such a case, the Secretary was empowered to impose a special 'antidumping' duty. The Act imposed no standards for determining injury, imposed no deadlines, and authorized no independent review of injury findings. Some commentators contended that the 1921 Act retained the antitrust objective of the 1916 Act and that the antitrust-type sanctions were dropped because of their lack of workability and not because of a divorcement of dumping and unfair monopoly practices in the Congressional mind. However, under the 1921 Act, dumping practices were subject to duties if they might injure US industries, even though they were not attributable to unfair competitive strategies approaching the level of antitrust violations. For instance, a prohibited dumping margin, the difference between fair market value and the US price, might result from simple currency fluctuations. Because material injury means 'harm which is not inconsequential, immaterial, or unimportant', duties could be assessed upon mere proof that a change in currency valuations threatened a US industry.[122] Furthermore, nothing barred the Treasury Secretary from considering other relevant factors, such as how enforcement might impact bilateral political and military relations.

The rapid shift towards the administrative approach adopted in the 1921 Act is a clear indication that US unfair trade legislation operated as a protective measure in support of the protective tariff in this historical phase. This generally held view was captured by one observer, who noted that: 'the dumping law has consistently been interpreted to protect competitors rather than competition, a goal directly at odds with fundamental antitrust policy'.[123] However, it also can be argued that the antidumping law probably developed somewhat differently than the framers intended and the common roots, at least in part, are important from a fairness perspective. Indeed, the concern with ensuring fair competitive conditions in international trade played an important role in the genesis of the unfair trade legislation, even if in its subsequent application the protectionist objectives often prevailed.

The 1921 Act was also supplemented by Section 316 of the 1922 Fordney–McCumber Act, which was mainly directed at infringements of intellectual property rights. With regard to products found to be imported under conditions of unfair competition, Section 316 authorized the President to impose either additional duties (from 10 per cent to 50 per cent *ad valorem*) or to exclude such products from entry into the USA. The purpose was to extend to import trade penalties against unfair methods of competition similar to those applied to interstate commerce by the 1914 Federal Trade Commission Act. Unfair methods of competition were deemed to be those 'the effect or the tendency of which is to destroy or substantially injure an industry, efficiently and economically operated in the United States'.[124] Congress also wanted to prevent the circumvention by foreign firms of the high tariff of the 1922 Act by unfair methods of competition. The remit of the provision was broad. As the Senate report on the bill stated: 'the provision relating to unfair methods of competition in the importation of goods is broad enough to prevent every type and form of unfair practice and is, therefore, a more adequate protection to American industry than any antidumping statute the country has ever had'.[125] As Senator Smoot put it: 'This section not only prohibits dumping in the ordinary accepted meaning of the word, ... but also bribery, espionage, misrepresentation of goods, full line forcing, and other similar practices frequently more injurious to trade than price cutting'.[126] Section 316 was repealed in 1930, but its substantive provisions were retained in Section 337 of the 1930 Tariff Act with limited amendments.[127] The penalties were made somewhat harsher, as exclusion from entry into the USA for infringing imports was the only action available under the Section 337.

The 1922 Fordney–McCumber Act introduced further flexibility in tariff-setting by allowing the Tariff Commission to recommend tariff changes to the President and authorizing the President to retaliate unilaterally against foreign tariff discrimination. With the objective of achieving equality of treatment for US goods in foreign markets, Section 317 of the Act (a forerunner to the current Section 301 of the Trade Act of 1974) provided for such retaliation against any foreign country that discriminated 'against the commerce of the United States, directly or indirectly, by law or administrative regulation or practice, by or in respect to any customs, tonnage, port duty, fee, charge, exaction, classification, regulation, condition, restriction, or prohibition, in such a manner as to place the commerce of the United States at a disadvantage compared with the commerce of any foreign country'.[128] The Tariff Act of 1909 had already authorized the imposition of penalty duties 25 per cent higher than the normal rates for the purpose of obtaining non-discriminatory treatment for US exports. Indeed, such rates were to apply unless the President was satisfied that a country was not 'unduly' discriminating against US exports. This provision did not allow for the possibility of modulating the penalty and for that reason it was never employed.[129] Such flexibility was introduced in 1922. The Tariff Commission would inform the President about foreign discrimination and offer recommendations.

As explained in the previous section, the President also was given authority to 'equalize the costs of production' of the USA and foreign producers by means of tariff adjustments. These adjustments were not to exceed 50 per cent in either an increase or reduction of existing rates.[130] The practice was to use the 'US selling price' for determining cost-equalizing tariff rates, so that prices of imports were raised by tariff to equal the final prices of domestically produced comparable and competitive goods. The Senate Finance Committee attributed foreign advantages, leading to the underselling of US firms to low wages, government subsidies, and lower taxation.[131] Section 317 was transformed without much change into Section 338 of the 1930 Tariff Act. Products imported in the vessels of a country discriminating against US exports were also subject to new or additional duties or exclusion from entry under Section 338.

The various unfair trade remedy provisions, as they developed between the 1890s and the 1930s, were certainly inspired by the prevailing protectionist attitudes of US legislature. However, they also reflected important fairness concerns, in particular, the objective that in international trade transactions, no party should take advantage of the other and appropriate undue benefits by means of unacceptable private or governmental practices: the ideal of 'fair' competition. Practices of this kind were considered unacceptable, as they conferred 'unfair' advantages, leading to benefits not commensurate with the respective contributions to the exchange and not in line with the normal market outcome.

3.2.3 Reciprocity and Equality of Treatment through Commercial Treaties

The third main issue that characterized US trade policy during the period under review was equality of treatment in foreign markets. The rebellion against Britain was a defining moment in many respects, including with regard to the new nation's commercial policy. During the period of revolution and confederation, the revulsion against the British restrictions, which, since the second half of the 17th century, had been maintained with the purpose of securing all the profits of colonial trade to English merchants and manufacturers, grew strong. Political freedom brought the desire for industrial and commercial freedom. Revolutionary leaders, such as Franklin and Jefferson, did not want autarky or the severance of commercial ties with Britain, but they sought access to foreign markets for US raw materials and agricultural products on the basis of reciprocity and non-discrimination, or, as it was generally referred to, 'equality of treatment'. In order to secure the freedom of trade, which seemed essential to prosperity, Adams, a convinced free-trader, was eager to use instrumentally the restrictions of commerce that he had deprecated. But as soon as Britain would yield, free trade could be inaugurated. In a 1785 letter, he clearly stated his position: 'The United States are willing to throw wide open every port in their dominions to British ships and merchants and merchandise, and I am ready on their behalf, to pledge their faith in a treaty to this effect, upon the reciprocal stipulation of this nation, that her ports will be equally open to our ships, merchants and produce'.[132] Early US statesmen generally believed that the offer of equal opportunity of access to the US market, in return for the removal of the discriminatory barriers that then prevailed in other countries, would bring about a generalized regime of liberal and equal treatment.[133] However, equal treatment would have to be denied to those countries that persisted in discriminating against trade with the USA. This is what fairness in international commercial relations meant at the Republic's inception.

During the US Revolution in 1778, the Continental Congress had sent emissaries, including important revolutionary leaders such as Franklin, to

France to seek diplomatic recognition and to negotiate commercial agreements. In September 1776, Congress had instructed his negotiators to 'endeavour ... to conclude treaties of peace, amity and commerce ... provided that ... the immunities, exceptions, privileges ... thereby stipulated, be equal and reciprocal'.[134] With Franklin's help, Adams drafted a model treaty to guide negotiators. Draft Art. 1 proposed that the subjects of either of the treaty partners pay only duties or imposts imposed on natives and 'enjoy all other ... rights, liberties, privileges, immunities and exemptions in trade, navigation and commerce' that natives or their companies enjoyed.[135] This was the broader understanding of 'equality of treatment', which corresponds to what is now generally referred as 'national treatment'. A similar provision was included a few years later in Art. IV, Section 2 of the Constitution, which reads: 'The Citizens of each State shall be entitled to all Privileges and Immunities of Citizens in the several States'. Thus, equality of treatment was considered necessary for trade within the USA, as it was for trade with foreign countries. Discrimination was seen as harmful both internally and externally.

If equality of treatment could not be attained, the second-best solution would be to seek trade conditions equal to those accorded to the most favoured third party, the 'most-favoured-nation (MFN) treatment'. The statement of principle contained in the 1776 Congress Plan was to be at the centre of future US trade policy. The USA's first trade treaty, the Treaty of Amity and Commerce with France of 6 February 1778, while failing to secure equality of treatment for the USA, committed in its preamble the two parties to 'fix in an equitable ... manner the rules that ought to be followed [in their] commerce' and to pursue 'the most perfect equality and reciprocity ... founding the advantage of commerce solely upon reciprocal utility and the just rules of free intercourse'.[136] In particular, the treaty contained an MFN clause in conditional form, stipulating that if one of the contracting parties should grant a special commercial favour to a third nation, the other party should enjoy the same favour only on allowing some compensation equivalent to that paid by the third nation.[137] This represented a discontinuity with the past, as until the time of the American Revolution, the MFN pledge had always appeared in its unqualified form (with no requirement of reciprocal compensation). No limitations were established regarding the circumstances under which concessions granted to other states should be extended as between the contracting parties.

While it appears that it was the French side that originally drafted the clause, the conditional interpretation was subsequently disputed by France and, in contrast, wholeheartedly embraced by the US side.[138] Secretary John Quincy Adams later stated that the preamble of the treaty with France was 'the foundation of our commercial intercourse with the rest of mankind, what the Declaration of Independence was to that of our internal government. The two instruments were parts of one and the same system matured by long and anxious deliberations of the founders of this Union in the memorable Congress of 1776'. And he added that it was the USA that first had proclaimed the political ideals of equality and independence, but also that it had placed for the first time 'the true principles of all fair commercial negotiation between independent states' on the 'diplomatic record of nations'.[139]

In subsequent treaties, US practice was somewhat varied, but there is no doubt that the conditional interpretation of the clause was the only one that was compatible with the general policy objectives of equality of treatment and reciprocity as understood and sought by Congress at the time. For instance, the 1782 Treaty with the Netherlands did not contain the conditional wording expressly. Concerning a dispute that had arisen with regard to a legislative act of the State of Virginia that had exempted French brandies imported in French and US vessels from certain duties to which like commodities imported in vessels from the Netherlands were left liable, and thus in breach of the MFN clause of the Treaty, John Jay, the Secretary of the Department of Foreign Affairs of the Confederation, reported to Congress as follows:

> It is observable that this article [the MFN clause in the Treaty with the Netherlands] takes no notice of cases where compensation is granted for privileges. Reason and equity however, in the opinion of your Secretary, will supply this deficiency. ... Where a privilege is gratuitously granted, the nation to whom it is granted becomes in respect to that privilege a favored nation ... but where the privilege is not gratuitous, but rests on compact, in such case the favor, if any there be, does not consist in the privilege yielded but in the consent to make the contract by which it is yielded. ... The favor therefore of being admitted to make a similar bargain is all that in such cases can reasonably be demanded under the article. Besides, it would certainly be inconsistent with the most obvious principles of justice and fair construction, that because France purchases, at a great price, a privilege of the United States, that therefore the Dutch shall immediately insist, not on having the like privileges at the like price, but without any price at all.[140]

The Confederation, with its fragmented trade policy, did not possess the leverage to achieve reciprocity and equality of treatment. As mentioned, this dissatisfaction was one of the arguments that weighted in favour of entrusting the conduct of trade policy with the US Congress. Pressure in this direction also was exerted by the business milieu. For instance, in 1784, Boston merchants stressed in an open letter that they considered it necessary 'to vest such powers in Congress ... as shall be competent to the great and interesting purpose of placing the commerce of the United States upon a footing of perfect equality with every other nation'.[141] A bargaining policy based on the conditional MFN treatment was considered as the only way to deal with European powers that frequently prohibited US trade or discriminated against US vessels and goods. The conditional policy was never regarded as discriminatory because it offered other countries' equality of opportunity to negotiate and obtain all the benefits that the USA might grant third countries. This approach was stated by President John Quincy Adams, who stressed that:

> this system [of conditional MFN], first proclaimed to the world in the first commercial treaty ever concluded by the United States – that of 6th February, 1778, with France – has been invariably the cherished policy of our Union. ... With this principle, our fathers extended the hand of friendship to every nation of the globe, and to this policy our country has ever since adhered. Whatever of regulation in our laws has ever been adopted unfavourable to the interests of any foreign nation has been essentially defensive and counteracting to similar regulations of theirs operating against us.[142]

More than a century later, the same considerations with regard to equality of treatment and reciprocity were voiced in 1898 by Secretary of State Sherman:

> It is clearly evident that the object sought in all the varying forms of expression is equality of international treatment, protection against the wilful preference of the commercial interests of one nation over another. But the allowance of the same privileges and the same sacrifice of revenue duties, to a nation which makes no compensation, that had been conceded to another nation for an adequate compensation, instead of maintaining, destroys that equality of market privileges which the 'most-favored-nation' clause was intended to secure. It concedes for nothing to one friendly nation what the other gets only for a price. It would thus become the source of international inequality and provoke international hostility.[143]

In an additional statement, Sherman stressed that: 'the [MFN] clauses are expressed in various forms of language ... but the intent is the same in all the conventions between civilized countries. ... That intent is to secure ... equality with all competing nations in the conditions of access to the markets of the other'.[144] This interpretation of the MFN clause reflects the objective of seeking fairness through reciprocity and the rejection of free-riding, two widely felt objectives among US policy-makers.

Thus, at the beginning of the Republic, the thrust of US trade policy was deeply influenced by fairness concerns. As seen on the import side, the protective tariff had among its objectives to fight back against foreign barriers (also through penalty duties). On the export side, the policy was to achieve equality of trade opportunities. President Washington, in his farewell address, expressed this position in the clearest fashion:

> Harmony, liberal intercourse with all nations are recommended by policy, humanity, and interest. But even our commercial policy should hold an equal and impartial hand, neither seeking nor granting exclusive favors or preferences; ... diffusing and diversifying by gentle means the streams of commerce, but forcing nothing; establishing with powers so disposed, in order to give trade a stable course,

to define the rights of our merchants, and to enable the Government to support their conventional rules of intercourse ... constantly keeping in view that it is folly in one nation to look for disinterested favors from another.[145]

Reciprocity and equality of treatment endured throughout the 19th century as the leading principles of US trade policy, as implemented through commercial treaties. The conditional construction of the MFN pledge, even in the case of treaties that did not include any explicit reference to it, remained a constant policy feature. A true exception was the 1850 USA–Switzerland treaty, in which case it could be demonstrated that the common explicit understanding of the parties at the time of conclusion was that the MFN pledge contained therein was unconditional. When a controversy arose in 1898, the USA admitted that the treaty was 'an exception to the otherwise uniform policy of the United States ... to treat the commerce of all friendly nations with equal fairness, giving exceptional "favors" to none' and the treaty was denounced.[146] As the USA's role in international trade grew, its treaty practice also became more influential. In the period between 1825 and 1860, European countries concluded various treaties, including the conditional MFN clause. The 1860 Cobden–Chevalier Treaty between Britain and France marked the turning point. After that, European powers used the unconditional form almost exclusively, except when dealing with the USA, while the latter clung to the conditional version until 1923. This practice remained independent of the degree of protection sought. In fact, the unconditional MFN pledge was used by high tariff countries, such as France and Russia, and moderate tariff countries, such as Switzerland and Belgium, as well as by free-trade Britain.

However, the divergence of interpretations with regard to the wording of the pledge gave rise to a large number of diplomatic controversies.[147] Furthermore, the US Tariff Commission recognized that over time:

> as separate and independent commercial agreements were entered into, the treatment accorded by the United States to different countries became not infrequently unequal. Special agreements and provisions were made in separate cases as they arose. Having begun with the intention to offer equality of treatment, and with the hope of securing such equality in return, the United States has nevertheless been led into commercial relations with individual nations of which the effect was inequality.[148]

In addition to broad commercial treaties, which included the MFN pledge but also covered a wide variety of other subjects (e.g., from diplomatic and consular relations to navigation, from immigration to protection of intellectual property), the USA pursued the negotiation of specific 'reciprocity agreements'. In such agreements, each party 'makes special concessions to the other with the intention that the transaction shall be looked upon as a particular bargain and with the understanding that its benefits are not to be extended automatically, generally, and freely to other States'.[149] However, the negotiation of such treaties proved very difficult. While the fairness objective *vis-à-vis* foreign countries was generally supported by Democrats as well as Republicans, the latter were much less disposed to sacrifice the protection of domestic interests for gains on the export side as well in order to further any broader foreign policy goal. In the period before the Civil War, the USA negotiated reciprocal market opening agreements with the Zollverein, Canada, Mexico, and Hawaii.

The necessary mutual exchange of concessions meant that some import-competing domestic businesses would allegedly suffer (because of the concession granted), for the purpose of benefiting some export-oriented domestic businesses. And the balance in terms of fairness of such initiatives stirred much controversy. Indeed, the quest for fairness in international trade through reciprocity and equality of treatment, one of the enduring policy objectives of the USA in its relations with other nations, had to contend with other powerful ideas and policy objectives, such as domestic protection and national security. Harry Wheaton, the US envoy in charge of negotiating with the Zollverein, saw the commercial treaty as an 'instrument of negotiation' to 'obtain equivalent concessions' from European countries in favour of US agricultural exports. Such an approach would 'eliminate some of the most objectionable features of our exaggerated tariff' and could be considered the 'first step towards a more liberal commercial intercourse between the different nations of Europe and the United States'.[150] Obviously, agricultural exporters backed the treaty, as did Democrats, while manufacturing interests and Republicans rejected it and managed to prevail in the Senate in 1844. Congress also was wary of losing its tariff-making power to the Executive. The Senate rejected the reciprocity treaties signed with Mexico in 1856 and Hawaii in 1859. The 1854 reciprocity treaty with Canada was approved, but the commercial advantages deriving from it were disputed. In the second half of the 19th century, various other treaties were negotiated, but only the one with Hawaii (of 1875) survived.

Issues of fairness with regard to trading partners, as well as between domestic interests, were always at the centre of the debate. In the Senate debate on the 1883 Mexican treaty,[151] the Chairman of the Finance Committee, Morrill, poignantly captured the issues in a resolution that he introduced in 1884, which stated: 'Resolved, that the so-called reciprocity treaties, having no possible basis of reciprocity with nations of inferior population and wealth, involving the surrender of immensely larger volumes of home trade than are offered to us in return, and involving constitutional questions of the gravest character, are untimely and should everywhere be regarded with disfavor'.[152] Consequently, until 1890 only two reciprocity treaties with Canada and Hawaii came into force.

In 1889, Republican Secretary of State Blaine tried to improve the State Department's negotiating leverage in order to promote foreign access for US products, particularly in Latin America, as he was convinced that the USA was hampered by high restrictions, while Latin American imports to the USA were largely admitted duty-free. The Pan-American conference to discuss trade and hemispheric affairs, which he had championed for a few years, was finally convened in that year. While Blaine initially favoured a continental customs union, the Conference finally recommended trade expansion through bilateral reciprocity treaties. Such support for the idea of reciprocity helped Blaine obtain negotiating authority from Congress. In the 1890 McKinley Act, Congress placed sugar (thus reducing his negotiating leverage *vis-à-vis* Latin American countries) and molasses on the free list (zero duty),[153] but also authorized the President to impose penalty duty on free imports from countries producing certain tropical products, such as sugars, molasses, coffee, tea, and hides that imposed 'unequal and unreasonable' duties on US exports. At the same time, the Act's reciprocity provision allowed the President to undertake commercial negotiations, albeit backed not by the prospects of making concessions, but by the possibility of imposing penalty duties. In this way, both protectionist and trade expansionist interests could be satisfied. With this weapon in hand, 10 executive agreements were concluded, including those with Brazil, Cuba, and Spain. Countries unwilling to cooperate, such as Colombia, Venezuela, and Haiti, were met with penalty duties.[154]

However, when the Democrats regained power in 1894, they repealed the 1890 tariff, as they considered the penalty duty generally ineffective and a source of international friction. They also terminated the reciprocity arrangements negotiated by the previous administration. In 1897, Republican President McKinley took office and, somewhat modifying his earlier negative posture in the House, urged Congress to re-enact the reciprocity provisions.[155] He advocated the 'opening up of new markets for the products of our country, by granting concessions to the products of other lands that we need and can not produce ourselves, and which do not involve any loss of labor to our own people, but tend to increase their employment'.[156] One of the earliest acts in the McKinley administration was the enactment in 1897 of the highly protective Dingley Tariff. The Act authorized not only penalty duties, but also reciprocal concessions, for the purpose of reducing foreign discrimination through negotiations. The President was empowered to negotiate two kinds of reciprocity agreements. The first type could only cover a few specific items, such as argols, brandies, wines, and champagnes; the second type allowed the President to cut import duties up to 20 per cent and transfer to the free list natural products of other countries as treaty concessions, which, however, still required Congressional approval. The McKinley administration reached nine such so-called 'argol agreements' with European countries. The argol agreements were negotiated primarily to eliminate discrimination against US exports in selected European countries, but they did not reflect any intention to reduce the protective level of the US tariff. However, the broader reciprocity agreements provided for by the Dingley Act, negotiated by former Congressmen and diplomat Kasson, did not pass the Senate's muster. In addition, European countries were particularly hostile to negotiations with the USA under such circumstances.

While in the context of a high protectionist tariff and with no disposition to negotiate significant reductions, the Republican approach to reciprocity indicated an increased attention to the international dimension of trade policy.[157] Times were changing, the US economy was increasing in size and expanding overseas[158] and McKinley, in his last speech, made at the Buffalo Pan-American Exposition on the 5th September 1901, gave voice to this change: 'God and man have linked the nations together. No nation can longer be indifferent to any other. ... The period of exclusiveness is past. The expansion of our trade and commerce is the pressing problem. Commercial wars are unprofitable. A policy of good will and friendly trade relations will prevent reprisals. Reciprocity treaties are in harmony with the spirit of the times. Measures of retaliation are not'. He also added: 'we must not repose in fancied security that we can forever sell everything and buy nothing. ... We should take from our costumers such of their products as we can use without harm to our industries and labor'.[159] The priority of producers' and workers' interests was thus maintained. The principle of no injury to the domestic industry once again was restated.

President Theodore Roosevelt, in his inaugural address in 1901 was on the same lines: 'Our first duty is to see that the protection granted by the tariff in every case is maintained, and that reciprocity be sought for so far as it can safely be done without injury to our home industries'.[160] However, while the Republican position was evolving, resistance to the reciprocity treaties remained strong in the Senate, and President Roosevelt was forced to abandon the so-called Kasson treaties. In the case of the reciprocity agreement with Cuba, after the war with Spain, Roosevelt considered that the USA had 'weighty reasons of morality and of national interest' for providing market opportunities for Cuban exports. He stood firm, despite the vocal opposition of domestic sugar interests. Interestingly, in this case the argument departed from the usual fairness pattern, as Roosevelt stated in his message to Congress: 'I ask this aid for her [Cuba] because she is weak, because she needs it, and because we have already aided her'.[161] The 1902 Treaty provided for a 20 per cent reduction in US duties on Cuban imports, including raw sugar, and reductions between 20 per cent and 40 per cent in Cuban rates on US products. In order to avoid the generalisation of the concessions to other MFN countries, the treaty specifically stated that the reductions were preferential. In its relations with less advanced countries, the USA also concluded several agreements, for instance with Egypt in 1884 and with Kongo in 1891, which granted no specific concessions but unilaterally extended the unconditional MFN without requiring like treatment in return. These were the very limited departures from a fairness approach based on equality of treatment and reciprocity in favour of countries that today would be referred to as 'developing'.

Republican President Taft, who succeeded Roosevelt, also was interested in moderating the tariff and furthering reciprocity. The Republican platform of 1908, like the Democratic platform of that year, called for a downward revision of the tariff. Nonetheless, the Payne–Aldrich Tariff Act, which Congress passed in 1909, was still a highly protective tariff. But with regard to reciprocity, it introduced minimum and maximum rates so as to facilitate bargaining. At the same time, President Taft tried to allay fears that the new dual tariff system would be used aggressively, leading to trade wars. He said that 'in order that the maximum duty shall be charged against the imports from a country, it is necessary that he shall find on the part of that country not only discriminations in its laws or the practice under them against the trade of the United States, but that the discriminations found shall be undue: that is, without good and fair reason'. Furthermore, he added that the approach of 'friendly negotiation' to secure the elimination of discriminatory treatment would be employed.[162] The Taft administration did not impose any penalty duties and was successful in negotiating a reciprocity treaty with Canada, which was strongly criticized along traditional lines. However, Taft managed to have the agreement approved by Congress, only to see it defeated in the Canadian Parliament because of broader political fears with regard to alleged 'US expansionism'.

An effective system to achieve equality of treatment in foreign markets and reciprocity was still very much an elusive policy objective for both Republicans and Democrats. Frank Taussig, a prominent international economist, friend of President Wilson, who replaced Taft, and Chairman of the newly created Tariff Commission, urged a 'determined and active effort' to keep US goods from being 'frozen out' of postwar foreign markets; also through an 'international policy of the open door – the same terms to all'.[163] In its study on *Reciprocity and Commercial Treaties*, the Tariff Commission emphasized 'equality of treatment [namely] that the United States treat all countries on the same terms, and in turn require equal treatment from every other country' as the guiding principle for US policy.[164] Indeed, President Wilson strongly supported the notion of the 'equality of treatment' and included it prominently in his Fourteen Points speech delivered to a joint session of Congress on 8 January 1918.[165] Wilson's project to ensure the 'world's peace' and 'justice and fair dealing' had an important economic component based on the liberalization of trade barriers, non-discrimination, and the maintenance of the necessary rules of international trade by means of international organizations governed by 'specific covenants'. But Congress was still averse to tariff reductions and not interested in international cooperation on economic matters, or more broadly institutionalized, multilateral cooperation, as demonstrated by the Senate's rejection of the League of Nations treaty.

The subsequent Republican administration of President Harding once again raised tariffs with the 1922 Fordney–McCumber Act, which also provided for the possibility of imposing retaliatory tariffs. This device was again meant to facilitate the negotiation of mutually advantageous commercial treaties. However, foreign discrimination was an enduring problem and in deciding on how to administer the new tariff law, Secretary of State Hughes proposed and President Harding accepted in 1923 to switch to the unconditional MFN approach when negotiating new commercial treaties. In the State Department's analysis, the conditional approach had led the USA to provide 'special concessions to some instead of equal treatment to all', which arouses 'antagonism, promotes discord, creates a sense of unfairness and tends in general to discourage commerce'. In contrast, the unconditional approach would 'eliminate conflicts, prevent charges of unfairness, promote commerce and improve international relations'.[166] In his instructions to overseas diplomatic missions, Hughes stressed that when the conditional approach was originally formulated in 1778, 'discrimination in commercial matters was the general rule among nations, and it was deemed advisable for the United States to adopt a policy of making concessions only to such states as granted in each case some definite and equivalent compensation'. However, as the principle of equality gained in acceptance, 'it is now considered to be in the interest of the trade of the United States, in competing with the trade of other countries in the markets of the world, to endeavour to extend the acceptance of that principle' through the adoption of the unconditional MFN pledge.[167]

Furthermore, in principle, the unconditional approach does not mean allowing treaty partners to free-ride on concessions that they have not reciprocated. As Viner explained:

> There is at least as complete and reciprocal an exchange of considerations between countries bound by an unconditional most-favored-nation contract as between countries in conditional most-favored-nation relations with each other. Under the unconditional form of the pledge there is in a sense an exchange of concessions at the moment of the coming into effect of the treaty, but this exchange receives its execution gradually throughout the life of the treaty through the immediate extension by each country to the other of the privileges, favors, or concessions which it may grant to other countries. ... [However,] it is possible ... that a country ... may deliberately refrain from making concessions to any country in order that it may avoid the obligation of extending such concession to other countries. Even

under such circumstances, ... country A has received from country B [the country refusing any positive concessions] the important and valuable pledge that no country will under any circumstances enjoy any privileges in B which will not be available in like measure to A. The guaranty to A of equality of treatment in B is a valuable consideration, in fact more valuable than any guaranty which it could receive under the conditional practice, even though in its execution it means merely that no worse treatment will be given to A's economic interests in B than to the interests of any third country and does not result in positive concessions to A of privileges not enjoyed by the latter prior to the signature of the treaty.[168]

Aside from such concerns, which were more directly related to fairness, there were obviously other commercial considerations at play. First,

it had for some time become increasingly difficult for the United States to secure renewal of old or the negotiation of new treaties on the conditional basis, and she [the US] was without commercial treaties and subject to serious tariff discrimination in several important countries.[[169]] Secondly, other countries were threatening to adopt for themselves the conditional practice ... Thirdly, American export trade had changed in character, and was now more liable to, and capable of being more seriously injured by, foreign tariff discrimination. ... In the past the United States was chiefly an exporter of raw materials and foodstuffs, which foreign countries could not do without ... [and] admitted free of duty or at low duties irrespective of American tariff treatment of their own products. ... American exports consisted now in large and increasing proportions of manufactured commodities, and foreign countries were able, and to an increasing degree willing, to impose heavy and discriminatory tariffs on such commodities.[170]

Clearly, in the post-World War I period, a number of European powers had adopted a policy of discrimination and quantitative restrictions, along with other restrictions in trade and also seized upon the US conditional approach for that purpose.

By 1933, a decade after its policy change, the USA had secured the unconditional MFN pledge[171] from 29 countries,[172] including some important trading partners, but not with Britain, Canada, France, and Spain. This was mainly because Congress was reluctant to agree to tariff reductions, which gave negotiators little leverage. Thus, US trade policy in this area between 1922 and 1933 was largely unsuccessful because 'though unconditional most-favored-nation treatment was promised, its purpose was defeated by the high single-column autonomous tariff'.[173] During the 1920s, reduction in tariffs was not considered to be a subject for negotiation. The tariff level was considered to be strictly a domestic concern. More generally, 'before 1922, the United States tariff, although negotiable in principle, had not been very negotiable in fact. After 1922, even the principle of negotiability was discarded'.[174] The treaties with Canada in 1854, Hawaii in 1875, Cuba in 1902, and the modest 'argol agreements' were the only examples of negotiated tariff reductions until the passage of the Trade Agreements Act of 1934.

The controversy with France exemplified the difficulty of reconciling a non-discrimination policy embodied in the unconditional MFN approach, reciprocity of benefits, and high tariff protection. When, in 1927, France increased its duties while at the same time announcing a reciprocity treaty with Germany that lowered them, the USA protested and proposed to enter into negotiations for a commercial treaty, which would ensure MFN treatment for the USA. But France refused, highlighting an important difference in the countries' respective approaches to international trade relations.

> The United States under its unconditional MFN policy regarded non-discrimination treatment as a principle of international conduct and not a matter for bargaining. To obtain unconditional MFN treatment for its exports, the United States was willing to grant unconditional MFN treatment to the exports of other countries, but nothing else. ... France regarded non-discriminatory treatment as something to be bargained against high tariff rates. Equality of bad treatment was not considered good enough to obtain French minimum rates.[175]

From the US perspective, fairness through non-discrimination could coexist with protection, while for France and other commercial partners, the conditions under which international trade should be conducted were all a matter of bargaining.

The domestic, non-negotiable character of the US tariff was reaffirmed as late as the 1933 World Monetary and Economic Conference, where Secretary of State Stimson made clear that the USA was unable to consider the question of tariff rates as they were 'purely domestic issues'.[176] However, while high and non-negotiable, the US tariff policy was not discriminatory as a matter of principle. 'With few exceptions the United States maintained a single-column tariff, so that de facto, if not de jure, United States policy, for the most part, amounted to one of non-discrimination'.[177] Only the tariff reductions made in the Canadian, Hawaiin, Cuban, and argol agreements were not generalized under the US conditional MFN policy. Furthermore, the Canadian, Cuban, and Hawaiian treaties were motivated by broader economic and political reasons, while the argol agreements were meant to eliminate discriminatory practices against US exports.

The first plans for reciprocal tariff reductions that were to bear fruit in the mid-1930s had already been advanced a decade before by Wallace McClure, an economist at the State Department, who suggested that tariff concessions could be negotiated bilaterally and then extended on an unconditional MFN basis, thus achieving 'moderation [in tariff] not as a free gift to other countries but in return for corresponding advantages'. After negotiating several such treaties, the most 'thorough method of achieving uniformity' was determined to be the negotiation of a single commercial convention open to all countries.[178] This plan found the support of Cordell Hull, who started to discuss with other Democrats in Congress, who in the late 1920s were still more favourable to legislated, as opposed to negotiated reductions in tariffs.

There is no question that from the early times of the Confederation until the 1930s, special business interests played a dominant role in trade policy-making. The way the institutional set-up for tariff writing had been developed, with Congress playing the decisive role, also helped increase the impact of these interests. However, fairness considerations were present all along and strongly contributed to shaping the debate, as is shown by the continuing reference to the notion in policy-makers' public statements. Together with protection, it was the dominant trade policy idea from the founding of the Republic until the 1930s. In terms of actual trade policy choices, fairness considerations were as important with regard to the protective tariff and unfair trade legislation as they were for export expansion and non-discriminatory access to foreign markets. Since the beginning of the Republic, the policy in these latter areas was that of securing equality of treatment and reciprocity of concessions. But as the importance of exports grew with the development of the US economy in the late 19th and early 20th centuries,[179] fairness concerns acquired increasing relevance in the area of commercial relations with foreign countries.

Furthermore, fairness issues always have had both a domestic dimension (e.g., consumers vs. producers, import-competing producers vs. export-oriented producers) and an international one, in terms of perceived foreign unfair practices. But as time passed, it was increasingly difficult to differentiate them, as Congressman McKinley did in discussing the 1890 tariff revision: 'I am not going to discuss reciprocity or the propriety of treaties and commercial agreements. ... This is a domestic bill; it is not a foreign bill'.[180] By the 1930s, fairness concerns had pervaded the whole trade policy debate and over time, it became increasingly difficult to disentangle domestic from international aspects.

3.3   SUMMARY

The principle of fairness, or the duty of fair play, as it has been posited in Chapter 2, requires all participants in schemes of social cooperation, such as international trade, from which they willingly benefit to contribute their fair share and to abstain from free-riding on the burdens shouldered by others. Fairness is thus concerned in particular with process (taking no undue advantage of other participants, operating under equality of conditions) and with how that process contributes to a fair outcome in terms of the distribution of burdens and benefits (no free-riding). The fairness idea, as embodied in the duty of fair play, is part of US economic ethos, and, as shown in this chapter, it has been reflected in the making of the country's trade policy ever since the Confederation period. Actually, the sense of unfairness that dominated the commercial relationship with the mother country, Britain, was one of the catalytic elements for the Revolution.

As the proceeding review of congressional debates and policies confirms, from the founding of the Republic until the 1930s, trade policy was mainly dominated by domestic political and economic issues, and, as such, the fairness concerns voiced in the debates had much to do with the desire to protect the home market against the perceived unfair practices of foreign traders, on which both parties agreed; and with the distribution of burdens and benefits that such protection (and the changes in its level) provided to different groups in society (mainly, producers vs. consumers and importers vs. exporters), on which politicians strongly clashed. Over time and in step with the progressive expansion of US foreign trade, the fairness of the conditions of competition faced by US traders abroad became an issue of growing importance.

Together with providing an additional justification for the protective tariff and, more specifically, for unfair trade legislation, fairness concerns were mainly translated into two (more operational) notions that have, ever since, played a key role in trade policy-making: equality of treatment (or non-discrimination) and reciprocity. If, in the domestic arena, fairness lent itself to arguments both in favour of increasing protection and moderating it, on the 'international' side, equality of treatment and reciprocity both aimed at achieving an increase in foreign trade and thus, indirectly at least, pointed towards openness in trade relations. However, a lack of equality and reciprocity could be used as a motive for retaliatory increases in barriers and penalty duties. The balancing factor resided in the 'no injury to domestic industry' principle.

Equality of treatment and reciprocity are connected. As one definition based on a study of the US presidents' public papers stated: 'Reciprocity is the granting by one nation of certain commercial privileges to another, whereby the citizens of both are placed upon an equal basis in certain branches of commerce'.[181] Furthermore, as the US Tariff Commission put it:

> a commercial agreement implies the giving of something for something. One of the greatest of the advantages which one nation may gain at the hands of another ... is the assurance that its subjects and its commerce will be treated as well by and within the jurisdiction of the other as are those of any third nation. Put negatively, this advantage may be gained in the form of an assurance against artificial exclusion or discrimination.[182]

Mutual assurances of this kind have generally been enshrined in commercial treaties by means of the MFN pledge, which was perceived to embody the process aspects of fairness (equality of treatment and thus competitive conditions and no discrimination leading to special advantages for some traders), as well as to contribute to a fair distribution of burdens and benefits from trade intercourse. Furthermore, the balancing of benefits was pursued not only with regard to tariff treatment, but also regarding any right, privilege, favour, or any other specified treatment, so that 'the party to whom it is extended shall conceive himself benefited by its acquisition and possession'.[183]

In order to ensure such a fair distribution of burdens and benefits and no free-riding, the USA not only relied on non-discrimination, but it also pursued a specific policy of reciprocity. Thus, sometimes it retaliated against foreign discrimination with penalty duties, seeking balance in the concessions granted and construing the MFN pledge for a long time as conditional and switching to the unconditional one only when its foreign trade interests had consolidated and the mutuality of advantages could be appreciated on a wider scale.

The period until the early 1930s was dominated by the protectionist objective, even if there were deep divisions in the US political landscape, for instance between Democrats and Republicans, manufacturing and agricultural interests, as well as import-competing and export-dependent industries, over the actual meaning and useful extent of protection. In this context, reciprocity could be enlisted to serve different purposes. Any tariff concessions or other commercial privileges, whether granted bilaterally or as a result of the unconditional MFN pledge, had to be perceived as abiding to the principle of reciprocity, which generally meant, because of the preference accorded to the interests of domestic producers, that tariff lowering was difficult. In this sense, the 'no injury' principle that dominated the domestic fairness concerns could be seen as part of the reciprocal balancing of advantages to be derived from international trade transactions. But reciprocity was also used to seek reductions in foreign trade barriers. However, until the 1930s, the reluctance to reduce tariffs restricted the negotiating leverage. To the extent that (barrier reducing) reciprocity was achieved, this was accomplished in the context of bilateral bargaining, with little concern for the stability and openness of the international economy as a whole.

NOTES

1. See H. McClosky and J. Zaller, *The American Ethos: Public Attitudes Toward Capitalism and Democracy*, Harvard University Press, Cambridge, MA, 1984.
2. Culture is taken here to mean the shared values and beliefs justifying desired social relations. Values are mainly conceived as the standards governing normative judgements. Ethos refers to the fundamental features that create a group's distinctive character.
3. See L. Hartz, *The Liberal Tradition in America: An Interpretation of American Political Thought since the Revolution*, Harcourt Brace Jovanovich, San Diego, 1955 [1991], p. 89.

4. See R. Hofstadter, *The American Political Tradition*, Knopf, New York, 1957 [1973], p. xxxviii.
5. See J. Madison, *The Federalist*, no. 10, in A. Hamilton, J. Madison and J. Jay, *The Federalist Papers* [1788], edited by C. Rossiter, Mentor, 1999, New York, NY, p. 48.
6. See B. Siegan, 'The Constitution and the Protection of Capitalism', in R. Goldwin and W. Schambra, eds., *How Capitalistic is the Constitution?*, American Enterprise Institute for Public Policy Research, Washington, DC, 1982, pp. 106–26.
7. 'The diversity in the faculties of men, from which the rights of property originate, is not less an insuperable obstacle to a uniformity of interests. The protection of these faculties is the first object of government. From the protection of different and unequal faculties of acquiring property, the possession of different degrees and kinds of property immediately results', in Madison, *The Federalist*, no. 10.
8. See McClosky and Zaller, op. cit., pp. 139–43.
9. See M. Diamond, 'Ethics and Politics: The American Way', in R. Horwitz, ed., *The Moral Foundations of the American Republic*, University Press of Virginia, Charlottesville, VA, 1986, p. 100.
10. See J. Locke, *The First Treatise on Government*, in J. Locke, *Two Treatises on Government*, edited by I. Shapiro, Yale University Press, New Haven, CT, 2003, Chapter 4, Section 42.
11. See R. Goldwin, 'Of Man and Angels: A Search for Morality in the Constitution', in R. Horwitz, ed., op. cit., p. 35.
12. See Miller, op. cit., pp. 555–93.
13. See McClosky and Zaller, op. cit. pp. 63, 81–2, 94, 121; Miller, op. cit., p. 565–6; and R. Bellah et al., *Habits of the Heart: Individualism and Commitment in American Life*, University of California Press, Berkeley, CA, 1996, pp. 25–6.
14. Herbert Croly, an influential liberal writer of the early twentieth century, observed that: 'American political thinkers have always repudiated the thought that by the equality of rights they meant anything like the equality of performance or power. The utmost varieties of power and abilities are bound to exist and to bring about different levels of individual achievement. Democracy ... requires an equal start in the race while expecting at the same time an unequal finish'. See H. Croly, *The Promise of American Life*, Bobbs-Merrill Co., Indianapolis, 1965, p. 181.
15. See T. Jefferson, 'Second Inaugural Address', in A. Koch and W. Paden, *The Life and Selected Writings of Thomas Jefferson*, The Modern Library, New York, 1944, p. 344.
16. See G. Hunt, ed., *The Writings of James Madison*, G.P. Putnam's Sons, New York, 1900, vol. 6, p. 86.
17. See *The United States Democratic Review*, October 1837, cited in J. Blau, ed., *Social Theories of Jacksonian Democracy*, Bobbs-Merrill Co., Indianapolis, 1954, p. 27.
18. See McClosky and Zaller, op. cit., Chapters 4 and 5.
19. See S. Bemis, *A Diplomatic History of the United States*, H. Holt and Company, New York, 1938.
20. See J. Goldstein, *Ideas, Interests, and American Trade Policy*, Cornell University Press, Ithaca, NY, 1993, p. 28.
21. See T. Jefferson, *Summary View of the Rights of British America*, Philadelphia, 1774 [1971], B. Franklin, Philadelphia; A. Eckes, 'U.S. Trade History', in W. Lovett, A. Eckes and R. Brinkman, eds., *U.S. Trade Policy. History, Theory and the WTO*, Armonk, NY and London, 1999, p. 56.
22. Quoted in W. Hill, *The First Stages of the Tariff Policy of the United States*, American Economic Association, Baltimore, 1893, pp. 85–6.
23. Id., p. 83.
24. Id., p. 84.
25. Id., p. 86.
26. See E. Stanwood, *American Tariff Controversies in the Nineteenth Century*, Houghton Mifflin, New York, 1903, p. 28. Again in a letter written in 1780 in reply to some questions regarding the hatred of the British, Adams stated: 'The Americans are animated by higher principles and better and stronger motives than hatred and aversion. They universally aspire after a free trade with all the commercial world, instead of the mean monopoly in which they

were shackled by Great Britain, to the disgrace and mortification of America, and to the injury of all the rest of Europe; to whom it seems as if God and nature intended that so great a magazine of productions, the raw materials of manufacturers, so great a source of commerce, and so reach a nursery of seamen as America is, should be open. They despise, sir, they disdain the idea of being again monopolized by any one nation whatsoever.' Quoted in Hill, op. cit., pp. 77–8. In 1784 in his message to the New York General Assembly, Governor Clinton stated: 'It is extremely difficult to hold any intercourse with a nation that will not suffer her commerce with other states to be governed by the principles of equality and reciprocity'. Quoted in Hill, op. cit., p. 94.

27. See V. Abramson and L. Lyon, *Government and Economic Life*, vol. II, The Brookings Institution, Washington, DC, 1940, p. 529.

28. 'Having in mind *foreign discrimination* and *commercial anarchy* that existed among the states, the framers of the Constitution provided that Congress should have the power to regulate foreign and interstate commerce, thus wiping out state tariff lines and creating a national market area behind a federal wall' (emphasis added). See C. and M. Beard, *The Rise of the American Civilization*, Macmillan, New York, 1930, p. 324.

29. 'Thus in the very beginning of the United States tariff legislation protection found the place which it has maintained, with little interruption, till the present day'. See Hill, op. cit., p. 112.

30. See F.W. Taussig, *The Tariff History of the United States*, G.P. Putnam's Sons, New York, 1923, p. 14.

31. See Stanwood, op. cit., pp. 40–41.

32. Hamilton remarked that 'the influence of habit, the fear of failure, the inequalities existing between nations in points of industrial organization, the granting of aid to established industries by rival nations, and the concerted action of competitors through the media of dumping, underselling, extension of long-term credit and other devices might easily ruin or seriously hamper the existence of any newly established industry'. Quoted in Goldstein, op. cit. p. 31.

33. See H. Syrett, ed., *The Papers of Alexander Hamilton*, vol. 1, Columbia University Press, New York, 1961, pp. 285–6.

34. Quoted in Stanwood, op. cit. p. 167–8.

35. Figures quoted in Eckes, op. cit., p. 60.

36. Clay coined the phrase 'American System' in an 1824 speech in support of the tariff. He stated: 'The greatest want of civilized society is the market for the exchange and sale of its surplus produce. This market may exist at home or abroad, but it must exist somewhere if society prospers. The home market is the first in order and paramount in importance. ... We must speedily adopt a genuine American policy. Still cherishing the foreign market, let us create also a home market, to give further scope to the consumption of the produce of American industry. Let us counteract the policy of foreigners, and withdraw the support which we now give to their industry, and stimulate that of our own country'. Quoted in F.W. Taussig, ed., *State Papers and Speeches on the Tariff*, Harvard University, Cambridge, MA, 1892, p. 265.

37. See, id., p. 61.

38. See Stanwood, op. cit., p. 201.

39. See, id., pp. 360–61.

40. For instance, the republican John Davis argued in Congress in 1837: 'The poor only ask you that you would pursue towards them an American policy – a policy which will give them good wages for their labor – and they will take care of themselves. They entreat you not to reduce them to the deplorable condition of the miserable population of foreign countries, by reducing their wages to the same standards. ... Break down the business in which it is employed by subjecting it to the direct competition with foreign pauperism; lessen the demand for labor by introducing foreign productions, and ... you will then have as poor and wretched a population'. Quoted in Goldstein, op. cit., p. 69.

41. See *Annals of Congress*, 18th Cong., 1st Sess., p. 649.

42. Tariff policy came more strongly than before to determine political and sectional divisions, and was the plaything of politics and presidential ambitions. Rapid economic changes

occasioned remarkable reversals of positions and of arguments on tariff policy by political leaders, and by states they represented, notably Calhoun from the South, by Webster in Massachusetts, and by Henry Clay speaking for the new western agricultural states'. See Abramson, op. cit., p. 547.

43. See Stanwood, op. cit., p. 389.

44. See Eckes, op. cit., p. 63.

45. Quoted in Goldstein, op. cit., p. 63.

46. See Goldstein, op. cit., p. 73.

47. The protectionist approach was, for instance, summarized by Senator Lodge in 1894 as follows: 'The protectionist theory is to discriminate by duties in favor of every article which can be grown or manufactured in the protected country in sufficient quantities for the use of the people, and everything which can not be grown or manufactured in sufficient quantities … should be placed upon the free list'. See *Congressional Record*, 10 April 1894, p. 3617.

48. See A. Isaacs, *International Trade: Tariffs and Commercial Policies*, R.D. Irwin, Chicago, 1948, p. 218.

49. See House Miscellaneous Document no. 210, 53rd Cong., 2nd sess., in J.D. Richardson, ed., *A Compilation of the Messages and Papers of the Presidents, 1789–1907*, Bureau of National Literature and Art, Washington, DC, 1908, p. 5169.

50. See, ibid., p. 5169.

51. See Stanwood, op. cit., p. 264. While this argument had strong political clout, in 1890 the House minority report stressed its weaknesses: 'The original argument in favor of protective duties was that they were necessary to foster infant industries by preventing ruinous competition from abroad until they could secure a hold in the home market and … a few years of public support would enable them to do this. But the present bill is based upon precisely the opposite view … that as industries grow older they grow weaker and more dependent upon the bounty of the government and the forced contribution of the people …; and accordingly the important increases in the rates of duty are made with a view of still further protecting the products of our oldest industries. … If it be true that these old industries need more protection now than they needed a hundred years ago, it must be because they have been existing under an unnatural and unhealthy system'. See House Report 1466, 1890, minority, p. 27.

52. See id., p. 23. 'They tell us that the tariff equalizes things all around; that its benefits are equally distributed. It does nothing of the kind. If a tariff equalized everybody it would unequalize itself. It would not be worth a cent if it equalized everybody, for it would leave them just where it found them. The reason for a tariff is the fact that it unequalizes. It gives to one and takes from another'. See Representative Mills, *Congressional Record*, 7 May 1890, p. 4265.

53. Already in 1883, President Arthur had asked Congress whether it would be 'advisable to provide some measure of equitable retaliation in our relations with governments which discriminate against our own'. Quoted in J.D. Larkin, *President's Control of the Tariff*, Cambridge, MA, Harvard University Press, 1936, p. 48.

54. See Abramson, op. cit., p. 574.

55. Quoted in W. Culbertson, *Reciprocity: A National Policy for Foreign Trade*, McGraw-Hill, New York, 1937, p. 173.

56. See Taussig, op. cit., p. 363.

57. In *The Wealth of Nations*, Adam Smith remarked that 'by means of glasses, hotbeds, and hotwalls, very good grapes can be raised in Scotland, and very good wine too can be made of them at about thirty times the expense for which at least equally good can be brought from foreign countries'.

58. See F.W. Taussig, op. cit., p. 363. The following exchange between Senators Aldrich and Bailey is quite telling: 'Mr Bailey: The Senator from Rhode Island would vote unhesitatingly for a duty of 300 percent. Mr. Aldrich: If it is necessary … to equalize the conditions, and to give the American producer a fair change for competition, other things being equal of course'. See US Congressional Record, 61st Cong., 1st Sess., 17 May 1909, p. 2182.

59. See Eckes, op. cit., pp. 64–5.

60. See Isaacs, op. cit., p. 214.
61. See, id., p. 215.
62. See D. Johnson and K. Porter, *National Party Platforms, 1840–1972*, University of Illinois Press, Urbana, 1973, p. 168.
63. See C. Hull, *The Memoirs of Cordell Hull*, Macmillan, New York, 1948, p. 52.
64. See J.D. Richardson, *Messages*, op. cit., p. 7872. In asking for the passage of the 1913 Tariff Act, President Wilson extolled the benefits that increased competition would bring. 'We are about to set them [businesspeople] free by removing the trammels of the protective tariff. Ever since the Civil War they have waited for this emancipation and for the free opportunities it will bring ... Some fell in love, indeed, with the slothful security of their dependence upon Government, some took advantage of the shelter of the nursery to set up a mimic mastery of their own within its walls. Now both the tonic and the discipline of liberty and maturity are to ensue. ... There will follow a period of expansion and new enterprise, freshly conceived'. See *Congressional Record*, 23 June 1913, p. 3.
65. In the same year, a federal income tax was passed, thus reducing the demand on tariffs to provide revenue for the state. Cordell Hull was the main author of the law.
66. See F.W. Taussig, 'The Tariff Act of 1913', *Quarterly Journal of Economics*, vol. 28, 1914, pp. 1–30. Representative Underwood, in reporting his tariff bill in 1913, said: 'Where the tariff rates balance the difference in cost at home and abroad, including an allowance for the difference in freight rates, the tariff must be competitive, and from that point downward to the lowest tariff that can be levied it will continue to be competitive to a greater or less extent'. Quoted in Culbertson, op. cit., p. 10. On this issue, Roosevelt wrote: 'We can create a competitive tariff, which means one which will put American producers on a market equality with their foreign competitors – one that equalizes the difference in the cost of production – not a prohibitory tariff back of which producers can combine to practice extortion upon the American public'. See F.D. Roosevelt, *Looking Forward*, William Heinemann Ltd., London, 1933, p. 186.
67. Cordell Hull was an advocate of the 'competitive tariff', which, albeit never fully elaborated, could be said to include the following elements: 'the fundamental justification for the tax was to provide government revenue, with little or no regard for protection of domestic industry; while American producers should be able to expect a reasonable profit, they were not warranted in complaining about fair competition; there would be no tariff shelter for monopolies and extortionate price policies; however, no efficient or economically justifiable industry should be endangered by abnormal imports; the free list generally should include essential imports, commodities not produced here, and things which this country mainly exports; maximum rates should be placed on luxuries'. See W. Allen, 'The International Trade Philosophy of Cordell Hull, 1907–1933', *The American Economic Review*, vol. XLII, 1953, pp. 113–14.
68. 'Logrolling' can be defined as a process of mutual favours and non-interference by which members of Congress sought protection for the industries they supported.
69. See Taussig, op. cit., p. 453.
70. See Johnson and Porter, op. cit., pp. 138, 66 and 78. What was meant with this formula is not always clear. For instance, Republican representative Dingley explained in 1894: 'A tariff should be a duty which covers the difference of the money costs of production and distribution here and abroad of an article which can be produced or made here substantially to the extent of our wants without natural disadvantage'. Quoted in R. Edwards, 'Economic Sophistication in Nineteenth Century Congressional Tariff Debates', *Journal of Economic History*, vol. 30, 1970, p. 827.
71. Between 1922 and 1929, more than 600 applications covering approximately 375 commodities were filed with the Tariff Commission, which managed to complete only 47 investigations regarding 55 commodities. See US Tariff Commission, *Thirteenth Annual Report*, 1929, p. 10.
72. See Representative Underwood, *Congressional Record*, 25 March 1909, p. 268.
73. For instance, this approach appears clear in the 1894 Democratic platform, which stated: 'Knowing full well that legislation affecting the occupations of the people should be cautious and conservative in method, not in advance of public opinion, but responsive to its

demands, the Democratic party is pledged to revise the tariff in a spirit of fairness to all interests. But in making reductions in taxes it is not proposed to injure any domestic industries, but rather to promote their healthy growth. ... Many industries have come to rely upon legislation for successful continuance, so that any change of law must be at any step regardful of the labor and capital thus involved. ... The necessary reduction in taxation can and must be effected without depriving American labor of the ability to compete successfully with foreign labor, and without imposing lower rates of duty than will be ample to cover any increased cost of production which may exist in consequence of higher rate of wages prevailing in this country'. See Johnson and Porter, op. cit., p. 66.

74. See Tariff Act of 1930, 46 Stat. 590.
75. See W. Kelly, ed., *Studies in United States Commercial Policy*, University of North Carolina Press, Chapel Hill, 1963, p. 4.
76. See E. Kaplan, *American Trade Policy, 1923–1995*, Greenwood Press, Westport, Conn. and London, 1996, p. 24.
77. See US Dept. of State, *Press Releases*, weekly issue no. 38, 21 June 1930, pp. 311 and 313.
78. See F. Fetter, 'Congressional Tariff Theory', *American Economic Review*, vol. XXIII, September 1933, p. 415.
79. See, id., p. 420.
80. In arguing for an increase in sugar duties, Senator Vandenberg stressed that such duty 'provide[s] the consuming public with an insurance policy against the inevitable price gouge and price extortion which is the result when we are at the despotic mercy of foreign sugar'. See *Congressional Record*, 5 March 1930, p. 4761.
81. See *Congressional Record*, 25 May, 1929, p. 1951.
82. Meltzer considered that 'the Hawley–Smoot tariff ... worked to convert a sizeable recession into a severe depression'. See A. Meltzer, 'Monetary and Other Explanations of the Start of the Great Depression', *Journal of Monetary Economics*, vol. 2, 1976, pp. 75–93.
83. See H.M. Hart, 'Processing Taxes and Protective Tariffs', *Harvard Law Review*, vol. 49, 1936, p. 612.
84. See P. Wright, 'The Bearing of Recent Tariff Legislation on International Relations', *American Economic Review*, vol. XXIII, September 1933, pp. 16–26.
85. See Hull, op. cit., p. 355.
86. See E. Dietrich, 'French Import Quotas', *American Economic Review*, vol. XXIII, December 1933, pp. 661–74.
87. See League of Nations, *Quantitative Trade Controls: Their Causes and Nature*, prepared by G. Haberler (in collaboration with M. Hill), Princeton University Press, Princeton, NJ, 1943, p. 17.
88. See Kelly, op. cit., p. 58.
89. Quotas were used to favour suppliers from countries giving better market access to the quota country's exports.
90. See League of Nations, *Quantitative Trade Controls*, op. cit., pp. 20–27 and League of Nations, *Trade Relations Between Free-Market and Controlled Economies*, prepared by J. Viner, Princeton University Press, Princeton, NJ, 1943, pp. 54–70.
91. See League of Nations, *Commercial Policy in the Interwar Period: Proposals and National Policies*, Geneva, 1942.
92. See League of Nations, *International Convention Relating to the Simplification of Customs Formalities*, Geneva, 3 November 1923.
93. See League of Nations, International Conference on the Abolition of Import and Export Restrictions, Geneva, 17 October to 8 November 1927, *Proceedings of the Conference*, Geneva, 1928.
94. Quoted in J. Viner, *Dumping: A Problem in International Trade*, 1923 [1966], Kelley, New York, p. 37.
95. Quoted in J. Garten, 'New Challenges in the World Economy: The Antidumping Law and the U.S. Trade Policy', *World Competition*, 1993, vol. 17, no. 4, p. 132.
96. See Tariff Act of 1890, Ch. 1244, Sec. 237, 26 Stat. 584.
97. The issue of bounty-fed sugar exports was also the subject of the 1902 Brussels Sugar Convention, which sought the abolition of bounties on the production and exportation of

sugar. See G. Pigman, 'Hegemony and Trade Liberalization Policy: Britain and the Brussels Sugar Convention of 1902', *Review of International Studies*, vol. 23, no. 2, 1997, pp. 185–210.
98. See Tariff Act of 1897, Ch. 11, 30 Stat. 205.
99. See 30 Cong. Rec. 318, 1987.
100. See W. Culbertson, *Commercial Policy in War Time and After*, New York, 1919, p. 141.
101. See Tariff Act of 1922, Ch. 356, 42 Stat. 838.
102. See Tariff Act of 1930, Sec. 303, 19 U.S.C. Sec. 1303, 1988.
103. See Sherman Antitrust Act, Ch. 647, Sec. 1, 26 Stat. 209, 1890.
104. See *United States v. Topco Assocs.*, 405 U.S. 596, 610 (1972).
105. See Viner, *Dumping*, op. cit.
106. See J. Davidson, *A Crossroads of Freedom: 1912 Campaign Speeches of Woodrow Wilson*, 1956, Yale University Press, New Haven, p. 156.
107. See H.R. Rep. No. 5, 63rd Cong., 1st Sess. 17, 1913.
108. See Taussig, op. cit., p. 448.
109. See Cong. Rec., Vol. 53, Pt. 15, App. (1916) 1911.
110. See Secretary of Commerce, *Annual Report 1915*, p. 43.
111. Id., pp. 40–41.
112. Id., p. 41.
113. See Cong. Rec., Vol. 53, Pt. 15, App. (1916) 1911.
114. See Revenue Act, Ch. 463, Sec. 800–801, 39 Stat. 798, 1916.
115. Also, the Assistant Attorney General Samuel J. Graham stated that the 'purpose' of the 1916 Act 'should be to prevent unfair competition. Just as we have said to our own people by the Clayton Act that they should not indulge in unfair competition, so we propose to say the same to the foreigner.' Letter from Samuel J. Graham, Assistant Attorney General, US Department of Justice, dated 30 June 1916 (published in *New York Times*, 4 July 1916, p. 10).
116. See D. Varga, 'Amending United States Antidumping Laws to Create a Viable Private Right of Action: Must Fair Trade be Free?', *Vanderbilt Journal of Transnational Law*, vol. 21, 1988, pp. 1033–6.
117. See H. Rep. No. 922.
118. See US Tariff Commission, *Annual Report of the United States Tariff Commission*, Washington, DC, 1919, p. 33.
119. See US Tariff Commission, *Information Concerning Dumping and Unfair Foreign Competition in the United States and Canada's Antidumping Laws*, Washington, DC, 1919, p. 12.
120. Id., p. 15.
121. See 59 Cong. Rec. 346, 1919.
122. See J. Dickey, 'Antidumping: Currency Fluctuations as a Cause of Dumping Margins', *International Trade Law Journal*, vol. 7, 1981–2, p. 67.
123. See P. Victor, 'Antidumping and Antitrust: Can the Inconsistencies be Resolved?', *New York University Journal of International Law and Policy*, vol. 15, no. 2, 1983, p. 350. See also Note, 'Rethinking the 1916 Antidumping Act', *Harvard Law Review*, vol. 110, 1997, p. 1555 et seq.
124. See Tariff Act of 1922, Ch. 356, Sec. 316, 42 Stat. 943–4.
125. See S. Rep. No. 595, 67th Cong., 2nd Sess. 3, 1922.
126. See Senator Smoot, 62 Cong. Rec. S. 5874, 1922.
127. See Tariff Act of 1930, Ch. 497, Sec. 337, 46 Stat. 590, 704.
128. The term 'foreign country' was defined to include 'any empire, country, dominion, colony or protectorate, or any sub-division or sub-divisions thereof (other than the United States or its Possessions) within which separate tariff rates or separate regulations are enforced'. This provision was aimed mainly at the preferences granted to Britain by its Colonies and Dominions.
129. In a letter to House Ways and Means Committee Chairman Underwood of 1991, Secretary of State Knox stressed that penalty duties should be varied in proportion to objectionable discrimination, so that 'the gravity of the offence should be met by a suitable remedy',

which could be in the form of an imposition of few additional duties, or the imposition of such duties on all of the offending country's exports, or in the worst cases, the prohibition of all imports. See US Tariff Commission, *Reciprocity and Commercial Treaties*, Washington, 1919, pp. 274–5.

130. See Taussig, op. cit., p. 481.
131. See A. Eckes, *Opening America's Market. U.S. Foreign Policy Since 1776*, University of North Carolina Press, Chapel Hill, 1995, p. 88.
132. Quoted in Hill, op. cit., p. 81.
133. Such barriers were reviewed, for instance, in the *Report on the Privileges and Restrictions on the Commerce of the United States in Foreign Countries*, prepared by Jefferson in 1793 on a request by Congress. See, Eckes, *Opening*, op. cit., p. 12.
134. Quoted in H. Davis, *America's Trade Equality Policy*, American Council on Public Affairs, Washington, DC, 1942, p. 5.
135. See Eckes, *Opening*, op. cit. p. 5.
136. Treaty of Amity and Commerce with France, 8 Stat. 12, T. S. No. 83 (1778); see D.H. Miller, *Treaties and Other International Acts of the United States of America*, Washington, DC, vol. II, 1931–1937, pp. 3–6.
137. Art. II of the Treaty reads: 'The most Christian King, and the United States of America engage mutually not to grant any particular Favour to other Nations in respect of Commerce and Navigation, which shall not immediately become common to the other Party, who shall enjoy the same Favour, freely, if the Concession was freely made, or on allowing the same Compensation, if the Concession was Conditional'. Id.
138. See V. Setser, 'Did Americans Originate the Conditional Most-Favored-Nation Clause?', *Journal of Modern History*, September 1933, pp. 319–23.
139. Quoted in Eckes, *Opening*, op. cit., p. 6.
140. Quoted in S. Crandall, 'The American Construction of the Most-Favored-Nation Clause', *The American Journal of International Law*, vol. 7, 1913, pp. 708–9.
141. See *Independent Chronicle*, Boston, 27 May 1784, quoted in W. Hill, op. cit., p. 96.
142. See Richardson, *Messages*, op. cit., p. 975.
143. Id., pp. 709–10. In 1888, the Supreme Court also confirmed this interpretation in *Whitney v. Robertson*, 124 US 190 ('the absence of an express provision for "compensation" does not imply that favors granted on a reciprocity basis are to be generalised').
144. Quoted in Davis, op. cit., p. 87.
145. See Richardson, *Messages*, op. cit., p. 223.
146. See *Foreign Relations*, 1898, pp. 740–48 and 1899, pp. 753–7. A similar problem arose with regard to the 1881 treaty with Serbia.
147. 'It is apparent that the United States in maintaining its own interpretation of this [MFN] clause, reserving the right to grant tariff concessions only in return for certain other concessions, and the right to decide whether concessions offered by other countries are equivalent to those obtained from any particular country, occupies a vantage ground as compared with a group of nations adhering to a different interpretation and granting to us the advantages of the clause which we, however, deny to them. All of this has led to exceedingly unfavourable comment on the part of the European countries which regard our attitude on the subject of the most-favored-nation clause as characteristically selfish'. See J.L. Laughlin and H.P. Willis, *Reciprocity*, The Baker & Taylor Co., New York, 1903, p. 15. 'The most-favored-nation clause in American commercial treaties, as conditionally interpreted and applied by the United States, has probably been the cause in the last century of more diplomatic controversy, more variations of construction, more international ill-feeling, more conflict between international obligations and municipal law and between judicial interpretation and executive practice, more confusion and uncertainty of operation, than have developed under all the unconditional most-favored-nation pledges of all other countries combined'. See J. Viner, 'The Most-Favored-Nation Clause in American Commercial Treaties', *The Journal of Political Economy*, February 1924, pp. 101–29.
148. See US Tariff Commission, op. cit., p. 9.
149. Id., p. 17.
150. Quoted in Eckes, *Opening*, p. 64.

151. The 1883 treaty with Mexico was ratified, but could not be implemented because Congress never enacted the necessary legislation.
152. See *Congressional Record*, 7 January 1885, p. 506.
153. The Republican decision to put sugar on the free list was due to their need to reduce the mounting budget surplus, an easy target of anti-protectionists, to which sugar tariffs were a large contributor.
154. Diplomatic pressure was applied to Brazil to grant to the USA preferential treatment for a number of products including wheat flour. Brazil granted such treatment autonomously, without any formal agreement, from 1904 to 1923, when the USA asked Brazil to extend unconditional MFN treatment, thus ending the longest-standing remnant of the penalty-preferential approach that it had followed since the 1890s.
155. The 1896 Republican platform stated: 'We believe the repeal of the reciprocity arrangements negotiated by the last Republican Administration was a National calamity, and demand their renewal and extension on such terms as will equalize our trade with other nations, remove the restrictions which now obstruct the sale of American goods in the ports of other countries and secure enlarged markets for the products of our farms, forest and factories. Protection and Reciprocity are twin measures of American policy and go hand in hand'. See Johnson and Porter, op. cit., p. 107.
156. Quoted in Eckes, *Opening*, p. 75.
157. Some Democrats recognized some policy convergence. Congressman Bell remarked: 'When the Democrats put an article on the free list, the Republican party shouts "Democratic free trade", while at the same time, when the Republican wants to put it on the free list, he has a little scheme which he calls "reciprocity", but which is simple free trade in its most cunning form under another name, under which the Republicans sometime even bribe other countries to join in free trade with us. Our friends talk as if they had just discovered reciprocity. Why, sir, it has been the principle of every political party'. See *Congressional Record*, 55th Cong., 1st Sess., Vol. 30, Pt. 1, p. 137.
158. 'As the protective system attained greater and greater strength abroad, American producers felt themselves subject to restrictions of increasing severity. The heavy duties imposed on our goods when entering European countries seemed to make it increasingly difficult for us to extend our markets. In South America we keenly felt the competition of Europeans, partly on account of their cheaper processes of production and partly because of the assistance granted European merchants by commercial legislation which enabled them to sell some of their goods more cheaply abroad that they did at home. ... Not until we began to feel the pressure of competition and to recognize that our merchants, too, might be able to enter successfully into international competition, should circumstances be made favourable, did reciprocity as a self-conscious system gain a considerable support'. See Laughlin and Willis, op. cit., pp. 27–8.
159. See Richardson, *Messages*, op. cit., p. 6621.
160. Quoted in Eckes, *Opening*, op. cit., p. 78.
161. Id., p. 79.
162. See Richardson, *Messages*, op. cit., pp. 7426–7.
163. See Eckes, *Opening*, op. cit. p. 87.
164. 'A great gain would be secured, now that the United States is committed to wide participation in world politics, if a clear and simple policy could be adopted and followed. The guiding principle might well be that of equality of treatment – a principle in accord with American ideals of the past and of the present. Equality of treatment should mean that the United States treat all countries on the same terms, and in turn require equal treatment from every other country. So far as concerns general industrial policy and general tariff legislation, each country – the United States as well as others – should be left free to enact such measures as it deems expedient for its own welfare. But the measures adopted, whatever they be, should be carried out with the same terms and the same treatment for all nations'. Possible exceptions were considered for bordering countries and in case of special political ties and responsibilities, such as in the case of Hawaii and Cuba. See United States Tariff Commission, *Reciprocity and Commercial Treaties*, Washington, 1919, pp. 10–11.

165. 'III. The removal, so far as possible, of all economic barriers and the establishment of an equality of trade conditions among all the nations consenting to the peace and associating themselves for its maintenance'. *Congressional Record*, Vol. 56, 1918, pp. 680–81. This principle was later transposed in the League of Nations Covenant: 'Article 23. Subject to and in accordance with the provisions of international conventions existing or hereafter to be agreed upon, the Members of the League: ... (e) will make provision to secure and maintain freedom of communications and of transit and equitable treatment for the commerce of all Members of the League'. The principle was considered by Viner 'empty because ambiguous and indefinite', see J. Viner, 'The Most-Favored-Nation Clause', in *Index* (Svenska Handelsbanken, Stockholm), vol. VI, January 1931, reprinted in J. Viner, *International Economics*, Free Press, Glencoe, IL, 1951, p. 95. It is also worth noting that the word used was 'equitable' and not equal treatment. On this issue see Chapter 5.
166. See Eckes, *Opening*, pp. 90–91.
167. Id., p. 91. Secretary Hughes, in a letter of 1924 to the Chairman of the Senate Foreign Relations Committee wrote: 'It was the interest and the fundamental aim of this country to secure equality of treatment but the conditional most-favored-nation clause was not in fact productive of equality of treatment and could not guarantee it. Moreover, the ascertaining of what might constitute equivalent compensation in the application of the conditional most-favored-nation principle was found to be difficult or impracticable. Reciprocal commercial arrangements were but temporary makeshift; they caused constant negotiation and created uncertainty. Under present conditions, the expanding foreign commerce of the United States needs a guarantee of equality of treatment which cannot be furnished by the conditional form of the conditional most-favored-nation clause. ... The time has come for demanding that conditions of commercial competition be placed upon a basis which will both assure our own interests and contribute to the peace of the world by eliminating unnecessary economic contention. As we seek pledges from other foreign countries that they will refrain from practicing discrimination, we must be ready to give such pledges, and history has show that these pledges can be made adequate only in terms of unconditional most-favored-nation treatment'. The letter is reproduced in *Foreign Relations*, vol. II, 1924, pp. 183–92 (quote on pp. 190–91).
168. See Viner, 'The Most-Favored-Nation Clause in American Commercial Treaties', op. cit., p. 105.
169. As of 1922 the USA had 'no commercial treaty with France, Russia nor the greater number of secondary states of Europe; no commercial treaty with Mexico, Chile, nor many other states of Latin America; and no commercial treaty with India nor the five self-governing British dominions'. Most of the treaties in effect were more than 50 years old. See W. Culberston, *Reciprocity; A National Policy for Foreign Trade*, New York, London, Whittlesey House, McGraw-Hill Book Company, 1937, p. 253.
170. See Viner, 'The Most-Favored-Nation Clause', op. cit., p. 106.
171. The 1925 Treaty between the USA and Germany on Friendship, Commerce and Consular Rights was the first to be signed and served as the prototype for the following treaties. Its Art. VII provided for the unconditional MFN treatment. It said in a relevant part: 'Each of the High Contracting Parties binds itself unconditionally to impose no higher or other duties or conditions and no prohibition on the importation of any article, the growth, produce or manufacture, of the territories of the other than are or shall be imposed on the importation of any other foreign country. Each of the High Contracting Parties also binds itself unconditionally to impose no higher or other charges or other restrictions or prohibitions on goods exported to the territories of the High Contracting Party than are imposed on goods exported to any other foreign country. Any advantage of whatsoever kind which either High Contracting Party may extend to any article, the growth, produce or manufacture, of any other foreign country shall simultaneously and unconditionally, without request and without compensation, be extended to the like article, the growth, produce or manufacture, of the other High Contracting Party'. See US Deptartment of State, *Treaty Series*, No. 725.
172. See US Tariff Commission, *Tariff Bargaining Under Most-Favored-Nations Treaties*, Washington, DC, Rep. No. 65, 2nd Ser., 1933, p. 3.

173. See Davis, op. cit., p. 110.
174. See Kelly, op. cit., p. 27.
175. See, id., p. 50.
176. See *Foreign Relations*, 1932, vol. I, p. 809.
177. See Kelly, op. cit., p. 33.
178. Quoted in Eckes, *Opening*, p. 94.
179. The internationalization of the US industry grew significantly in this period, with the proportion of moderate and highly export-dependent manufacturers increasing to 63.6 per cent of US industry in 1909. See Lake, *Power, Protection, and Free Trade*, op. cit., p. 146.
180. See *Congressional Record*, 7 May 1890, p. 4250.
181. Quoted in Laughlin and Willis, op. cit., p. 2.
182. See US Tariff Commission, op. cit., p. 396.
183. Ibid.

4. The fairness idea in the development of the multilateral trade regime

4.1 THE RECIPROCAL TRADE AGREEMENTS PROGRAMME

As noted, before 1934, US commercial policy had been characterized by autonomous, single-column protective tariffs. Congress set duty rates unilaterally and not as a result of bargaining with other countries. The rates were generally rising, with the debate revolving around the fairness of the distribution of benefits and burdens afforded by such protection to domestic producers and consumers. But the rates applied equally to all countries (with the exception of Cuba, which received preferential treatment and a few other minor deviations). Extending equal treatment to all countries, the USA sought equal treatment in return, and, to this end, penalties could be instituted in cases of discrimination against US commerce, dumping, and other unfair trade practices. This search for reciprocity was partly construed as a matter of national and producer interests, but also in good measure as an issue of fairness between domestic and foreign competitors.

The presidential election of 1932 produced a key evolution in US trade policy. With the victory of Franklin D. Roosevelt, the focus of trade policy broadened from import politics (restricting imports through tariff legislation) to include decisively export politics, with a focus on opening up foreign markets. The process already had started in previous years, but the new administration brought it to full fruition. Part of the reason for the refocusing was the emergency situation of the depression, which had drastically reduced US foreign trade, but, more structurally, it was related to the consolidation of the USA as a continentally integrated industrial powerhouse. The outward orientation adopted in trade policy was also part of the general shift towards internationalism that characterized the Roosevelt administration.

This change was not immediately evident during the campaign, when Roosevelt followed a prudent approach meant to satisfy both protectionists and free-traders, calling for a reduction in protection, which could facilitate his domestic platform intended to boost wages and prices. Throughout the 1920s, the Republican administrations of Harding, Coolidge, and Hoover believed in low taxes and high tariffs. The foreign economic policy of the new administration remained uncertain during the first months after the election, due to the President's preoccupation with domestic issues and a sharp divergence in its advisors' views. In particular, both the National Recovery Act (NRA) and the Agricultural Adjustment Act (AAA) included provisions authorizing the President to restrict imports where they adversely affected domestic industry or agriculture.[1]

However, with a Democratic President and Congress, changes in trade policy were expected as part of the Roosevelt 'New Deal' programme. 'The spirit of the New Deal reform, [sought] in this field to correct the gross inequities of the Hawley–Smoot tariff and to secure a tariff constructed with some consideration for the consumer'.[2] In December 1933, a White House statement said: 'Now the time has come to initiate the second part of the [recovery] program and to correlate the two parts, the internal adjustment of production with such effective, foreign purchasing power as may be developed by reciprocal tariffs, barter, and other international arrangements'.[3] In June 1934, under the leadership of Secretary of State Hull, the Reciprocal Trade Agreements Act (RTAA)[4] was signed into law. Cordell Hull, a committed free-trader, played the role of a true policy entrepreneur within the Roosevelt administration. His personal commitment to open US trade, while preserving fair conditions of competition internationally, was decisive enough to overcome many resistances. The act, and the approach to policy-making it embodied, was a dominant feature of US commercial policy well into the post-World War II period and, in some respect, to this day, as well as the main source and reference for the creation of the multilateral trade regime.

Formally, the RTAA was an amendment to the Hawley–Smoot Tariff Act of 1930, and indeed its main elements had precedents in the Republican trade legislation of the preceding 40 years. The congressional delegation of power to the President to adjust the tariff within prescribed limits was already present in the Tariff Acts of 1922 and 1930. The magnitude was different, as the new legislation gave the President the authority to reduce any tariff rate as much as 50 per cent when negotiating reciprocal trade agreements with foreign countries. These were considered 'agreements' and not treaties in constitutional terms, so that they did not require the Senate's approval. Again, this latter feature had already been provided for, to a modest extent, in the Acts of 1890 and 1897.

The RTAA's aims were mainly to secure the removal of restrictive foreign trade barriers to US exports and thereby increase domestic employment[5]; to scale down excessive US tariff rates; to check the trends towards discriminatory trade practices among foreign countries and the bilateralization of trade; and to restore a commercial system based on equality of treatment. In this respect, Congress officially accepted the unconditional interpretation of the MFN clause adopted in 1923 by the Executive. In order to achieve these aims, the Act authorized the President, 'whenever he finds ... that any existing duties or other import restrictions of the United States or any foreign country are unduly burdening and restricting the foreign trade of the United States', to negotiate executive agreements with foreign countries based on reciprocal trade concessions.

Although the legislation acknowledged that tariff reduction might help stimulate domestic and international economic growth, it was not a repudiation of protectionism. As Assistant Secretary of State Sayre put it: 'If the American standard of living is to be maintained, we must trade. This does not mean 'free trade'. No responsible government is advocating that doctrine today'. A simple, unilateral reduction of tariffs, although it had been sought at times by the Democratic Party, was not a politically feasible option, because it would have been seen as unfair, especially at a time when the Depression made it imperative to boost exports activities.

> By unilateral action on the part of Congress we could reduce the barriers which we ourselves have set up against an increased flow of imports; but we would not thereby gain immediate reduction of foreign trade barriers, nor would we thereby secure ourselves against discrimination on the part of foreign nations against American goods. Joint action is the only feasible course; we must adopt a policy of 'bargaining our way' into the markets of the world.[6]

Hence,

> the objective of the program was not the adoption of 'free' trade at home, or the insistence upon the removal of all governmental controls abroad; rather it was the more moderate aim of gradually moving, on a democratic basis, toward freer trade at home and freer and less discriminatory practices abroad, so that the United States commerce might be conducted on the basis of competitive decision and private initiative.[7]

The RTAA helped create a public constituency in support of trade liberalization. But this constituency was small compared to the number of Americans who supported protection. The idea that protectionism preserved US jobs was so embedded in US polity that the government had to portray the RTAA as a temporary measure that would increase employment. The preamble of the Act noted that it was designed to 'restore the nation's standard of living', create jobs, and increase US citizens' purchasing power. Polls revealed that few Americans at the time understood the rationale for, or the costs and benefits of, multilateral trade agreements.[8]

Congress debated the RTAA for four months. Although some members opposed the legislation for protectionist reasons, many others had difficulty reconciling this new approach with the USA's democratic (congressional) tradition of determining trade policy. They objected to what they saw as an unconstitutional delegation of legislative power from the Congress to the Executive. These members alleged that the act infringed on Art. I, section 8, and Art. II of the Constitution. Moreover, they worried that 'the vesting of authority in one man, who would have to rely mainly upon the advice of others, was unwise'.[9] Some opponents feared that Congress was being forced to give advance approval for any agreements into which the President might enter.[10] Some members argued that the trade agreements were in fact treaties, which required ratification by two-thirds of the Senate. Finally, much attention and Republican opposition was directed towards the proposed repudiation of the equalization of costs of production approach as an instrument for determining proper tariff rates.

The issue of Congressional control did not disappear in the following years and also received important support from the ranks of the Democratic Party. The law kept the Executive on a tight leash, forcing him to return to Congress every three years to obtain renewed authority, as well as feedback on the agreements he had made. The law was designed to ensure that the State Department, the chief negotiator of trade agreements, would be responsive to specific sectors' needs and would balance export promotion with import protection. In exchange for guarantees that no significant sectors of the population would suffer sustained injury, the executive branch was given the power to pursue a sustained policy of trade liberalization. Moreover, special interests retained much of their ability to influence trade policy considerations.[11]

In order to fulfil Roosevelt's promise that 'no sound and important American interest [would] be injuriously disturbed' by trade agreements,[12] tariffs could only be reduced selectively on a product-specific basis. Tariff reductions ('concessions', as they were called) were granted in return for equivalent concessions by other nations and 'only after exhaustive study show[ed] that they [would] not result in material injury to any group of American producers'. Thus, the RTAA built freer trade policies upon sector-specific protection. Policy-makers could not use this act to make economy-wide cuts in tariffs. The high Hawley–Smoot duty rates became the general tariff schedule, which could be utilized in tariff bargaining, and the lowered rates arrived at by agreement constituted the conventional or minimum rates. The selective approach to the tariff laid out in the RTAA was one of its most important features. It meant that separate consideration had to be given to each of the thousands of rates in the tariff law, with varying reduction or no reduction at all, as suggested by an examination of all relevant considerations, such as the height of the rate, the competitive strength of the protected industry concerned, and the probable effect a duty reduction would have on it. During the hearing on the bill, Secretary Hull spoke of 'singling out items that could be made the subject of profitable arrangements', and of 'picking out one item very carefully here, another commodity there very carefully ... so that instead of anybody being injured, the American people would be helped'.[13]

This was part of the Administration's commitment to the principle of no serious injury to domestic industry. This principle was implicit in the manner in which the legislation contemplated tariff negotiation, namely, on a selective, product-by-product basis. It was debated in Congressional hearings and adopted as a matter of administrative policy by the Executive until the mid-1940s.[14] In 1942, the no-injury principle took the form of an escape or safeguard clause in the trade agreement with Mexico. The provision stated that: 'if, as a result of unforeseen developments and of the concessions granted on any article ..., such article is being imported in such increased quantities and under such conditions as to cause or threaten serious injury to domestic producers of like or similar articles the Government of either country shall be free to withdraw the concessions, in whole or in part, or to modify it' by increasing the duty or imposing a quota.[15] But until 1947 there was no specific procedure to invoke escape clauses in trade agreements entered into by the USA. In 1945, during the discussion of the RTAA extension bill, the administration pledged to Congress to include a general escape clause of the kind agreed to with Mexico in any future trade agreement. As no procedure was provided for, complaints were handled as all other trade agreements issues, by the interagency Trade Agreements Committee chaired by the State Department. However, it appears that very few complaints were lodged, leading to the dissatisfaction of various import-competing industries, which considered a safeguard mechanism essential in the context of the downward trend in tariff set in motion by the RTAA.[16]

As a result of the Republican victory in November 1946, the issue became even more prominent, with Congress threatening to curtail the President's trade negotiating authority. President Truman reiterated the pledge of previous presidents that 'domestic interest will be safeguarded in this process of expanding trade. ... The government does not intend, in the coming negotiations, to eliminate tariffs or to establish free trade. All that is contemplated is the reduction of tariffs, the removal of discriminations, and the achievement, not of free trade, but of freer trade.'[17] After a discussion with the Republican Congressional leadership, President Truman resolved the matter with the issuance of an Executive Order in 1947, establishing formal procedures for considering complaints by domestic industries and the use on their behalf of escape clauses provided for in trade agreements.[18] The Order entrusted the Tariff Commission with the tasks of investigating injury complaints, holding public hearings, and recommending action to the President 'in the light of the public interest'. Based on its investigation, the Commission would determine whether the reduction of a duty in a trade agreement had led to increased imports and caused or threatened serious injury to a domestic industry. The withdrawal or modification of tariff concessions was allowed only to the extent and for such time as was necessary to prevent the injury. The Order also required the inclusion of an escape clause in all future agreements, so that the withdrawal or modification of concessions could be permitted 'if, as a result of unforeseen developments and of the concessions granted by the United States on any article in the trade agreement, such article is being imported in such increased quantities and under such conditions as to cause, or threaten, serious injury to domestic producers of like or similar articles'.

The fear that import competition could cause serious injury to domestic producers also led to the introduction of a so-called 'peril-point' procedure in the RTAA extension legislation of 1948. This provision required the Tariff Commission to determine in advance of negotiations the precise tariff level that could be safely agreed to without the threat of injury. The President was not bound by these determinations, but if tariffs were cut below the peril point, he was required to provide Congress with an explanation. This approach was reminiscent of the cost-of-production formula and assumed that tariffs could be scientifically determined. The provision was disputed by the administration, which doubted the Tariff Commission's ability to reach such determinations without having to overshoot on the suggested rates. Furthermore, such an approach posed the usual fairness concern, as it would tend to privilege import-competing interests. The minority report of the House Ways and Means Committee stressed this issue by pointing out that 'the Tariff Commission ... would be required to consider only the interest of domestic producers, without regard for, and representation of, the broad interests of American industry, labor, farmers, and consumers, and American financial and foreign policy'.[19]

While perhaps contrary to the original wish of Secretary Hull and his supporters, but once cast in the US political context, the RTAA did not aim to introduce a free-trade policy, or even a general low-tariff policy, but only a policy of altering tariffs to the degree necessary to gain concessions for US exports without hurting domestic producers. But the approach chosen to ensure that domestic producers were not subject to unfair import competition differed significantly from that adopted previously. Despite the temporary flashback of the 'peril-point' provisions, the protection of domestic interests was not to be pursued through the cost-of-production equalization formula, as embodied in Sections 315 and 336 of the 1922 and 1930 Tariff Acts, which generally meant high tariffs. The USA's export interests had become preeminent. The chief instrument to open foreign markets was reciprocal trade agreements, which implied negotiable tariffs and the possibility of agreeing to tariff reductions. In this context, fairness among the various producers (export-oriented and import-competing) were to be ensured by the principle of 'no serious injury to domestic industry', as now embodied in mandatory inclusion of the safeguard clause in trade agreements. Tariff-setting had completely ceased to be a purely domestic matter and had become an international one subject to negotiations.

This also provided an important boost to the realization of the principle of unconditional equality of treatment to which US trade policy was firmly anchored.

> Ever since the days of George Washington, the policy of equality of treatment to all, tested and proved by years of experience, has been the very cornerstone of American commercial practice. It is founded upon justice and fairness, and therefore it will be enduring. On it rests our 'open door' policy. It lies at the foundation of innumerable claims and protests which the State Department makes whenever discrimination can be proved against American commerce.[20]

And by lower tariffs, the principle could no longer be dubbed 'equality of treatment before the closed door', as it was referred to in France.[21]

The RTAA had as a major objective to restore equality of treatment as a dominant principle in international trade relations. With US export capacity in continuous ascendance, this condition of trade was very beneficial to the USA. When tariffs, even high tariffs, were the main regulator of international trade, equality of treatment meant that competition among foreign suppliers would, at least, not be hindered by discrimination and political and bureaucratic interference. But with the growth of discriminatory, direct controls, such as quantitative restrictions, import and export licensing requirements, government trade monopolies, and foreign exchange controls, trade was in disarray.

At the same time, 'equality was a democratic ideal, a principle of *laissez-faire* capitalism, the basis of "decent, honorable, and fair commercial relations"', and, as such, it strongly appealed to the US ethos.[22] 'The principle of the most-favored-nation treatment in international commerce is essentially the ideal of applying between the countries of the world the same equality in the market which exists within the United States'.[23] However, the preoccupation with the fairness of a non-discriminatory policy in terms of the distribution of benefits and burdens and the risks of free-riding had not disappeared.

Secretary Hull's views prevailed within the administration, but not without controversy, and the RTAA reaffirmed the policy of unconditional MFN treatment. The law read:

> The proclaimed duties and other import restrictions shall apply to articles the growth, produce, or manufacture of all foreign countries, whether imported directly, or indirectly: Provided that the President may suspend the application to articles of growth, produce, or manufacture of any country because of its discriminatory treatment of American commerce or because of other acts or policies which in his opinion tend to defeat the purpose set forth in this section.

The language of the law covered not only *de jure* but also *de facto* unconditional treatment, thus extending the application of reduced tariff rates to countries not party to an agreement with the USA providing for such treatment. A general exception to the MFN principle was that of regional tariff relations.[24]

However, in keeping with US exporters' interests and with the ideal of equality, the RTAA authorized the President to exclude any country found to be discriminating against US products from the benefits of the lower tariffs established in the trade agreements. This power was sparingly used. Only Germany was permanently excluded in 1935 and Australia was denied MFN treatment in 1936 because of discrimination against US goods, in particular, motor cars. Once Australia modified the offending measures in the following year, its MFN benefits were restored.

Both before and after the RTAA's enactment, voices inside and outside the administration criticized the equality-of-treatment approach. In particular, George Peek, previously the administrator of the AAA and then special advisor to the President on foreign trade, opposed the unconditional MFN and favoured bilateral dealing and even barter to expand trade and promote domestic recovery. 'Peek perceived that cheap labor nations like Japan would become free riders and take advantage of unconditional most-favored-nation-treatment to gain access to the U.S. market without providing reciprocal access at home'.[25] He also considered that lower tariffs and unconditional MFN conflicted with the aims of the NRA and the AAA, which were intended to increase domestic prices and gave the President the authority to block imports that interfered with this objective. He negotiated several agreements that conflicted with the principle of equality of treatment, including a barter agreement with Germany for disposing of US cotton. Secretary Hull strongly disagreed, and the President accepted his view that the proposed agreement should not be approved. As a result, Peek resigned in 1935. This episode shows the influence of ideas. Both Hull and Peek pursued the expansion of US trade, but the former supported non-discrimination as the policy that would ensure fair competitive conditions in international trade, while the latter militated in favour of discrimination and bilateralism, as a matter of expediency.

Hull won the battle of ideas within the administration and the non-discrimination policy remained on course. However, fairness also meant that the President could suspend the application of trade agreement concessions on the grounds of foreign discrimination against US trade. At the same time, however, the possibility offered by the RTAA to suspend reduced rates because of the trade partner's 'other acts or policies', which could mean high but non-discriminatory tariffs or other trade barriers, was disregarded as a matter of policy.[26] Reductions in high foreign tariffs should be sought only through negotiations and offers of reciprocal concessions in terms of US tariffs, not by leveraging threats to increase duties.

Nonetheless, it was clear that the unconditional MFN approach could give rise to free-rider behaviour on the part of some trade partners. In order to counter that, the State Department applied the 'doctrine of the principal supplier', which meant that the country that was the chief source of supply for a certain commodity was given a tariff reduction on this commodity, provided that such concessions would not cause injury to domestic industries, and that reciprocal concessions were obtained in the course of negotiating the trade agreement. This approach was clearly meant to restrict free-riding on the MFN clause, as in general third countries (not party to the reciprocal trade agreement) would be receiving benefits that were of limited value, as they were not main exporters of the concession commodity. This represented a key element of the trade agreements programme, clearly motivated by the familiar US concern for fairness, which was later transposed in the postwar trade regime. Furthermore, reciprocal trade agreements negotiated under the RTAA generally provided for the right of either party to withdraw a concession, if, contrary to expectation, a third country proved to be the major beneficiary and an undue increase in imports occurred as a consequence. The other party then was free to terminate the agreement. Obviously, the principal supplier approach suffered from a number of limitations that could only be cured in a multilateral negotiation. In particular, small countries were rarely chief suppliers, and sometimes there was no principal, but various important suppliers.[27]

While views on the actual positive effects of the RTAA varied,[28] about 60 per cent of US foreign trade was conducted with trade agreement countries in 1938 and 1939. Between 1934 and the outbreak of World War II, the US had concluded 20 trade agreements. More than 3,000 concessions were obtained, covering approximately 75 per cent of US agricultural exports and about 50 per cent of industrial exports. On average, total exports to trade agreement countries increased more than 60 per cent in the years 1938–39, as compared to 1934–35, while the increase of exports to non-agreement countries was only above 30 per cent. And 'there appears to be general agreement that these results were obtained without serious injury to any American industry. ... One hundred and thirty of the 160 largest concession items were imported from countries which were our "principal suppliers." These 130 items accounted in 1939 for approximately 82 percent of all imports on which duty reductions had been made'.[29] Still, the Republicans' view of the Hull programme was rather negative. For instance, already in the debates for the 1937 extension, Senator Vandenberg had criticized the administration, as he considered that the trade agreements already negotiated had failed to bring just compensation for the privileges extended by the USA to foreign nations.

The 'no-injury' principle and the equality of treatment were particularly important to ensure that the distribution of benefits and burdens from international trade and any trade agreement were perceived to be fair. Moderate tariff duties were established with the belief that the domestic economy's welfare demanded such protection, and tariff reductions to the advantage of consumers and export-oriented industries were to be made, ensuring that no injury to the domestic producers would be caused. Equality of treatment guaranteed that imports came from the lowest-price sources and exports went to the market where they were priced the highest, again to the advantage of all parties concerned, both consumers and producers. Discriminatory treatment abroad was to be met with similar treatment at home.

However, such a scheme appeared to work satisfactorily, as long as tariffs were the main instruments governments used to regulate trade.

> In the various commercial agreements concluded by the United States under the Trade Agreement Act of 1934 ... the essential objective has been the restoration and expansion of world trade upon the basis of the principle of equality of competitive opportunity. In practice this has meant, among other things, an attempt to revitalize the unconditional most-favoured-nation principle into an instrument of external economic policy applicable not only to tariffs but to all forms of trade control.[30]

Indeed, already in the 1920s and 1930s countries were using many discriminatory devices. 'The pre-depression concept of "equality of treatment" meant in essence, freedom of competition among foreign countries for a nation's import trade. But when market forces are eliminated as the decisive factor in buying, the old concept of equality goes with them'.[31] For instance, widely used 'import quotas ... lend themselves more readily to violation of the equality of treatment principle, and involve a greater degree of interference with the ordinary process of the free market'.[32]

The USA at least tried to limit the use of direct trade controls and to apply the MFN clause to them, as the prospect of completely eliminating them appeared remote at the time.[33] In all reciprocal trade agreements (except with Belgium), future import quotas on the articles mentioned in the concession schedules were forbidden, except under special circumstances. In all other cases, the question was how to ensure a 'fair' share of import quotas. For this purpose, the Department of State devised the following criterion of fairness: 'If quotas can be reconciled with non-discriminatory treatment, this term must be defined as meaning the allotment to any foreign country of a share of the total quantity of any article permitted to be imported, equivalent to the proportion of the total importation of the article which that foreign country supplied during a previous representative period'.[34] A 'representative period' was further defined as one in which no discriminatory policies were in effect and no abnormal circumstances were at work to curtail imports from the USA.

On this basis, the USA negotiated quota allocations with a number of countries. Obviously, this criterion only vaguely approximated a situation in which all foreign countries may compete on equal terms – the same tariff rate – for a nation's import trade. Apart from the difficulty of identifying a representative period, quota allocation on this basis cannot give consideration to changing competitive conditions. However, the representative period is 'probably the only general formula which provides even a remote approximation to the desired result which after all is the assurance of a share in the total imports of a commodity which the United States would supply in the absence of quantitative restrictions'.[35]

Government restrictions on foreign exchange posed similar problems. As a result, a number of trade agreements included provisions for equal treatment in the allocation of foreign exchange. In some agreements, there was only the guarantee of fair treatment, while in others, more precise rules were included, so that the share of foreign exchange made available by the treaty partner for commercial transactions was to be equivalent to the share in a previous, representative period. Import monopolies also posed thorny problems. The USA sought equality of treatment by requiring that purchases be made based on commercial considerations.[36]

However,

> combating these new devices with the most-favoured-nation clause was like fighting a mechanized army with bows and arrows. The most-favoured-nation principle was based on the conception of international trade between competitive market economies. Exchange restrictions and quantitative limitation were the methods of a system of State-controlled trade from which market forces were largely eliminated. 'Discrimination' was of essence of this system.[37]

In a policy environment in which simple tariffs had already begun losing importance and the international interaction of other policies was becoming apparent, the need to find a common understanding and reference model for acceptable and fair behaviour in trade relations was emerging. The move towards a more moderate tariff system and the continued emphasis on equality of treatment contained in the RTAA allowed the USA to champion the principles of *laissez-faire* liberalism, which were in tune with the prevalent philosophy of capitalist USA. In contrast, economic nationalism, discrimination, and preferential bargaining 'means the shifting and adjustments of the currents of world trade, not in response to the operation of fundamental economic laws of supply and demand, but in accordance with the arbitrary and political decisions of public officials'.[38]

The application of general, free-market principles that inspired the RTAA, and its focus on non-discrimination and reciprocity, was not without some inconsistencies and deviations. In the area of industrial goods, the US negotiators sometimes managed to achieve larger export quotas than the representative period principle would have suggested; they also reclassified items under different tariff headings so as to nullify the working of the unconditional MFN clause, obtained goods from treaty partners that voluntarily applied export quotas towards the USA to limit import competition, and used disguised protective duties in the form of excise taxes. Furthermore, under the NRA, import quotas were introduced for a few commodities, such as liquor, lumber, and petroleum. However, overall, these deviations were of limited importance.

The same cannot be said of the policy chosen in the area of agriculture.

> Under the [New Deal] farm program the government has attempted to stabilize farm income through measures of governmental intervention in the market – measures that in recent years have increasingly led to the use of import restrictions, export subsidies, and increased tariff protection in the form of import fees. Under the trade agreements program the government has sought to stimulate the freer flow of international trade, principally by seeking agreement with other countries to reduce or remove governmental barriers of the same type employed in connection with the domestic farm program.[39]

Import quotas and export subsidies for farm products were used relatively little before World War II, mainly in two instances: in 1939, with regard to cotton and in 1941 to wheat. However, even though the Secretary of Agriculture Wallace argued that the USA was only trying to preserve its 'fair' share of world trade, disagreement arose between him and Secretary of State Hull, and a good deal of distrust was engendered in foreign countries with regard to the direction and motives of US trade policy.

The trade–agricultural policy conflict was due to a rather important disagreement. US agricultural policy subjected trade policy to the achievement of domestic policy objectives. In particular, it was aimed, at least in part, towards changing the distribution of income between farm and non-farm producers. Various policy-makers, Secretary of Agriculture Wallace among them, harboured a fairness-related concern that agriculture was being discriminated against.

> Agriculture receives less than its due share of the national dividend, urban industry an excessive share. ... Burdens of tax and interest bear more heavily on agriculture than on industry. The farming classes find themselves unable to maintain the advancing improvement in the standard of living. Foreign trade has declined and this decline has fallen disproportionately on agriculture, both before and during the depression.[40]

In this respect, agricultural policy pursued the broad objective of 'parity'. Starting with the Agricultural Adjustment Act of 1933, Congress sought to raise market prices for a number of commodities to reach 'parity prices'.

These were based on the notion that the agricultural sector should garner prices, and thus lead to farmer incomes, close to those found in the industrial sector, or at least, close to those prevalent at a time when the agricultural sector was relatively prosperous.[41] Government intervention to alter the distribution of income generated by the competitive process was an important element in US farm policy. Secretary Wallace emphasized this point, stating the administration's commitment 'to getting the farmer, the laborer, and the industrialist such share of the national income as will put each in a balanced relationship with the other' and to produce 'a supply and demand situation which will get the farmers their normal share of national income'.[42] As such 'the ideological underpinning of trade liberalisation – that is, that government should rely on markets to set price and quantity – was never accepted as a tenet of agricultural policy'.[43] The conflict between these two philosophies, that of the trade agreements programme, which relied on the fairness of the competitive market system, and that of the farm policy, which included a significant redistributive element through government intervention, was the harbinger of an enduring tension within the trading system that emerged after World War II. In this case, Hull lost the battle of ideas, and the principles of non-discrimination and (contribution-based) reciprocity had to incorporate important exceptions to cater to the farm policy's objectives.

In conclusion, the Hull programme certainly was motivated by the USA's specific interests in supporting the domestic process of economic recovery. This meant adopting the necessary legislative and policy changes to boost the export sector. The new course in trade policy did not lead to a complete renunciation of protectionism, only to its reduction. But it meant the adoption of a 'freer' trade policy, one in which state intervention in international trade was to be limited and the free play of market forces ensured.[44] The concepts of equality of treatment, non-discrimination, and no injury to domestic industry fit well with this approach, together with providing an answer to the traditional fairness concerns in terms of the distribution of burdens and benefits among the different economic actors in international trade.

Furthermore, two main developments characterized the policy shift of the 1930s. First, with the full acceptance of the negotiability of tariffs, trade policy definitively became an international (bargaining) issue.[45] And second, tariffs became just one, and perhaps not the most important, among many instruments for the control of foreign trade. The fairness concerns that, until then, could be debated and arbitrated within Congress mainly by modifying tariff rates, so as to balance (never fully satisfactorily) the interests of the various groups (import-competing and export-oriented industries and domestic consumers), now had to be played out in the international arena. It was no longer a matter of autonomously setting tariffs to equalize the costs of production and applying them in a non-discriminatory way. In light of the increasing interconnectedness of the international economy, trade policy had become – in large part – a matter of negotiations with foreign countries, not only on tariffs, but also on a much broader array of issues and instruments. Non-discrimination needed to be applied somehow to quantitative restrictions and other trade controls. Tariffs needed to be negotiated down without causing injury to domestic industries. To some extent, the interests of foreign countries also were to be taken into account. The fairness of all these actions needed to be benchmarked. The free-enterprise system and the free-market economy, which had often been part of the debate in earlier years (at times quite specifically, as when discussing the anticompetitive features of dumping or the link between monopolies and high tariffs), took centre stage as the reference point for fairness in international trade. This was very far from a spotless application of textbook, neoclassical economics doctrine. The market model was fully politically and socially 'embedded'.[46] And indeed, much flexibility needed to be applied, as the tension, particularly between trade and farm policies, had to be accommodated.

4.2   FAIRNESS CONCERNS IN THE DEVELOPMENT OF THE GATT SYSTEM

President Roosevelt called Cordell Hull the 'Father of the United Nations',[47] and for his contribution to the creation of the world organization he was awarded the Nobel Peace Prize in 1945. However, not less important was his contribution to the establishment of the multilateral trading system and the GATT, particularly through the role he played in forging the new trade policy orientation that emerged in the USA as a result of the passage of the RTAA, one of his main successes in US politics. Together with advocating a more liberal trade policy for the USA, Hull was also a champion of a multilateral approach to international trade relations.

Already, during the First World War, Hull had introduced into the US House of Representatives a resolution calling upon President Wilson to propose to the governments of all commercial nations the convocation of an international trade conference for the purpose of establishing a permanent international trade agreement congress.[48] Hull suggested that this body should consider 'all international trade methods, practices, and policies, which in their effect are reasonably calculated to create dangerous and destructive commercial controversies or bitter economic wars'; the formulation of trade agreements 'designed to eliminate, prevent, and avoid the injurious results and dangerous possibilities of economic warfare'; and the promotion of 'fair and friendly trade relations among all nations of the world'.[49] He considered the postwar period a most propitious time to convene an international trade conference, leading to the formation of a permanent international body to establish 'a code of commercial ethics'.[50] During the following years, Hull continued to advocate international cooperation in the field of trade relations. He was the principal author of the 1932 Democratic electoral platform, which stated: 'We advocate ... reciprocal tariff agreements with other nations, and an international economic conference designed to restore international trade and facilitate exchange'.[51]

Indeed, a major shift in policy towards a more internationally minded posture was already in the making in the Republican Party. In his Lincoln Day address in February 1933, President Hoover stated:

> The American people will soon be at the fork of three roads. The first is the highway of cooperation among nations, thereby to remove the obstructions to world consumption and rising prices. This road leads to real stability, to expanding standards of living, to a resumption of the march of progress by all people. It is today the immediate road to relief of agriculture and unemployment, not alone for us but for the entire world.[52]

The link between the USA's economic health and that of other nations was beginning to be perceived.

Hull had an opportunity to act on his ideas when he was nominated Secretary of State in March 1933. Already, before the passage of the RTAA, Hull had travelled to England to participate in the London Economic Conference with the objective of convincing the attending nations to reduce trade barriers. Negotiators achieved a modest compromise, whereby each nation would take steps to improve trade relations. However, while the Conference was under way, Congress increased tariffs on several agricultural products, thus undermining Hull's negotiating stance. Furthermore, at that point, President Roosevelt had not yet embraced Hull's approach and was fully absorbed by domestic recovery priorities. But Hull continued his battle and managed to convince the President, gaining his support in the effort to wrestle more control over trade policy-making from Congress. The passage of the RTAA sealed an important political victory that set the stage for a significant shift away from protection and in favour of more openness in US trade policy. But the main tenets of non-discrimination and reciprocity, necessary – in the prevailing US policy-makers' view – for international trade to be considered as fair, remained unchanged.

As seen, the notion of fairness was a constant concern of US legislators and policy-makers during the various phases in the development of US trade policy. Fairness was a preoccupation of the Founding Fathers even before the birth of the Republic, and it persisted throughout the entire 19th and early 20th centuries. Fairness was generally considered compatible with and even required a measure of protection (in cases of serious injury) for home industries and workers, as well as equality of treatment and non-discrimination in foreign markets. Often at issue was instead how to organize such protection so that the various economic actors in the domestic arena would not be discriminated against and no one would take unfair advantage of anyone else.

Vis-à-vis foreign competitors, the issue was how to ensure that trade yielded reciprocal advantages, which meant seeking equal concessions (no free-riding) and non-discrimination. Certainly, until the end of the 19th century, the US approach to fairness was a mainly domestic, inward-looking one, with little regard for the international implications of trade policy. But with the continuous development of the nation's economy and the momentous events of the time in international political and economic relations, the approach to fairness also started to evolve. The emphasis on reciprocity grew, the merits of the unconditional interpretation of the MFN clause were recognized, and the importance of moderating the tariff and using it for bargaining purposes was increasingly debated. The inequities engendered by the Tariff Acts of 1922 and 1930 and the negative effects on external trade interests and third countries could no longer be ignored. While the immediate exigencies of the economic emergency were certainly primordial, the RTAA supporters had always seen the Act in a broader context. Assistant Secretary of State Sayre stressed this point when he wrote:

> we must make the Act an instrumentality for throwing the weight of American power and influence against the disastrous world movement towards economic nationalism. Our objective must be to encourage and to make possible, so far as we can, the breaking away by other nations from the vicious circle in which they are caught, and their return to a more liberal and constructive commercial policy.[53]

In a sense, the RTAA consolidated the movement towards an internationalization or a multilateralization of the US notion of fairness, which had started significantly with a conversion to the unconditional version of the MFN pledge in 1923. With that shift, the USA had accepted that the policy of equality of treatment could not be considered only in a narrow, bilateral manner, but needed to put all countries on the same footing. In order to be treated equally in foreign markets, the USA had to extend the same favour it gave bilaterally to any specific country to all other partners. Non-discrimination (i.e., the absence of preferential treatment) then would lead to a fair distribution of benefits that foreign countries could obtain through trading with the USA.

But at the same time, there was also an increased recognition that the very height of the US tariff was harmful to foreign interests (with highly unequal economic effects across countries) and thus was not conducive to the (reciprocal) lowering of foreign trade barriers constraining world-competitive US exporters. An international trade system where equality was the leading principle required a generalized and non-discriminatory lowering of barriers. However, the risk of free-riding on the unconditional MFN clause was not forgotten. As a result, the lowering of tariffs was to be accomplished selectively, using the 'chief supplier' principle, and to be accompanied by various safeguards, so as not to cause injury to domestic producers. Foreign discriminatory treatment was addressed by allowing the suspension or withdrawal of concessions.

All of these fairness-related preoccupations found their way into the debates and negotiations that led to the creation of the multilateral trade system. In this regard, the RTAA set the pattern for the GATT, as its intellectual progenitor. At a very broad level, the RTAA's objective was, as one contemporary commentator put it, to achieve 'a world system in which governments, while they limit their total import trade as they see fit, leave the distribution of that trade among foreign countries to the competition of private producers unhampered by discriminatory treatment'.[54] And indeed, the same interpretation could be applied to the GATT.

The economic and social interconnectedness among countries – that both the Depression and the war had brought into sharp focus – provided the backdrop and part of the impulse to develop plans for a new economic order after the hostilities had ended. The RTAA was the document that all planners in the State Department and elsewhere had on their desktop. And they soon realized that while they might have preferred to have an even broader legislative vehicle, there was no chance to extract from Congress any further concessions in terms of trade policy-making. As such, the RTAA not only set the GATT's intellectual parameters, but also the legislative mould in which the international regime had to be cast.

At Hull's instigation, detailed planning for this regime started under the stewardship of State Department officials Leo Pasvolsky and Harry Hawkins in late 1940. Their efforts were aimed at linking international trade liberalization and economic growth and job creation. The exigencies of the war effort led the State Department to cooperate with the British government. The 1942 lend–lease agreement provided an opportunity to win the British government's support for postwar economic planning, by leveraging the help that the US government had decided to extend to friendly nations fighting the Axis powers.[55] While the British Government always remained much cooler with regard to postwar non-discriminatory liberalization, which it feared would mean the dismantling of imperial preferences and thus the loss of the advantages it brought to its economy, the process of transatlantic cooperation continued. In August 1941, Roosevelt and Churchill issued a joint declaration, the Atlantic Charter, whose Point Four proclaimed that non-discriminatory trade relations would be the guiding principle for international trade, but that existing obligations (such as the imperial preferences) would be respected.[56]

However, despite the apparent meeting of minds, from the US point of view (in particular the State Department's perspective), non-discrimination and reciprocal trade liberalization were the cornerstones of the future trade order, while the British government placed much more emphasis on the need for government intervention, also in the trade field, in order to promote employment.

Indeed, in the British–American debates, a fundamental ideological difference started to emerge during the war years.[57] From the US perspective (or at least from the perspective of the planners and the more free-trade-inclined representatives in government and Congress), multilateral, non-discriminatory trade would mean expanding the free-market system, which characterized the national (continental) US economy, to the whole world. This required that tariffs and other trade barriers be reduced reciprocally and the benefits and costs fairly distributed, so that no party to international trade would be allowed to free-ride, for instance, by enjoying preferential treatment. This system was both economically efficient and ethically fair, and in line with the long-standing trade policy tradition of the country. As Gardner put it: 'non-discrimination … was a doctrine approved generally within the American Administration and widely supported in the nation at large. … Well before the Second World War … equality of treatment had become firmly entrenched as a fundamental tenet of American policy'.[58]

From the British perspective, government intervention, regulation, and planning had a much larger role to play, including in international trade, which could be steered with the help of trade controls and bilateral arrangements. A regulated approach, rather than the US style of capitalism, was needed. Pragmatically, a deep and across-the-board opening of the US market, as well as of other key export markets, was considered necessary to envisage any change to the imperial preference system. '[T]here was little sympathy with the State Department's advocacy of non-discrimination. Lowering trade barriers was accorded greater priority than non-discrimination'.[59] The Dominions generally shared this view. 'Whereas the Americans endorsed multilateralism as an end in itself to promote private enterprise and prosperity, the British cared only that trade volume increased. For the British, regulation of commerce was the safe route to growth'.[60]

In the context of the war effort, these differences were played down, but they remained at the core of the difficulties in negotiating the postwar trade regime. Obviously, much debate continued also within the USA on the future shape of trade policy. Controversy persisted on the traditional issue of the extent of protection to be afforded to domestic interests, particularly to firms and workers, and on the control over policy-making, with many in Congress rather distrustful of the Executive's approach. But the need to pursue non-discrimination and reciprocity (even 'more effective' reciprocity in the minds of the protectionist members of Congress) was not in doubt. As mentioned in the previous section, the protection of agriculture was the one area where a different approach had prevailed, with the public regulation of markets holding sway. For other commodities, 'selectivity' in tariff reduction remained a political imperative in the USA. Even a radical diminution in the imperial preference, as the British side was proposing in 1943, was not enough to entice the USA into an across-the-board tariff reduction.[61]

After much discussion within the administration, especially among the State Department planners,[62] and with the British counterparts, the process was formally set in motion in November 1945, when the original 'Proposals for Expansion of World Trade and Employment' were issued by the State Department.[63] The idea was for a small group of trading nations to simultaneously negotiate trade agreements and then encourage additional agreements with other countries. In the words of Leddy, one of the Proposals' drafters, this was 'an attempt to cut the cloth of our postwar commercial policy so as to fit the legal pattern of the Trade Agreements Act and still permit bold and rapid action'.[64] Meanwhile, in December 1944, the appointment as Assistant Secretary of State for Economic Affairs in charge of trade policy negotiations of William Clayton, a businessman and Southern Democrat who fully shared this approach, was important. He took up the role of policy entrepreneur for the postwar multilateral trade regime that had been Hull's until his retirement because of ill health in November 1944.

The Proposals contained suggestions for rules to govern trade barriers, restrictive business practices, and inter-governmental commodity agreements and outlined an institutional structure for an International Trade Organization (ITO). Several issues proved rather controversial. The link between trade and employment policies, particularly dear to the British side, was acknowledged by including two separate proposals, stressing the connection between the two objectives and urging that measures to be taken in the two areas should not conflict. The language was vague enough to cover the substantive differences between the US and British approaches. The two countries also agreed to eliminate quantitative restrictions, but both Britain's wish to allow them in cases of balance-of-payments difficulties and the USA's desire to retain them in the agricultural field were accepted. Finally, the Proposals sealed the agreement to use bilateral negotiations on tariff reductions on many goods at the same time, a crucial requirement to fit the RTAA mould, and to foresee the gradual phasing out of the imperial preferences, albeit after certain exceptions were made. Already at this stage, a two-track approach had been accepted. One track would build on the RTAA's aim to achieve immediate trade barrier reductions, through bilateral negotiations and the unconditional MFN clause. This led to the conclusion of the GATT, as an interim agreement (and a liberalization 'early harvest' of sorts). The other would link trade and employment and construct a broader system, going beyond commercial policy *stricto sensu*, as well as a new international organization, the ITO, which would ultimately subsume the GATT and be the institutional home of future trade and tariffs negotiations.

The governments of several countries expressed their general support for the Proposals, and at its first meeting in February 1946, the Economic and Social Council (ECOSOC) of the United Nations passed a resolution at the request of the USA, calling for an international conference on trade and employment, which would consider the establishment of an ITO.[65] To this end, the ECOSOC established a Preparatory Committee of 19 countries to arrange for the conference and to prepare a draft charter for the ITO. For this purpose, in September 1946, the USA elaborated a more detailed 'Suggested Charter for the International Trade Organization'.[66]

The intellectual approach of the Proposals and the Suggested Charter was rather plain. As one contemporary commentator put it, they aimed at

> organizing world trade so that private enterprise can survive and thrive. It is arguable, to be sure, that world prosperity can be maximised and international friction minimized if primary reliance is placed – within carefully defined areas – on the initiative of free enterprise in a free market. In fact, this has been the conceptual core of the State Department's policy since 1934.[67]

In the same vein, another contemporary noted that:

> the United States has, since 1934, steadily adhered to a policy aimed at restoring multilateral, competitive trade, originating in private enterprise, and conducted on the basis of equal trading opportunity. There is no reason to doubt that this official policy is firmly rooted, both in the economic advantage of the United States and in the political beliefs of the majority of its people.[68]

The crucial interplay between ideas and interests was clearly stressed. If one were to consider only interests, it would be more difficult to understand the USA's insistence on non-discrimination. With its overwhelming power in the aftermath of the war, the USA could have leveraged better deals in a bilateral context. But the engrained notions of fairness and equality of treatment, like the Weberian switchman, put the USA on the multilateral track.[69]

The international code of trade behaviour that the USA was championing contained the main attributes of fairness – non-discrimination and reciprocity (no free-riding, but also no injury to domestic producers). These were increasingly considered the cornerstones of competitive international trade. But, as it had been the case for the implementation of the RTAA, the proposed regime did not amount to free trade. It meant a system in which barriers to trade in industrial products were to be non-discriminatory and lowered to moderate levels (but not eliminated), the interests of domestic producers were to be safeguarded, and agriculture would be in good measure carved out, because of the strong political opposition to a reduction in protection. This was the traditional approach of the trade agreements negotiated under the RTAA, where non-discrimination was a first-order objective and the reduction of trade barriers a second-order one.

Important in this debate was the consideration that some protective instruments, such as quantitative restrictions and exchange controls, supplant the free market entirely, while others, especially tariffs, have an impact on relative prices, but still make use of the market mechanism, and as such could be acceptable if contained within reasonable limits. This approach, while never fully consensual, had virtues that appealed to the main political currents in US polity at the time. Non-discrimination was important to the multilateralists and free-traders, such as Cordell Hull and his associates; reciprocity was key for the protectionists, as it at least ensured that any concession would have to be balanced and accompanied by safeguards against serious injury to domestic producers; and both non-discrimination and reciprocity were in line with the general US attachment to the capitalist system. Free markets and competitive trade were seen as the hallmarks of the US economy and a foundation of US democracy. This was particularly important at a time when the ideological rift between the two economic and political systems in the East and West were starting to become wide and threatening.

The USA's pursuit of its own conception of fairness in the construction of the international trade regime was not an easy one, because of the difficulties and policy inconsistencies in its own camp[70] and due to the opposition it faced from its partners, primarily, but by no means only, Britain. These problems and differences first emerged, as seen, in the discussions of the Atlantic Charter. They continued, unabated, thereafter during the negotiations that led to the adoption of the GATT and the conclusion of the ITO Charter, and certainly contributed to the final rejection of the latter. Ultimately, the US approach was to prevail, at least as far as the GATT was concerned, thanks to the strength of the ideas held by such important policy entrepreneurs as Hull and Clayton and their associates (a kind of 'epistemic community') and to the skills and commitment of its negotiators, who could obviously rely on the USA's overwhelming political and economic power at the time, but also, as will be recalled below, its pragmatic disposition to compromise.

The Preparatory Committee met in London in October–November 1946. Two further meetings were held in 1947 in Lake Success (New York) and Geneva, and the final conference took place in Havana between November 1947 and March 1948. Before the Havana conference, a tariff conference was carried out, which led to the conclusion of the GATT in Geneva in October 1947.

Many contentious issues were hotly debated during these negotiations. But surely among the most important and controversial was the prominence given to the principle of non-discrimination. For instance, the protracted argument over the Imperial Preferences revolved around the design of an exception to the non-discrimination rule (as well as the reciprocal balancing of the lowering of Imperial Preferences on one hand and the high US tariff rates on the other). The disagreement over the proper government role in pursuing growth, development, and employment through trade instruments, again, had an equality-of-treatment component, as the policies generally envisaged to seek such objectives entailed, at the time, discriminatory measures of and heavy interferences with market forces.

Already, the Draft Charter that had emerged from the London meeting provided that countries should enter, upon request, 'into reciprocal and mutually advantageous negotiations ... directed to the substantial reduction of tariffs and the elimination of import tariff preferences'.[71] Following the US approach already contained in the Proposals, this meant that no new preferences were to be introduced and that negotiated MFN reductions would reduce existing margins of preferences gradually, with a view to their final elimination. The exception to non-discrimination in this instance was to be only a transitory one. While agreed upon in principle, this approach remained controversial in Britain and proved difficult to implement when actual tariff negotiations stared in the spring of 1947.

The USA entered the tariff negotiations with the greatest tariff-reducing authority ever delegated to the Executive: 50 per cent of the 1945 tariff levels. However, the negotiating method was to remain based on bilateral and selective tariff reduction deals, to be multilateralized through the operation of the MFN clause. The USA did not accept the across-the-board tariff reduction procedure favoured by Britain.[72] In addition, the administration had to agree to the inclusion of an 'escape clause' in every trade agreement, providing for the withdrawal or modification of concessions that caused or threatened to cause serious injury to a domestic industry. However, with a large tariff reduction authority, Clayton was convinced that enough bargaining power was at his disposal to achieve the elimination of the Imperial Preferences, as increasingly demanded by the then Republican-controlled Congress.

The negotiations started on a bad note, as the US Congress passed a bill providing price support for the domestic wool industry and an increase in the wool tariff. This development risked completely derailing the negotiations, as wool was one of the major commodities on which Britain and Australia were seeking increased access in the US market. At Clayton's request, President Truman intervened, vetoing the bill and authorizing Clayton to offer instead a 25 per cent tariff reduction. But the problems were not over. The US negotiators proposed to reduce tariffs to the maximum of their delegated authority on a vast number of items, which meant a virtual liquidation of the Hawley–Smoot tariff and a return to the levels of the 1913 Underwood Tariff. On its side, Britain offered less significant reductions, often smaller than one-third of the existing preferential margins, as British negotiators considered that in the negative economic situations of the time, the close cooperation with Commonwealth countries could not be weakened. In assessing the proposed deal with the USA, what counted in the end was the benefit arising from increased trade flows, not tariff concessions for items that had no immediate commercial interest. And in that context, the difficult supply capacity of the British industry was an important factor. It was on that broader basis that reciprocity should be assessed.

Faced with strong British opposition, Clayton and the US delegation had to choose between breaking up the negotiation, which most likely would have meant the end of cooperation in trade matters (and with it the project of establishing a behavioural code for fair commercial relations) and the acceptance of only a limited decrease in the discriminatory practice contained in the Imperial Preference. Clayton chose this latter course. The final deal brought about a significant reduction in US tariffs and more limited concessions by Britain in the preferences it enjoyed in the Dominions, which was partly compensated by greater concessions in the preferences the Dominions received in the British market and by a ban on new preferences. However, and most importantly, the Geneva talks also sealed the accord on a broader set of rules governing international trade relations, as embodied in the GATT. Almost unnoticed, the postwar multilateral trade regime was born and the US imprint is unmistakable. The GATT was largely based on the draft rules included in the commercial policy chapter of the broader Charter that was being negotiated in preparation for the UN Conference on Trade and Employment that was about to begin in Havana.

Another thorny set of issues in the negotiations of the ITO Charter involved the relationship between trade liberalization (on the basis of non-discrimination and the reciprocal reduction of trade barriers) and both employment and development. With regard to the employment issue, the USA recognized the importance of high levels of employment and effective demands to achieve an expansion in world trade. However, it considered that such objectives were neither completely nor primarily in the hands of governments and, unlike the reduction of trade barriers, were not amenable to binding international commitments.[73] Furthermore, government interference with market forces was always a matter of concern in the USA, as shown from the troubled history of the 1945 Full Employment bill, which business and Congressional conservatives strongly opposed.[74] The Suggested Charter thus proposed that each country should 'take action designed to achieve and maintain full employment within its own jurisdiction through measures appropriate to its political and economic institutions'.[75] This approach was basically confirmed in the Havana Charter, which also stressed that action in this area was necessary in achieving the Charter's general purpose (Art. 2).

Even more controversial was the issue of including a safeguard clause that could release affected countries from their multilateral obligations and allow the introduction of trade restrictions in case of deflationary pressures. Such an 'employment escape clause' was strongly supported by Australia, and equally strongly resisted by the USA, which felt it was directly targeted by the proposal, as the only country that actually could create a new economic slump. In the end, the Havana Charter obligated surplus countries to take measures to correct situations that might create employment difficulties in other countries. Failure to do so could be invoked under the Charter's 'nullification and impairment' provisions and thus lead to a release from Charter obligations, including in the area covered by the commercial policy chapter, thus potentially allowing the introduction of trade restrictions. Furthermore, more flexibility to use quantitative restrictions was assigned to countries in balance-of-payments difficulties. While discrimination in the application of such restrictions was to be transitory, there was no assurance that this transition would expire in the near future.[76]

In this respect, and more generally, it is important to note that the Charter's negotiation was not undertaken in isolation. Decisions taken in that context were also heavily influenced by other, parallel negotiations and events in international economic relations. The prospects of establishing a multilateral trade regime anchored to fairness principles was in the end acceptable to many European countries because they saw the opportunity of regaining their trade capacity in a reasonable period of time, particularly through the help of the Marshall Plan. As Brown observed:

> Many of the escapes and exceptions to general Charter rules, particularly the balance-of-payment exceptions, were formulated in practical recognition of [European] difficulties. It is easy to imagine in retrospect that the limitations and safeguards surrounding these exceptions would have been extremely difficult if not impossible to negotiate had it not been for the hopes and expectations associated with the Marshall Plan. Without these limitations and safeguards the Charter would probably have been so weakened as to be unacceptable to the United States. Without the Marshall Plan, the general commitments of the Charter would probably have proved unacceptable to many European countries.[77]

However, the balance-of-payments problem was only one of the many concerns important to the developing countries participating in the negotiations, and there was no Marshall Plan in sight to help them develop.[78] As a result, they vigorously asserted the importance of promoting economic development, an issue that had been given little attention in the Anglo-American postwar planning.[79] Countries such as Australia, Brazil, Chile, and

India insisted that economic development should be included as one of the new regime's main objectives and that enough flexibility should be allowed for them to pursue their development policies. In this respect, the Havana Charter included 'economic and social progress and development' among the objectives to be pursued (Art. 1). To this end, signatories of the Charter committed to 'national and international action ... to foster and assist industrial and general economic development, particularly of those countries which are still in the early stages of industrial development'. At the Havana conference, in particular, developing countries claimed full freedom in their trade policy. This meant that in order to promote industrialization, they should remain free, *inter alia*, to raise tariffs, use import quotas, and create preferential systems. To the US delegation and that of many other industrial countries, these were exorbitant, unacceptable requests.

The measure of flexibility for development finally included in the Charter (but in the main not incorporated in the GATT) was generally won against the opposition of the USA, but also of Britain, which conversely, in the area of employment, actually advocated such flexibility for government action. Despite US opposition towards tariff preferences, developing countries obtained that, albeit under rather strict conditions, 'new preferences could be granted in the interests of economic development ...' (Art. XV). Furthermore, developing countries demanded to be allowed to use quantitative restrictions to allocate scarce foreign exchange for those imports most needed for their development plans. As noted, in the US view, quantitative restrictions were considered particularly offensive, as they meant discrimination and political interference: 'Under a quota system the direction of trade and the sources of imports [are] rigidly fixed by public authority without regard to quality, cost or price. Under a tariff, equality of treatment of all other states can be assured. Under a quota system, ... there must inevitably be discriminations amongst other states'.[80]

Developing countries took a different approach. For instance, India remarked: ' ... our plans are of an expansionist character ... but it will only expand if we take a rational view of the whole problem of trade regulation, and instead of rejecting certain methods of regulation on grounds which are not applicable to Indian conditions, make full use of them for the purpose of building up our economy'. Even more broadly, India stressed that: 'it is essential that the nation's economic development should not be left wholly to the operation of the private enterprise and of unchecked competition, whether internal or external'.[81] At the 1946 London meeting, developing countries secured the right to use quantitative restrictions to promote economic development (subject to negotiations with affected trading partners for possible compensations). This was basically the compromise that was retained in the GATT. However, developing countries considered that insufficient.

Difficult negotiations continued at Havana, and they finally won more flexibility in the Charter, through a very complex set of provisions. Briefly, in the case of commodities covered in a trade agreement, the Charter provided that prior consent must be obtained from other parties to that agreement. For commodities not covered by any obligation, consent must be obtained from other ITO members that would be affected or permission must be requested through the ITO and would be authorized, if such quota were not deemed more trade restrictive than any other reasonable or practicable alternative. Developing countries also obtained the possibility of establishing regional preferential agreements, with a view to providing adequate markets for the industries or agricultural sectors to be developed. Guiding principles for approval were consultation, mutual accommodation, and the avoidance of unnecessary injury to the interests of other ITO members.

The controversy over quantitative restrictions for industrialization purposes dovetailed with that regarding subsidies as a policy instrument. The USA's position was that production subsidies were a preferable means of protection, as opposed to quantitative restrictions, as they could, by lowering prices, increase international trade.[82] Furthermore, their 'cost is clear and taxation can distribute [their] cost equitably among those who benefit'.[83] However, for instance, Brazil argued that it considered subsidies as harmful as quotas, since they could both lead to oversupply and unfairly displace some countries' exports,[84] and Cuba stressed that subsidies were useless for developing countries that could not afford them.[85] From the developing countries' side there was a sense that, also in this instance, the design of the international rules would not be suited to their needs and circumstances. The original GATT contained only a notification and consultation requirement for subsidies, as the issue had not been settled when the agreement was concluded. The Charter instead included provisions (Art. 25–28) that were fully inspired by the original US position, as put forward in the Proposals and Suggested Charter. The approach was to prohibit export subsidies (i.e., subsidies which result in the sale for export at prices lower than the comparable price in the domestic market), as these – in the traditional US countervailing duty approach – were 'regarded as an unfair method of competition'[86] likely to injure domestic producers of like goods, and to allow production subsidies, subject to notification and consultation requirements. In addition, the Charter included a provision dealing with primary commodities that banned the use of subsidies to acquire 'more than a fair share of world trade in that commodity'.[87] Amendments to the GATT that entered into effect in 1957 took over some of the Charter's provisions.

The controversy over investment that erupted at the 1947 Geneva meeting of the Preparatory Committee also related to issues of discrimination, which was central to the fairness debate. Investment issues were left conspicuously outside postwar planning. It was mainly at the instigation of US business that the issue of investment was later included as negotiations were already under way. In particular, the omission of any reference to the treatment of foreign investment in the London draft was a matter of concern to US business, and the US delegation took up the matter in the subsequent Geneva Preparatory Committee meeting. At the time, developing countries were quick to realize the importance of investment for development and suggested many amendments to the US proposal, all in the direction of affirming the right to discriminate between investors and legitimizing the right to expropriate foreign investments without paying full compensation to the owners. The USA's business initiative had backfired. In Havana, the US delegation had to expend no small effort to fight off some of what it considered the most dangerous proposals. However, in the final language of the Charter, members only undertook 'to give due regard to the desirability of avoiding discriminations between foreign investments', thus leaving the door open to the use of discriminatory treatment.[88]

In conclusion, at the end of the protracted and difficult negotiation phase of the multilateral trade regime, two international instruments had emerged: the GATT and the Havana Charter. As is well known, the former, meant to be only a provisional, tariff reduction agreement, continued to exist for almost 50 years, while the latter, which had designed a much broader edifice, substantively and institutionally, was stillborn, since it failed to be ratified by the USA and, as a consequence, by the other major players. Both documents were clearly influenced by the USA's notion of fairness, based on non-discrimination and reciprocity as the guiding principles for international trade relations. But they also incorporated important differences in this respect, which contributed to their opposite fates.

4.3   THE RESULTS OF THE NEGOTIATIONS: THE GATT AND THE HAVANA CHARTER

The GATT was originally a trade agreement designed to record the results of a tariff conference that at the time was envisioned as the first of a number of such conferences to be conducted under the auspices of the impending ITO. The Truman administration was under pressure to conclude tariff reduction negotiations before the President's authority to negotiate under the RTAA, as extended, expired in June 1948. Recognizing the mounting hostility to liberal trade policies in Congress, the USA suggested that tariff negotiations be undertaken at the same time, but independently of, the ITO negotiations. As seen, difficult talks took place until the end of October 1947, which led to the conclusion of the GATT. The Agreement consisted of two parts: the general provisions, mainly selected articles from the commercial policy chapter of the 'Geneva draft' of the ITO Charter, and schedules of tariff concessions. The link between the two was strong, as the tariff concessions could be easily 'nullified' if fair trade rules were not established and adhered to. The GATT entered into force on 1 January 1948 by means of a Protocol of Provisional Application. At the Havana Conference, which ended in March 1948, and later in the year, several changes were made to the Agreement's provisions.

As the intricate and heavy preparatory work suggests, the GATT is a complex document, the product of intense negotiations and compromises. However, the US imprint is evident in many respects, starting from the very objective to establish a code of international behaviour based on fairness as a defining element and market-based competition as the economic reference model. This approach permeates both the GATT and the Commercial Policy chapter (Chapter IV) of the Havana Charter. As Secretary of State Acheson put it: 'the code of fair trade practices set forth in the Charter is a code designed to help achieve an international trading system in which traders may buy and sell where they please – the system economists call 'multilateral trade' – the system under which private enterprise and free competition has the best chance to prosper'.[89] And indeed, the principles of non-discrimination, reciprocity, and fair competition are firmly enshrined in the rules of the GATT.

The principle of non-discrimination is embodied in the provisions relating to the unconditional MFN treatment of foreign products (Art. I and II) and national treatment of foreign products once imported (Art. III). The unconditional MFN obligation contained in Art. I applies not only to border measures (e.g. tariffs), but also to internal measures affecting imports and exports: 'any advantage, favour, privilege or immunity granted by any contracting party to any product originating in or destined for any other country shall be accorded immediately and unconditionally to the like product originating in or destined for the territories of all other contracting parties', both 'with respect to customs duties and charges of any kind imposed on or in connection with importation or exportation or imposed on the international transfer of payments for imports or exports, and with respect to the method of levying such duties and charges, and with respect to all rules and formalities in connection with importation and exportation, and with respect to all matters referred to in paragraphs 2 and 4 of Art. III', namely 'internal taxes and other internal charges' applied to like domestic products as well as 'laws, regulations and requirements affecting the internal sale, offering for sale, purchase, transportation, distribution or use' of imported products.

With the exception of the certain longstanding historical preferences, which were saved by the so-called 'grandfather clause' of Art. I (especially the British Imperial Preferences), Art. II confirms that tariff concessions are to apply to all contracting parties and not only to the party with which each concession was negotiated. The traditional freedom to enter into (discriminatory) customs unions and free-trade areas is safeguarded by Art. XXIV. Furthermore, under Art. II, a GATT contracting party making a tariff concession is committed (except as otherwise specifically provided) not to impose other duties or charges that would tend to offset that concession. Similarly, many GATT provisions are meant to ensure that other trade measures do not undercut tariff concessions.[90] The principle of non-discrimination also extends to the administration of non-tariff trade barriers, such as quantitative restrictions (which are generally prohibited, under Art. XI, subject to specified exceptions), government procurement rules, and exchange controls. The most important exceptions are that quantitative restrictions may be maintained for balance-of-payments purposes (Art. XII–XV), that they may be used in support of certain domestic agricultural programmes, particularly those which, by raising domestic prices above the world market price, tend to create an incentive to import (Art. XI), and that they may be employed by developing countries, under specific conditions, in pursuit of their economic development plans or in response to foreign exchange problems (Art. XVIII).

While the MFN obligations ensured that a country could not discriminate externally between different contracting parties, Art. III ensured that it could not discriminate internally. The national treatment provision requires the equal treatment of imported foreign products and like domestic products in regard to internal taxation and regulation. Thus, for instance, internal taxes are not to be imposed at a higher rate on imported goods than on domestically produced goods. Furthermore, all general government measures affecting foreign trade must be published before their application 'in such a manner as to enable governments and traders to become acquainted with them' (Art. X), thus limiting the opportunity to circumvent or offset existing obligations. Several GATT articles also require the notification of specific trade measures, with a view to increasing the transparency of trade policy-making.

Reciprocity, together with equality of treatment (non-discrimination), is another key operational principle necessary, from the US perspective, to ensure fairness in international trade relations, and as such, it has been incorporated as a cornerstone of the GATT. As non-discrimination provisions aim, in general, to prevent the granting of special privileges to either foreign or domestic products, the principle of reciprocity seeks to avoid unbalanced concessions in negotiations. The GATT Preamble specifically refers to reciprocity when it calls for the conclusion of 'reciprocal and mutually advantageous arrangements directed to the substantial reduction of tariffs and other barriers to trade and to the elimination of discriminatory treatment in international commerce'. The initial, reciprocal balancing of concessions as negotiated in the various bilateral tariff reduction deals is recorded in the national Schedules of Concessions annexed to the GATT. Art. II(b) then provides that imported products shall be exempt from 'all other duties and charges of any kind' in excess of those recorded in the Schedules. Tariffs as negotiated at 'reciprocal and mutually advantageous' levels are thus bound.[91] The same reciprocity concept expressed in the Preamble is repeated in Art. XXVIII bis with regard to (further) tariff negotiations.

If then parties wish to modify a tariff concession, a new agreement needs to be concluded with the party with which the concession was initially negotiated (and with other parties having a principal supplying interest) and this with a view to maintaining 'a general level of reciprocal and mutually advantageous concessions'. If no agreement can be reached, the affected parties can withdraw concessions 'substantially equivalent' to those initially negotiated (Art. XXVIII).[92] Furthermore, if the balance of benefits and burdens resulting from tariff negotiations and, more generally, from all the provisions of the Agreement were to be affected over time, even without a breach of any obligation, Art. XXIII provides for a complaint mechanism aimed at 'ensuring continued reciprocity and balance of concessions in the face of possibly changing circumstances'.[93]

The provisions on non-discrimination and reciprocity are fundamental to ensuring fairness in international trade relations. Non-discrimination means no free-riding, since countries have to extend the benefits of any bilateral lowering of trade barriers to all other countries and cannot benefit from exclusive reductions or other advantages to increase bilateral trade flows, thus bringing such flows more in line with comparative advantages and market forces, which ultimately would determine the distribution of trade benefits and burdens. Similarly, countries could not afford domestic products with a better treatment than foreign products, with the exception of the tariff duties, which are subject to progressive reduction. In principle, tariffs are the only fully legitimate mechanism to regulate foreign trade, a long-standing US position, and the balance of reciprocal tariff concessions should not be undercut by other restrictive measures that would diminish or negate such concessions (thus affording a free-ride). Transparency provisions also are meant to help to guarantee such a result.

This is the main fairness approach adopted in the GATT, which is fully in line with the prevailing US understanding of the notion. However, as seen in previous sections, the fairness discourse in the USA, increasingly over time, had been couched in terms of a requirement of fair competition. Indeed, fair or market-based competition is perceived as the economic system that would better ensure the realization of reciprocity and no free-riding, particularly when the aspects beyond tariff negotiations are taken into account. As a result, the GATT also embodies the principle of fair competition.[94] In this respect, for instance, when discussing the value determination of imported goods for customs purposes, the GATT directly refers to the price formed 'in the ordinary course of trade under fully competitive conditions' (Art. VII). Furthermore, 'the principle of "commercial consideration", or support for values of the free market versus government interventionism, is implicit in the entire framework of the GATT. The term is mentioned specifically in Article XVII, where state-controlled enterprises are enjoined to act according to "commercial consideration" ...'.[95]

The GATT does not purport to preordain market results; rather, it focuses on general rules and trade barrier reductions that can increase trading opportunities and generate market outcomes. In this respect, it does not attempt to define strict reciprocity requirements (for instance, in terms of depth of tariff cuts, trade coverage, loss of tariff revenues, or projected new market opportunities). The Agreement tries to ensure reciprocity by setting out behavioural rules for governments, also with regard to those instances in which governments may want to intervene to correct perceived market failures or modify the distribution of benefits and burdens as a matter of fairness. The general approach retained in the GATT is that the more market-distorting a trade policy instrument is, the more stringent are the constraints applied to it. As a result, domestic governmental intervention in the form of production subsidies (Art. XVI:1), consumption taxes and non-discriminatory internal regulations (Art. III) are permitted because they are considered to interfere the least with the price system. MFN tariffs, while subject to negotiated reduction, are preferred to trade preferences and quantitative restrictions, which instead can distort or paralyse the price system. 'The admissibility of antidumping and countervailing duties (Art. VI) and the prohibition of export subsidies (Art. XVI:B) reflect the same premise that the pattern and structure of international trade should be determined by undistorted market competition and that the benefits of trade are maximized if decisions to import or to export are taken by citizens themselves responding to market forces and informed by market prices'.[96]

If market-based competition is the GATT's reference system to ensure fairness in international trade relations, the traditional US preoccupation to guarantee fairness among different groups of domestic producers – import-competing and export-oriented ones – also finds its place in the Agreement. The objective is to make sure that tariff concessions, while helping some producers, do not result in serious injury to others. The mechanism is the inclusion of safeguard provisions along the lines of the Mexican clause, which the US Congress had asked the President to incorporate in all trade agreements under the RTAA programme. Then, if a tariff concession unexpectedly leads to serious injury to a domestic industry, the affected contracting party may have recourse to Art. XIX in order to withdraw that concession (and raise back the tariff duty), to the extent and for such time as may be necessary to remedy the injury. In the absence of any agreement otherwise, the contracting party to which the concession was originally granted is then entitled to withdraw equivalent concessions.

While many compromises had to be reached in the form of flexibilities and exceptions, the basic thrust of the GATT followed the original US objectives, as included in the plans for the postwar reconstruction of the international trade regime. In particular, it reflected the 'dogged judgement that the most satisfactory basis for trade is world-wide and unmanaged competition'.[97] Competitive trade meant non-discriminatory and reciprocally advantageous trade, the requirements of a fair trading system. The same approach inspired, from the US side, the broader negotiation of the ITO Charter. But if exceptions and loopholes had already partly tainted the GATT, including because of the USA's own policy inconsistencies and ever-strong protectionist sentiments (the treatment of agriculture in the GATT remains emblematic in this respect), the Charter, with its much broader scope, was even more bedevilled by the need to satisfy contrasting ideas and approaches on how the trade regime should be designed. Quite interestingly many of the issues which the Charter addressed, from competition policy to foreign investment, and that were left out of the GATT, remained a matter of debate and controversy over the years and have become particularly contentious in the WTO for similar reasons. As Gardner put it: 'the two major sponsors of the ITO sought to incorporate in the Charter a detailed statement of their favourite economic doctrines. The United States pressed formal undertakings for the elimination of Imperial Preference, quantitative restrictions, and discrimination of all kinds. The United Kingdom pressed equally detailed undertakings to protect domestic policies of full employment'.[98] Developing countries also, albeit much less successfully, pushed for the recognition of their economic and developmental needs. All this made for a very difficult compromise.

The Havana Charter consisted of 106 articles divided into nine chapters. The Commercial Policy chapter from which the GATT was largely taken was accompanied by others dealing with such broad matters as restrictive business practices, intergovernmental commodity agreements, international aspects of domestic stabilization policies, economic development, and international private investment, as well as the institutional provisions for the ITO and the settlement of disputes. With regard to restrictive business practices, each member agreed to take all possible measures to ensure that both private and public enterprises did not engage in practices that could restrain competition, limit market access, or foster monopolistic control in international trade. Upon a member's complaint, the ITO was to investigate the matter and make recommendations for remedial actions. The provisions on restrictive business practices thus gave formal recognition to 'the principle of competition in international markets' but stopped short, as the Charter's critics emphasized, of outlawing cartels *per se*.[99]

With regard to commodity agreements, ITO members agreed to limit their use for the regulation of primary commodity markets. Such agreements (cartel agreements of sorts), which allowed the control of production, exports, imports, or prices, could be used only for commodities produced under strictly specified conditions and in situations of widespread surplus and distress. Also, these agreements were to be subject to several requirements in terms of duration, periodic reviews, open participation, availability of supply, and progressive adjustment so as to promote the restoration of free markets.

With respect to employment and stabilization policies, each member agreed to take action designed to achieve and maintain full and productive employment and a growing demand through measures appropriate to its political, economic, and social institutions. Furthermore, in case of maladjustments in the balance of payments that might endanger domestic employment programmes, ITO members agreed to cooperate, while remaining free to decide which measures to take. As far as economic development was concerned, members agreed to promote it both through cooperation and the action of international agencies. Each developing country was to be free to subsidize new industries. And with regard to commodities not covered by a trade agreement commitment, it would be free to impose new tariffs or to increase existing ones. But in cases in which a member wanted to use an instrument that was disallowed, such as a quantitative restriction, it needed to obtain permission from affected ITO members. Thus, restrictive measures were not to be used for protecting infant industries without international approval. In the field of foreign investment, signatories agreed to provide adequate security for existing and future investments, not to impose unjust requirements on the ownership of such investments, or other unreasonable conditions. While these provisions were not further specified, and could be open to dispute, signatories did *not* commit to avoid discriminatory treatment. Finally, the ITO was to have an articulated institutional structure composed of a Conference of the member states, an Executive Board of 18 members, specialized technical commissions, and an international secretariat headed by a Director-General. Disputes arising between ITO members were to be settled by consultation, arbitration, or decision by the Executive Board. The Board's decisions could be referred to the Conference for review.

From this brief overview, it seems clear that the proposed Charter had a very broad reach that went well beyond the stated objectives of US postwar planners. While they strenuously defended the Charter as consistent with the overall approach of creating a system based on non-discrimination and reciprocity that supported fair, market-based competition,[100] the opposition to the ITO project proved very strong, to the point that at the end of 1950, the

Truman administration decided to quietly shelve the initiative.[101] Only the commercial policy chapter (somewhat modified) survived, as embodied in the GATT.

As late as April 1950, Secretary Acheson still advocated that:

> by joining the ITO, member nations will accept the principles of non-discriminatory, competitive, multilateral trade, governed primarily by the forces of the market place. These are the principles in which the United States believes and which it has advocated. Only if these principles are accepted and widely lived up to can the private trader have a real opportunity to conduct his business on a fair, competitive basis.[102]

In his January 1950 State of the Union address, President Truman still called for Congressional approval of the Charter. However, the vast majority of the business community, which generally shared the administration's enthusiasm for non-discriminatory and competitive world markets, turned against it. In a sense, the Charter fell victim to its own stated objectives, by not living up to them in the eyes of US business. This, together with a changed world setting and new foreign policy priorities, not least the Korean War and the Marshall Plan, as well as the fact that the GATT was already delivering results in terms of reducing trade barriers, rang the Charter's death knell.

The stress that business and other groups placed on the Charter's shortcomings with respect to the key elements of fairness in international trade – non-discrimination, reciprocity, and ultimately market-based competition – shows the importance that they attached to them. Indeed, they were not only an emanation of a particular political and bureaucratic faction, with Cordell Hull as the main instigator and policy entrepreneur, but they represented a policy approach broadly shared by those parts of the US polity that had an interest in international trade relations.[103] And this was still in the presence of important differences with regard to the appropriate level of protection (through market-conforming tariff duties) to be afforded to the domestic industry, and the acceptation of the need for a specific (and different) treatment of agriculture.

However, across the political spectrum, both highly protectionist groups and (the majority of the) liberal ones found themselves united in the cry against the Charter as a document that, in the words of the National Foreign Trade Council, a strong supporter of the RTAA programme, 'does not reflect faith in the principles of free, private, competitive enterprise'.[104] Even the liberal and internationally minded business representatives came out against the Charter for a number of reasons. They believed that it was 'too heavily laden with the ideological and practical paraphernalia of government regulation and control, so that it would not help, and very likely hinder, the development of private enterprise'[105]; that it would be of little help in removing foreign trade barriers and that by sanctioning various objectionable practices through exceptions it would even strengthen some of them (i.e. import quotas); that it provided legitimization to commodity agreements, considered as harmful, government-sponsored cartels; that it would provide too little discipline for restrictive business practices and an unfair advantage for enterprises active in jurisdictions where cartels were generally tolerated; and that it would provide little if any protection to US investors, who still could be discriminated against in their foreign operations.[106]

The Executive Committee of the US Council of the International Chamber of Commerce summarized the prevailing criticisms with particularly stark language. The Charter, it stated,

> is a dangerous document because it accepts practically all of the policies of economic nationalism; because it jeopardizes the free enterprise system by giving priority to centralized national governmental planning of foreign trade; because it leaves a wide scope to discrimination, accepts the principle of economic insulation and in effect commits all members of the ITO to state planning for full employment. From the point of view of the United States, it has the further very grave defect of placing this country in a position where it must accept discrimination against itself while accepting the Most-Favored-Nation treatment to all members of the Organization.[107]

Obviously, some of this criticism could also be levelled at the GATT, particularly because it had retained many of the exceptions to the principle of non-discrimination and did not eliminate the possibility of free-riding. However, what is important to stress is that there seemed to be no major disagreement on the importance of ensuring fairness in international trade, through its main operational attributes: non-discrimination and reciprocity. Ensuring fairness was to be one of the main objectives of any multilateral trade regime. The difference between proponents and opponents of the Charter was that the former accepted its shortcomings mainly as necessary compromises to achieve international acceptance and on balance considered the Charter as a step forward,[108] while the latter simply considered that, as negotiated, the Charter was not good enough, and some of its features were actually potentially dangerous and needed to be rejected outright.[109]

4.4   A SELECTIVE LOOK AT THE EVOLUTION OF THE GATT SYSTEM

The preceding analysis showed that fairness considerations played a central role in the creation of the GATT regime. The system is based on a vision of fairness that relies on market forces for its realization. Equality of treatment (non-discrimination) and reciprocity ensure that the distribution of benefits and burdens in any exchange – be that an agreement on the exchange of tariff concessions or the establishment of rules for future behaviour, or be it the sales of goods across national borders under such rules and tariff treatment – is based on comparable, respective contributions, so that free-riding is avoided. From a philosophical perspective, this is akin to the model of commutative justice that prevails in arm's-length exchanges. From an economic perspective, this approach is best approximated in a situation of market-based competition. The market system generates fair outcomes, and, as such, it could be deemed to be just. Distortions, including government interventions, should, in principle, be eliminated. This appears to have been the prevailing fairness vision at the inception of the GATT, even making allowance for all the inevitable exceptions and loopholes, including those due to the unrelenting protectionism that has affected the policies of all contracting parties, the US *imprimis*.

Viner clearly had recognized this problem when he wrote with regard to the Charter's negotiation: 'the pattern of international legislation on complex matters cannot reasonably be expected to be tidier than the patterns with which we are familiar in the field of domestic legislation. No economic principle has universal appeal. No government has objectives single enough and simple enough to enable it to avoid mixing its principles'.[110] What is interesting is to see whether in the development of the system, this notion of fairness (with market-based competition as the ideal reference model) has been confirmed, even though, keeping in mind Viner's admonition, this journey could be expected to be neither straightforward nor entirely consistent in any area.

The evolution of the rules on subsidies and safeguards, which culminated in the Uruguay Round of trade negotiations, provides interesting test cases. The rules that are meant to stem and in some cases prohibit the use of subsidies can be characterized as 'market-corrective'. Conceptually, they assume that granting subsidies represents a special advantage for a particular group of producers that would not have been present had such producers been operating under 'normal' conditions of competitive markets and non-distortion by government. Their unacceptability derives from the unfairness that results between two groups of producers located in two different countries. Safeguard rules instead can be characterised as 'protected adjustments', allowing for the imposition of import restrictions to limit or eliminate unacceptable or undesirable (unfair) effects felt by a particular group of domestic producers as a result of trade liberalization that the government has negotiated, presumably in order to create market opportunities for some other groups of domestic producers, which thus reap the benefits. While the situations are different, the agreed rules rest in both cases upon 'basic market principles. Implicitly or explicitly, they posit certain norms of economic behaviour by governments, both foreign and domestic. The usual, 'normal' condition is assumed to be non-intervention'.[111] While neither set of rules can fulfil all the requirements of textbook, efficiency-maximizing policy instruments, as virtually no real life – domestic or international – policy tool does, they both still maintain fair, market-based competition as their main reference point.

Such consistency with the general approach espoused by the USA, which runs across virtually all the Uruguay Round agreements, also helps in understanding why the WTO package was finally accepted by the Congress. This was particularly important at a time when market orthodoxy, as epitomized by the Washington Consensus, was running quite high among policy-makers.[112]

4.4.1   The Case of Subsidy Rules

As seen in Chapter 3, the treatment of subsidies has been a contentious issue in trade policy for a long time. Generally consisting of government grants to suppliers of goods and services, subsidies have long been used as a means of both regulating the economy and promoting national policies. Subsidies may alter market prices and costs and may create a wedge between foreign and domestic prices, thus distorting international competition and affecting the contribution-based distribution of benefits and burdens of international trade. At the same time, however, subsidies can correct market failures and thus enhance economic welfare in the subsidising country.[113]

Public policy reasons invoked when granting subsidies are diverse, and economic analysis does not always play a major role in decision-making. Such motivations include the encouragement of export of domestic goods and services, as well as their protection against import competition; the promotion of the use of domestic products and services; the development of less economically advanced regions; the support of infant or ailing industries or industries whose existence is deemed to be in the national interest; the preservation of employment, even in instances where the economic viability of the particular industry or enterprise is questionable; the maintenance of incomes of specific groups of producers, such as farmers, or of consumers, for instance through subsidized food prices; or the provision of services deemed of public utility.

Recourse to subsidies as a form of government intervention in the market has created a great deal of controversy at the international level, owing in large measure to the distortions of trade and investment that subsidies may bring about and the subsequent welfare losses for the international economy, as well as for individual national economies.[114] The relative merits and legitimacy of subsidies as policy instruments has always been controversial because of the different conceptions of the government's proper role in the economy. Whereas subsidies may be regarded in some countries as an illegitimate distortion of international trade, in others they may be considered a necessary instrument of public policy. Hence, subsidies have become a natural, albeit complex, subject matter for international negotiation and regulation. Since its inception, the multilateral trading system has recognized the need to provide some measure of transparency and discipline in this area. To counter the effects of foreign subsidisation, a number of countries, such as the USA, have traditionally responded by developing countervailing duty (CVD) procedures. This has led the international rules on subsidies to become linked to the multilateral (mainly procedural) control of unilateral, countervailing measures.

The GATT rules on subsidies have evolved over time. In the original treaty, Art. XVI (Subsidies) contained only a consultation and notification provision. In 1955, additional provisions on export subsidies (Art. XVI, Section B) were added, introducing the distinction between 'primary' and 'nonprimary' products. Export subsidies on 'nonprimary' products were prohibited if they resulted in an export price that was lower than the comparable domestic price. The commitment with respect to 'primary' products, including agricultural products, was only to 'seek to avoid' the use of export subsidies, so as not to lead any party to have 'more than an equitable share of world export trade' in the subsidized product. This was also partly the result of the particular treatment reserved for agriculture within the GATT. An 'Illustrative List of Export Subsidies' was adopted in 1960.

The GATT contains no specific provisions on domestic subsidies, although, quite early, it became GATT practice to consider the granting of subsidies to goods subject to bound tariffs as a ground for claiming nullification or impairment of benefits. Subsidies were in fact considered as capable of altering the competitive relationship between imported and domestic goods, thus affecting the reasonable expectations of benefits to be derived under the General Agreement and entitling the aggrieved party to compensation.[115] Besides, Art. VI allowed the imposition of countervailing duties (in excess of Art. II-bound duties) on products that had benefited from a subsidy, whether or not it was directly related to export or resulted in an export price lower than the exporting country's domestic price, but only to the extent necessary to redress the injurious effects of subsidized imports.

The regulation of subsidies was broadened significantly with the negotiation of the 1979 Tokyo Round Subsidies Code.[116] The latter was 'plurilateral' in character (i.e. only binding upon the countries that decided to sign on to it) and never commanded wide acceptance among developing countries.[117] The 1979 Code made the treatment of export subsidies more stringent by prohibiting them without regard to their differential effect on prices. As for domestic subsidies, the Code provided the first international law discipline on the matter. It recognized that domestic subsidies could cause injury to industries or serious prejudice to the interests of another signatory 'in particular where such subsidies would adversely affect the conditions of normal competition'. In such cases, the Code required parties to 'seek to avoid causing such effects' (Art. 11). The Code then provided for consultation and dispute settlement procedures. In addition (or instead), an importing country remained free to impose countervailing duties upon determining that a domestic industry had suffered (or was threatened by) material injury as a result of the subsidy.

A new, comprehensive Agreement on Subsidies and Countervailing Measures was negotiated in the framework of the Uruguay Round, which ended in 1994.[118] In terms of coverage, the new Agreement certainly represents a significant improvement over its Tokyo Round predecessor. Being part of a single undertaking, all WTO Members are now under the same set of obligations. The basic concepts of the Tokyo Round Code have been retained. Certain types of subsidies are prohibited, while other types should not be used in ways that harm trading partners or threaten to do so. If they nevertheless have such effects, the affected trading partner is entitled to take offsetting actions, in the form of countervailing duties, subject to specific procedures.

The new Agreement also has introduced a number of important new disciplines. It finally fulfils one of the unmet Tokyo Round objectives by defining 'subsidies',[119] and distinguishing them as being 'specific' or 'non-specific'.[120] The former are defined as those whose access, formally or in fact, is limited to certain specific enterprises, industries, groups of enterprises or industries, or to enterprises in a specific geographical region. Conversely, 'non-specific' subsidies are those that are in effect generally available to, and broadly distributed among, all enterprises or industries in a country.[121] *De jure* non-specificity (i.e. formal general availability) may be challenged on a number of grounds, including the track record of the granting authority and the actual concentration in the use of a subsidy programme.

The Agreement then proceeds to divide subsidies into three categories: prohibited, actionable, and non-actionable. The third category was provisional and lapsed at the end of 1999. Prohibited[122] subsidies are non-agricultural[123] ones, which are based on export performance ('export subsidies') in law or in fact[124] and those contingent upon the use of domestic rather than imported goods. Developing and transition economies enjoy less stringent terms.[125] A WTO member that feels confronted with a prohibited subsidy may seek remedy by first consulting with the allegedly offending party.[126] If no 'mutually acceptable solution' is found within 30 days, the matter may be submitted to the WTO Dispute Settlement Body (DSB) for panel referral and adjudication. If the subsidy is found to fall in the prohibited category, the remedy provided for is its immediate withdrawal. Failing that, countermeasures are to be authorized.

Actionable are those 'specific' subsidies that cause 'adverse effects to the interests of other members'[127] by injuring their domestic industry, nullifying or impairing their benefits under the GATT (in particular tariff concessions), or causing them serious prejudice. The latter may occur when the effect of the subsidy is to displace or impede imports of like products into the subsidizing member's market or export to a third-country market.[128] Serious prejudice may also arise when the effect of the subsidy is a significant undercutting by the subsidized products as compared with the price of a like product of another WTO member in the same market, or finally, in the case of primary products, when the effect of the subsidy is to increase the world market share of the subsidizing country over its previous, three-year average. Remedial action procedures follow closely those provided for in the case of prohibited subsidies. The remedy in this case would be the withdrawal of the subsidy or the removal of its adverse effects.

Part V of the Agreement concerns the use of countervailing duty measures on subsidized, imported goods. It sets out disciplines on the initiation of countervailing cases, investigations by national authorities, and rules of evidence. The provisions are not particularly different in substance from the disciplines agreed to in the Tokyo Round Code. The general approach remains unchanged. In order to impose a countervailing duty, a member country needs to prove the existence of a subsidy, an injury to a domestic industry, and the causality linking the former to the latter.[129] The concept of 'injury to domestic industry' is used in the same way in the countervailing-measures context as it is for the purpose of determining the existence of adverse effects and thus the actionability of a subsidy.[130] The determination of injury is based on an examination of the volume of the subsidized imports and their effect on prices in the domestic market for like products and the consequent impact of these imports on the domestic producers of such import-competing products.[131] In making this assessment, the investigating authority must consider a number of factors, including the size of the increase in subsidized imports, the extent of price undercutting and price depression, and 'all relevant economic factors and indices having a bearing on the state of the industry'.[132]

Voluntary undertakings are a permissible means of terminating CVD investigations. They should lead to the elimination or limitation of the subsidy, or the removal of its injurious effects through a price increase of the subsidized imports.[133] In any event, CVDs 'shall remain in force only as long as and to the extent necessary to counteract subsidisation which is causing injury'[134] and shall be terminated no later than five years from imposition (or from the most recent review), 'unless the authorities determine ... that the expiry of the duty would be likely to lead to continuation or recurrence of subsidisation and injury'.[135]

The Agreement on subsidies represents an important exercise in international governance in the field of multilateral trade relations. Unlike the Uruguay Round Agreement on antidumping measures, it goes well beyond a multilateral attempt to control, through procedural rules, the use of one of the 'contingent protection'[136] instruments – CVD actions – available to governments. Two major goals seem to have characterized the negotiation. One group of countries, featuring most prominently the USA, considered the development of subsidy disciplines as a central objective, while others sought greater control over the use of countervailing measures as their primary goal.[137] The development of subsidies rules as 'market-corrective' devices is in line with the fair competition principles embodied in the GATT since its inception. In this sense, the Agreement aims to eliminate or correct distortions arising out of the specific economic behaviour being regulated, namely that of governments granting subsidies.

Subsidies may create distortions of the market process for allocating resources. They do so when they alter the price and cost information that enterprises receive, leading to an inefficient use of resources.[138] By granting subsidies, governments may, in fact, confer 'artificial' competitive advantages, and alter and distort competitive conditions by favouring domestic firms in home or export markets and hampering foreign ones in internal markets, thus ultimately distorting market outcomes. The benchmark or standard for assessing the distortive potential of these government practices seems to be a pragmatic notion of 'normal competition' or the 'normal competitive process',[139] based on the interaction of market agents' 'skill[s], foresight and industry',[140] as well as the 'natural' competitive advantages they enjoy.[141] In this sense, competition is the kind of rivalrous relationship between firms that would prevail in the absence of a government's distortive actions. Protecting the 'competitive process' appears to be quite consonant with protecting 'competitive relationships' and the 'conditions of competition', which is how the basic provisions of the General Agreement have been consistently interpreted.[142] The concept of 'normal competition' was used in the Tokyo Round code and again in the preparatory work of the Agreement. In the Uruguay Round, the same approach was accepted in the area of services, as Art. XV (Subsidies) of the General Agreement on Trade in Services explicitly recognized that 'in certain circumstances, subsidies may have *distortive* effects on trade in services' (emphasis added).[143]

At the international level, market distortions induced by specific government behaviour, including subsidization, manifest in the form of distortions of trade and investment flows and decisions.[144] However, government interventions are widespread in today's economies. They are directed in many instances to improve the efficiency of national economies by correcting, and compensating for, market distortions or failures and by helping firms to internalize externalities and to develop (e.g. in the case of 'infant industries').

Furthermore, sovereign nations may decide to seek additional goals that stem from their specific societal preferences.[145] Thus government intervention may be required in order to pursue important policy objectives, including high levels of health or environmental protection, the preservation of some traditional activities, and the achievement of high standards in labour conditions. The relative value attached to the various objectives may differ across countries. Government action in pursuit of societal preferences, values, and other public sector objectives ultimately may be considered efficiency- and welfare-enhancing from each national community's perspective.

Hence, the crux of the matter comes in disentangling distortive actions from efficiency-enhancing ones[146] and, from a fairness perspective, determining whether such actions allow selected competitors to appropriate benefits from international trade that are not commensurate to their contributions, but are due to the unfair advantage granted to them by their respective governments. This is unacceptable, as it compromises the reciprocal and fair distribution of burdens and benefits from international trade that derives from mutually advantageous market openings (e.g. tariff bindings) and undistorted, market-based exchanges. When the international community decides to tackle the regulation of one important form of government behaviour, subsidies, with a view to increasing world trade and efficiency through the reduction of distortions to the market outcome, it is confronted with the challenge of establishing a standard so as to discern acceptable from unacceptable actions. The standard or reference model used to draw the line seems to be that of 'normal competition' referred to earlier, as adjusted to accommodate those public policy goals that the international community considers welfare- and efficiency-enhancing and thus legitimate. Such a standard seems to underlie the approaches and disciplines agreed upon in the Agreement.

First, the Agreement introduces a 'specificity test', which tries to distinguish between generally available programmes deemed not to afford advantages to any specific enterprises, nor to create distortions and inefficiency, and specific, targeted, programmes capable of affecting the costs and revenues of individual firms relative to competitors. The dividing line between the two categories is in practice quite blurred. The test is obviously a short-cut to avoid a painstaking review of all programmes and their eventual distortive potential. Moreover, the Agreement makes an allowance for *de facto* specificity, trying to remedy the potential lack of comprehensiveness of too formal a distinction between 'specific' and 'non-specific' subsidies.[147] Many *de jure*, generally available programmes could in fact have a specific and distortive impact. The notion of *de facto* specificity brings them within the Agreement's regulatory reach. In contrast, 'specific' programmes, which may well have efficiency-benign consequences, are widespread in many jurisdictions.[148] Hence, they are generally included in the 'actionable' category, which calls for more in-depth scrutiny, reminiscent of a 'rule-of-reason' analysis under domestic antitrust law.

Second, in order to assess the distortive, or anticompetitive, effects of government subsidisation just alluded to, and as a requirement for remedial action, the Agreement establishes an 'effects test'. In particular, the effects are qualified as 'adverse' on the interests of other members.[149] Whereas the 'specificity test' tries to separate efficient from inefficient subsidies by analysing the subsidies' characteristics and their distortive potential, the 'adverse effects test' aims to determine the kinds of trade distortive effects the Agreement is meant to regulate and provide a remedy for. In so doing, it also affords the reason why the multilateral trading system needs to be cognizant of subsidy practices and define the scope of international disciplines. Quite consistently with the approach already embodied in Art. XVI (Subsidies) of the GATT, the only pertinent 'adverse effects' are those affecting international trade. Subsidies whose economic effects remain confined within national borders are of no consequence to the multilateral system and do not fall under its regulatory competence. The same approach was followed in the 1957 Treaty of Rome, establishing the European Economic Community. Art. 92 prohibited 'any aid granted by a Member State ... which distorts competition' by favouring certain enterprises, provided that an effect on trade is shown. As is clearly indicated in Art. 92, and as the Subsidies Agreement should be interpreted in order to maintain consistency with the system's distortion-reducing objective, the only relevant trade effects for determining adverse effects should be those capable of distorting the international competitive process.[150] Thus, in order to establish the existence of 'adverse effects' two elements would need to be present: first, an effect on international trade, and second, a distortion of the international competitive process.

Art. 3 (Prohibition) of the Agreement forbids subsidies contingent on export performance and the use of local content. This *per se* prohibition is motivated by the accord among WTO Members that these types of subsidies are inherently trade- and competition-distorting. Thus, there is no need to proceed with the 'adverse effects' on trade and competition inquiry and a *per se* treatment is in order. The only apt remedy is then the subsidy's withdrawal, as provided for in Art. 4 (Remedies). However, 'actionable' subsidies require the adverse effects analysis to be conducted before a remedy can be granted. Members are to refrain from using subsidies that cause adverse effects on other members. If they nonetheless do so, their actions can be challenged under the WTO dispute settlement procedures. It then becomes necessary to ascertain the existence of those effects before a remedy can be granted. Art. 5 defines three kinds of 'adverse effects': nullification and impairment of benefits, serious prejudice, and injury to the domestic industry. No particular difficulty seems to arise with the first category. GATT jurisprudence has recognized that subsidies may alter and distort the competitive relationship between domestic and imported products so as to nullify or impair the reasonable expectation of benefits under the Agreement.[151] By offsetting an efficiency-enhancing reduction of a distortive trade barrier, usually in the form of a bound tariff concession, subsidizing governments both restore the distortion of trade and circumvents an international obligation.[152] By providing an 'artificial advantage' to domestic producers, governments thus tamper with the international competitive process.

'Adverse effects' also arise when a subsidy creates 'serious prejudice' against the interests of another WTO Member. Here again, the emphasis appears to lie on the subsidy's effect on the international competitive process. A WTO member can complain and seek remedy if a subsidy is impeding its exports of a like product in the market of the subsidizing WTO Member or in a third-country market. It is up to the adjudicating body to decide whether the resulting trade effects are creating the kind of prejudice the Agreement is meant to remedy.[153] In this context it needs to ascertain whether the trade distortion was caused by the advantage granted by the subsidizing government. The analysis is thus more complex than in prohibited subsidies cases, where distortive effects are considered inherent to government action.

Much more problematic is the last category of 'adverse effects'. Such effects are deemed to arise when 'injury to the domestic industry of another member' takes place. The term 'injury' is used here in the same sense as in Part V of the Agreement, which regulates countervailing measures imposed by member countries.[154] The focus on the effects of import competition on specific competitors, the 'domestic industry', inherent in the injury concept, appears difficult to reconcile with the objective of preserving the 'normal competitive process' that the Agreement seems to embrace. 'Injury to the domestic industry' cannot be equated to the distortion of the international competitive process. Injury to competitors is not the same as injury to competition. It is inherent in the process of competition that some firms prosper while others do not. Domestic competitors may suffer injury because of import competition, without necessarily implying that any distortion to the 'normal competitive process', arising from 'artificial' advantages accorded by the subsidizing government, has taken place. The very fact that imports occur produces, in almost all cases, a displacement of sales of domestically produced goods.

The provision of a subsidy, specific to a firm or an industry on the one hand, and the existence of injury to the domestic industry on the other, does not necessarily mean that the former has caused the latter.[155] What would be important to prove is that the subsidy has indeed provided the recipient firm or firms with an 'artificial' competitive advantage, affecting its cost and revenue structures, and that this action has distorted the 'normal competitive process', resulting in injury to the domestic industry. Consideration of this link appears to be crucial in the causation analysis, and for the possibility of obtaining a remedy.[156]

An approach that focuses on the injurious effect on domestic industries is typical of contingent protection instruments, such as countervailing measures. Although their rationale may include fighting distortive practices,[157] over time, such instruments have taken on, much more distinctly, the function of softening the undesirable effects of import competition on domestic competitors. These 'adjustment' objectives, when not 'captured' by protectionist motives, are entirely legitimate for sovereign nations, albeit debatable on purely economic grounds. The US practice in the area of countervailing duties is often criticized on these grounds, as a way for special interests to shield themselves from foreign competition.

To summarize the argument, the Uruguay Round Subsidies Agreement may be interpreted as providing rules for the elimination of market distortions arising from the use of one important public policy instrument: subsidies. This would keep the Agreement's objective in line with the market- and competition-based notion of fairness prevailing in the multilateral trading system. The standard, which appears to underpin the Agreement, is that of 'normal competition' based on market and efficiency principles. The economic behaviour of governments in the international marketplace needs to be assessed against this standard. But due account is to be taken of the various efficiency-enhancing interventions that governments carry out. This implies that only a subset of subsidies is deemed to be *per se* distortive. All other subsidies that cause adverse trade effects, and thus fall under the purview of international regulation, require a rule-of-reason-like analysis before a remedy can be granted. This approach is consistent with the position, taken by the USA in the Suggested Charter about 50 years earlier, that export subsidies should be banned *per se*, while domestic subsidies should be evaluated based on a 'serious injury to other countries' analysis.

4.4.2   The Case of Safeguard Rules

Reciprocal trade liberalization increases import competition, as well as market opportunities in foreign markets. But competition creates winners and losers, and this, as a matter of fairness between different producers in the domestic economy, gives rise to a need for safeguards to ensure that the balance of benefits and burdens from trade remains balanced. This is the approach traditionally followed by US trade policy, which has been transposed in the GATT. While the latter includes a number of rules allowing for the introduction of safeguard-type measures,[158] Art. XIX (Emergency Action on Imports of Particular Products) provides the main safeguard mechanism. It permits the adoption of a safeguard measure by a GATT Contracting Party when, as a result of 'unforeseen developments' and the effect of GATT obligations, including a tariff concession, the product in question is being imported into its territory in such increased quantities and under such conditions as to cause or threaten 'serious injury' to domestic producers.

From the start, the interpretation of Art. XIX has been bedevilled by interpretative uncertainties, which may have contributed to its limited use.[159] These uncertainties include the concepts of unforeseen circumstances, GATT obligation, product, industry, serious injury, time frame, and characteristics (relative or absolute) of the increase in imports, as well as the modalities of safeguarding, such as the nature of permissible remedies, their discriminatory or non-discriminatory application, and the compensation requirement. For many years, GATT Contracting Parties have sought to reform the safeguards regime. Unsuccessful negotiations to reform Art. XIX were conducted during the Tokyo Round. A quite similar agenda was picked up again during the Uruguay Round, with countries finally being able to strike a deal, the Agreement on Safeguards,[160] which clarifies a number of issues and reinforces the safeguards discipline.

Originally, the Art. XIX safeguard measures were to be taken only in case of emergency, and only as long as necessary to counter that emergency. If, due to developments unforeseen at the time of entering into a GATT obligation, a contracting party were exposed to a surge in imports that was injurious to its domestic industry, it could temporarily 'escape' from its GATT commitments and adopt import relief measures. Neither the GATT obligation concept nor the nature of the permitted relief was defined. The former certainly refers to tariff concessions, but may also encompass other liberalization measures, such as the elimination of a quantitative restriction. As for the import relief, various measures, such as tariff increases and quantitative restrictions, have been used.

Early GATT practice seems to suggest that the issues GATT drafters were mainly trying to address were short-term, as well as seasonal, import surges.[161] In effect, the prerequisite of an 'emergency' situation linked to trade liberalization was soon relaxed, and this condition is no longer mentioned in the Safeguards Agreement.[162] Thus, the main rationale for safeguard actions under the new WTO system has become that of easing 'structural adjust-ment'.[163] However, safeguards do not, as a matter of legal compulsion, need to be accompanied by some adjustment process.

Import competition, while benefiting domestic consumers by providing cheaper alternatives and incentives to use local factors of production more efficiently, may also hurt domestic producers, at least in the short term, thus posing the well-known fairness issue as between domestic groups partici-pating in different capacities in international trade. While the competitive process plays itself out, import-competing domestic firms and workers need to adjust. Import restraints are one of the safeguard mechanisms that virtually all governments – not just the USA, who was only its early proponent – want to maintain at their disposal in order to provide respite to adjusting industries and thus to ensure overall fairness. Adjustment may take two different forms: import-competing domestic firms may transfer their resources out of existing production to alternative uses, or domestic firms may restructure and regain their ability to compete with imports in the same line of business. In both cases, the temporary import relief is meant to facilitate the process.

Unlike in the case of antisubsidy actions, safeguard measures are not predicated upon the alleged existence of any foreign anticompetitive conduct, granting an artificial competitive advantage, and thus distorting the 'normal' competitive process that should govern a 'fair' international trade. The adjustment objective that informs the safeguards regime is not *in principle* consistent with a market-based, competition model. An approach that tampers with market forces in order to influence which firms survive and which do not is at odds with such a model. The legitimate effects of successful import competition are what a safeguards regime tries to override, or at least modify.[164] Furthermore, in most cases, it is quite difficult to ascertain whether a surge in imports is really injuring a domestic industry. For example, factors determining the relative market shares of foreign and domestic competitors are numerous, including consumer tastes and incomes, technology, product quality, foreign and domestic input prices, and movement in exchange rates. Thus if an increase in imports is really the effect of different causes at play, it is doubtful that trade restrictions are an efficient, first-best response; this would seem to be particularly the case when distortions and other factors of domestic nature are mainly responsible for the injury. If the policy objective is to facilitate adjustment, then this is usually best accomplished through a package of different instruments, closer to the inefficiency sources. Such instruments may include government assistance and tax relief, which offer the additional advantage of having a less direct impact on foreign competitors.

However, an adjustment-motivated safeguards regime is not devoid of market-conforming justifications from the perspective of the invoking country. Import restrictions impose efficiency losses, which need to be compared with displacement and other social costs that the safeguard measure may be able to reduce or eliminate,[165] or with the benefit of restoring an internationally competitive producer in the market. The import restraint allows import-competing domestic firms to temporarily raise their prices, reaping supra-competitive profits, which can be used to finance the adjustment process. In such a cost–benefit analysis, it is thus important to weigh the social preference attached to reducing domestic factors such as dislocation or transition costs against the ensuing consumer welfare losses. There may be good economic as well as fairness-based reasons to avoid concentrated losses for a particular vulnerable group (e.g. textile workers in an underdeveloped region), at the expense of a large number of consumers, who would have to give up some small trade gains (and pay moderately higher prices for the protected textile products). In this sense, the existing safeguards regime also confirms the traditional – decreased but never overcome – protectionist favour for producers' over consumers' interests, in the presence of adjustment problems, as in other circumstances.[166]

Hence, while safeguards, in principle, contrast with the goals of market-based competition, the economic adjustment purpose, underpinning the use of temporary trade restrictions in favour of import-competition-affected domestic industries, provides some common ground.[167] Absent this important fairness-inspired justification would relegate safeguard measures to the domain of ordinary protection. Although a number of problems still remain, the new disciplines established by the Safeguards Agreement have the merit of both emphasizing the adjustment objective and of forestalling the potential use of safeguards for protectionist purposes. The ban and progressive phase-out of a long-standing protectionist tool, voluntary export restraints (VERs), was an important achievement in terms of regaining legal certainty and transparency in the area of safeguards, as well as reining in an important and abundantly used protectionist weapon. A number of other substantive constraints have been introduced in the Agreement, in order to decrease the distortive impact of safeguards. They include limits on the duration and extension of safeguard measures, as well as their progressive liberalization and reapplication limits.[168]

Safeguards should be applied only for the time and to the extent 'necessary to prevent or remedy serious injury and to facilitate adjustment'.[169] Such crucial obligation is not specified or accompanied by more detailed disciplines, except for the requirement that competent authorities show 'evidence that the industry is adjusting' at the time when they are to decide on an extension of a safeguard measure.[170] This is a critical shortcoming if governments, pressured by uncompetitive domestic industries, are able to offer protection that is de-linked from any effort and prospect of adjustment.[171]

Beyond this, the Agreement does not seem to have significantly reinforced or clarified either standards or requirements for action. A country invoking a safeguard measure must show the occurrence of an imports surge and a causal nexus between this event and serious injury. Consolidating previous GATT practice, the increase in imports may be either absolute or relative (to domestic consumption), while no indication of the reference period is given. Industry and product definitions remain vague, allowing for interpretations that may render the determination of surge and injury easier. The definition of serious injury, as 'a significant overall impairment in the position of a domestic industry', remains open-ended.[172] The concept of 'threat of serious injury' is not specified and remains ambiguous. There is also no indication of how to determine causality. Although the burden of proving injury is clearly on the safeguard-invoking country,[173] mere temporal coincidence between increased quantities of imports and injury could even suffice.[174] Hence, existing requirements do not seem to be particularly difficult to meet. Under the surge, serious injury, and causality standards, countries retain a wide discretion to justify eligibility for safeguard relief.[175]

Moreover, the Agreement has endeavoured to make the application of safeguard measures more attractive, with a view to encouraging their use in place of alternative measures. In particular, under not-well-defined circumstances, safeguard measures may be taken in a discriminatory (selective) fashion.[176] For the first three years of a safeguard measure, exporting countries' right to retaliate, in case of disagreement over compensation, is withheld. Safeguard measures can be taken in the form of import quotas and may also be administered by the exporting countries, thus shifting the administration cost of the measure.[177]

The choice of the import relief instrument, its discriminatory or non-discriminatory application, and the compensation due are among the thorniest issues in the debate on safeguards, which shares much of the same difficulties that characterize the general discussion on discrimination in the trade regime more broadly. As mentioned, all trade restrictions affect the international competitive process. But unlike non-prohibitive tariffs, quotas hold the potential of entrenching domestic monopoly power and are thus particularly inimical to the market-based, competitive model. Once relieved from the competitive pressure of imports, which cannot exceed the quota, dominant domestic firms may exert their power over prices. In addition, tariffs have the advantage of raising revenues to be employed by the government in the pursuit of adjustment.[178]

The implementation modalities of trade restrictions also have a number of consequences for the international competitive process that are difficult to appraise. Applying safeguards selectively and discriminatorily against the most efficient foreign producers amounts to penalizing those competitors that have proven to be the most successful in providing better goods at a lower cost, one of the core elements of market competition. It also distorts the international allocation of resources affecting the relative competitive position of the various suppliers. In contrast, non-discriminatory quotas avoid the diversion of trade towards unconstrained third countries, create a powerful constituency, the world-trading community, provide pressure for the early removal of the trade restriction, and allow some degree of competition. In fact, importers continue to buy an albeit limited quantity from the cheapest source of supply, while foreign exporters keep on competing for sales. Consumers, though, may still have to pay higher, scarcity-induced prices.

But the administration of non-discriminatory quotas presents a number of problems as well. Global (non-country-allocated) quotas often are managed on a 'first-come, first-served' basis. Such a system may foster rent-seeking activities, with some suppliers obtaining larger shares than their competitive strength would command. A quantitative restriction based on historical shares, which is permitted, albeit not preferred under GATT rules,[179] may end up favouring established, less dynamic suppliers over the most competitive ones. Finally, non-selective trade restrictions affect the totality of trade flows, as well as the 'side-swiping' exporters that may not be contributing significantly to the serious injury and the ensuing adjustment problems.[180]

The efficiency impact of compensation is also controversial. Given the desirability of promoting adjustment, it is not evident that a safeguard measure truly taken for adjustment purposes should be compensated or retaliated against. In this regard, it has been argued that 'reciprocity ... also means mutual dependence, mutual responsibility and co-operation. Surely it is destructive of the spirit of reciprocity ... for a country in an emergency to be obliged to pay for taking *bona fide* temporary action, to negotiate such a payment, and to be threatened with retaliation if it does not offer enough'.[181]

In conclusion, the Agreement on Safeguards has the merit of emphasizing 'structural adjustment and the need to enhance rather than limit competition in international markets'[182] as the objective of any safeguard restraint, although this has not been translated in any strict obligation. It has provided some important, temporal limits and progressive liberalization requirements on the application of safeguards, diminishing their protectionist potential. It has forbidden the use of VERs, previously tolerated in the multilateral trading system, while easing the recourse to lawful safeguards by both consolidating governments' discretion to invoke them and providing some measure of flexibility on selectivity and compensation issues. However, the same latitude may be used for purely protectionist motives, relegating the adjustment goal to the sideline. It is on the tension between the promotion of adjustment and the mere protection of injured domestic competitors that the contribution of the Safeguards Agreement in ensuring fair, market-based competition in the multilateral trading system ultimately can be judged.

4.5 SUMMARY

Fully in line with US postwar planning objectives and long-standing tradition, the GATT regime is predicated upon the acceptance that fair dealing is a necessary standard of a thriving trading system. The centrality of non-discrimination and reciprocity principles and the attending rules attest to that. However, fairness cannot apply only across countries. Benefits and burdens also must be fairly apportioned between different groups within each country, so that nobody is seen as taking advantage of the international trade arrangements at the expense of others. The safeguard clause included in the GATT was an effort in this direction. From a fairness perspective, this is the essence of the 'embedded liberalism compromise'. If non-discrimination and reciprocity could provide a relatively easy behavioural benchmark with regard to tariffs, through (principal supplier) bilateral negotiations, coupled with the operation of the unconditional MFN clause, much more complicated was to gauge the behaviour of governments in many other areas, from quantitative restrictions to state-trading enterprises, to the granting of subsidies and so on. It is in this sense that the market reference became particularly useful. Indeed, the system of economic relations that better approximates the realization of non-discrimination and reciprocity/no free-riding is the free market, competitive mechanism. Hence, fair trade is a competitive, market-based trade. As seen, elements of this vision found their way into the original rules of the GATT, and the approach consolidated with the evolution of the system over time.

Surely, the criticisms levelled at the commercial policy provisions of the Charter, and thus also at the GATT, in terms of the many lapses and exceptions, are partly justified. As any international agreement, the GATT is a product of compromise, and as such it can be viewed from different perspectives and assessed in different ways. As Gerard Curzon wrote: 'the GATT for the American was Article I; for the Europeans, it was Articles XII and XXIV'.[183] Even more importantly, the USA's position was characterized by significant inconsistencies, due to its need to appease important interest groups, which led to the introduction of some important exceptions to the general principles. Clair Wilcox, the chief US negotiator of the Charter and the GATT, recognized this openly, when he stated that: 'the United States has championed active competition in open markets, but it has taken pains to insure, in many cases, that competition will not be too active and that markets will not be opened too wide'. After citing several examples, including the Buy American Act of 1933 and the tied credits of the Export-Import Bank, he remarked that US agricultural policy was clearly 'inconsistent with our belief in private enterprise, and with our efforts to restore a freer trading system'.[184] However, the key importance for the system of the notion of fairness, as pursued by the USA by means of the principles of non-discrimination and reciprocity, is unmistakable. In line with Viner's admonition that no economic policy principle has universal appeal,[185] exceptions and inconsistencies were a price that had to be paid.

However, from the examples of the rules' evolution in the areas of subsidies and safeguards, it seems possible to argue that the centrality of the fairness idea with market-based competition as its reference model has endured. This approach, with a weighty baggage of policy inconsistencies and backsliding, has been championed by the USA over the years. In many cases, to be sure, the fairness idea has been used rhetorically and instrumentally to serve the interests of specific industries, firms, or other groups. However, the lineage of the idea, its deep roots in the nation's ethos, and the persistence with which policy-makers have employed it over the years (or better the centuries) attests to its independent effect on specific rule design and the formation of the trade regime more broadly, as well as its development over time.

Beyond that, it is also important to recognize that fairness is not an idea like any other. The perception of fairness is crucial for the legitimacy and thus the compliance pull of any regime, as it is generally seen as a major element of any *just* social arrangement. A modicum of consensus on what fairness implies among a regime's participants is thus necessary. However, as with the vast majority of political ideas, fairness lends itself to contradicting interpretations and opposing policy prescriptions that do not impugn its importance in shaping policy- and rule-making, but surely need to be reckoned with, as the existence of conflicting fairness perceptions sap any regime's legitimacy. Hence, in the following chapter, this study will turn to two competing understandings of fairness in the trading system.

NOTES

1. These two acts, adopted in 1933, represented the main attempt of the 'first New Deal' at recovery through domestic planning. The NRA fixed domestic prices and wages, thus undermining the competitiveness of US industry, with public works supposed to compensate for lost foreign markets. The AAA was meant to increase commodity prices by restricting production and cheap imports, which otherwise would undermine the effort. For a penetrating analysis of the New Deal and its Constitutional history, see C. Sunstein, *The Second Bill of Right: FDR's Unfinished Revolution and Why We Need It More Than Ever*, Basic Books, New York, NY, 2004.
2. See W. Lockwood, *The Foreign Trade Policy of the United States*, American Council of Pacific Relations, New York, 1936, p. 25.
3. Quoted in J. Wilkinson, *Politics and Trade Policy*, Public Affairs Press, Washington, DC, 1960, p. 3.
4. Public Law No. 316, 73rd Cong.
5. Secretary Hull told the Ways and Means Committee that 'the primary objective of this new proposal is both to reopen the old and seek new outlets for our surplus production, through the gradual moderation of the excessive and more extreme impediments to the admission of American products into foreign markets'. See *Hearings* on H.R. 8430 before the House Committee on Ways and Means, 73rd Cong., 2nd Sess., 1934, p. 4.
6. See F. Sayre, *America Must Act*, World Peace Foundation, Boston and New York, 1936, pp. 6 and 34.
7. See J. Letiche, *Reciprocal Trade Agreements in the World Economy*, King's Crown Press, New York, 1948, pp. 19–20.
8. See H. Cantril, *Public Opinion, 1934–1946*, Princeton University Press, Princeton, 1951, pp. 122 and 124, opinion polls no. 4, 6, 7 and 19.
9. See H. Tasca, *The Reciprocal Trade Policy of the United States: A Study in Trade Philosophy*, University of Pennsylvania Press, Philadelphia, 1938, pp. 33–8.
10. J. Day Larkin, *Trade Agreements: A Study in Democratic Methods*, Columbia University Press, New York, 1940, pp. 11–12.

11. The Executive was required to publicly announce his intention to negotiate a trade agreement and interested parties could present their views. For this purpose, a special Committee for Reciprocity Information was created.
12. See Larkin, op. cit., p. 69.
13. See *Hearings* on H.R. 8430 before the House Committee on Ways and Means, 73rd Cong., 2nd Sess., 1934, p. 24.
14. 'From 1934 to 1942 the methods of avoiding damage took the form of (a) interdepartmental administrative procedures designed to assure the careful weighing of facts and probabilities with respect to proposed tariff concessions; (b) the use of qualified concessions, i.e., tariff reductions on foreign merchandise limited to types, quantities, grades, or seasonal periods of importation, which offered less competition with domestic production than unqualified concessions would have; (c) the use of special escape clauses aimed at specific risks, such as foreign currency devaluations, which encouraged imports by lowering their prices in terms of dollars; and (d) willingness to renegotiate concessions that occasionally turned out to be more painful than expected'. See J. Leddy and J. Norwood, 'The Escape Clause and Peril Points Under the Trade-Agreements Program', in Kelly, op. cit., p. 124.
15. See Art. XI, Reciprocal Trade Agreement between the USA and Mexico, US *Executive Agreement Series*, No. 311.
16. See Leddy and Norwood, op. cit., pp. 125–6.
17. Quoted in Eckes, *Opening*, op. cit., p. 159. In a letter to the Speaker of the House Senator Rayburn, in May 1945, President Truman wrote: 'I have had drawn to my attention statements to the effect that this increased authority (i.e., to reduce the tariff of another 50%) might be used in such a way as to endanger or "trade out" segments of the American industry, American agriculture or American labor. No such action was taken under President Roosevelt and Cordell Hull and no such action will take place under my Presidency'. Quoted in O. Strackbein, *American Enterprise and Foreign Trade*, Public Affairs Press, Washington, DC, 1965, p. 32.
18. See Executive Order 9832, 25 February 1947, Prescribing Procedures for the Administration of the Reciprocal Trade Agreements Program, 12 *Federal Register* 1363, subsequently superseded by Executive Order 10082, 5 October 1949, 14 *Federal Register*, 6105 as emended in 15 *Federal Register* 6901.
19. See US Congress, House Committee on Ways and Means, *Report to accompany H.R. 6556*, 80th Cong., 2nd Sess., Rep. No. 2009, 24 May 1948, p. 5.
20. See Sayre, op. cit., p. 40.
21. See W. Diebold, *New Directions in our Trade Policy*, Council on Foreign Relations, New York, 1941, p. 27.
22. See Diebold, op. cit., p. 25.
23. See A. Taylor, *The New Deal and Foreign Trade*, Macmillan, New York, 1935, p. 219.
24. This exception covered, for instance, the agreements with Central American countries and excluded from the application of the MFN clause, the advantages offered by the USA to Cuba and the Philippines, and the tariff arrangements among Central American republics.
25. See Eckes, op. cit., p. 146.
26. See Leddy and Norwood, op. cit., p. 95.
27. In this case, the same concession was sometimes offered simultaneously to each country or limited reductions were offered in sequence to the various suppliers in order to maintain bargaining leverage. And, sometimes a commodity as defined in the tariff schedule was subdivided into several categories (so-called 'tariff specialization'), in order to identify the principal supplier country.
28. See, for instance, Eckes, op. cit., pp. 140–77, for a critical review.
29. See Letiche, op. cit., pp. 26–32.
30. See H. Tasca, *World Trading Systems: A Study of American and British Commercial Policies*, International Institute of Intellectual Cooperation, Paris, 1938, p. 7.
31. See Diebold, op. cit., p. 34.
32. See J. Viner, 'Conflicts of Principle in Drafting a Trade Charter', *Foreign Affairs*, July 1947, p. 618.

33. For instance, Art. II of the Agreement with Brazil provided that should 'either Government establish or maintain any form of quantitative restriction or control of the importation of any article, the growth, produce or manufacture of the other country, it will give the widest possible application to the most-favored-nation principle and will administer any such prohibition or restriction in such a way as not to discriminate against the commerce of the other country'. See Reciprocal Trade Agreement between the USA and Brazil, *Executive Agreement Series*, no. 82, 1936.
34. See Department of State Press release of 6 April 1935, quoted in Diebold, op. cit., p. 31.
35. See Tasca, op. cit., p. 13.
36. For instance, Art. VIII of the Agreement with Switzerland read: 'In the event that the United States of America or Switzerland establishes or maintains a monopoly for the importation, production or sale of an article or grants exclusive privileges, formally or in effect, to one or more agencies to import, produce or sell an article, the Government of the country establishing or maintaining such monopoly, or granting such monopoly privileges, agrees that in respect of the foreign purchases of such monopoly or agency the commerce of the other country shall receive fair and equitable treatment. It is agreed that in making its foreign purchases of any article such monopoly or agency will be influenced solely by competitive considerations, such as price, quality, marketability, and terms of sale'. See Reciprocal Trade Agreement between the USA and Switzerland, 9 January 1936, *Executive Agreements Series*, no. 90, 1936.
37. See H. Arndt, *The Economic Lessons of the Nineteen-Thirties*, Oxford University Press, London, 1944, p. 85.
38. See F. Sayre, 'Address before the National Convention of the United States Junior Chamber of Commerce at Columbus, Ohio, 28 June 1935', quoted in Lockwood, op. cit., p. 28.
39. See J. Leddy, 'United States Commercial Policy and the Domestic Farm Program', in Kelly, op. cit., p. 174.
40. See Taylor, op. cit., pp. 13–14. See also H. Wallace, 'American Agriculture and World Markets', *Foreign Affairs*, vol. 12, no. 5, 1934, pp. 216–30.
41. The Agricultural Adjustment Act of 1933 aimed at re-establishing 'prices to farmers at a level that will give agricultural commodities a purchasing power with respect to articles that farmers buy, equivalent to the purchasing power of agricultural commodities in the base period'. The Soil Conservation and Domestic Allotment Act of 1936 reaffirmed the broad objective of parity, but the Congressional declaration of policy mentioned 'parity of income' between agricultural and non-agricultural producers as being the desirable objective. See, id., pp. 176–7 and in general L. Goodwyn, *The Populist Moment: A Short History of the Agrarian Revolt in America*, Oxford University Press, New York, 1978.
42. See H. Wallace, *New Frontiers*, Reynal and Hitchcock, New York, 1934, pp. 29 and 231.
43. See Goldstein, op. cit., p. 155.
44. This point was immediately apparent to contemporary commentators. See, for instance, Lockwood, op. cit., p. 5: '[The RTAA] differs significantly from other aspects of the New Deal in that it seeks to diminish rather than to increase the amount of government intervention in economic life, and to restore in greater degree the self-adjusting mechanism of the free market'.
45. This was also a result of exchange rate instability and competitive devaluations, which followed the collapse of the gold standard in 1931.
46. For an interesting legal enquiry on the the 'market' concept see M. Torre-Schaub, *Essai sur la Construction Juridique de la Catégorie de Marché*, L.G.D.J., Paris, 2002.
47. See Hull, *The Memoirs*, op. cit., p. 1717.
48. See H.J. Res. 63, 65th Cong., 1st Sess., *Congressional Record*, Vol. 55, 23 April 1917, p. 991. Hull reintroduced the resolution in February 1920.
49. See *Congressional Record*, Vol. 57, 21 February 1919, p. 3960. In a speech to Congress on 10 September 1918, Hull also expressed his view in these words: 'Believing as I have that the best antidote against war is the removal of its causes rather than its prevention after the causes once arise, and finding that trade retaliation and discrimination in its more vicious forms have been productive of bitter economic wars which in many cases have developed into wars of force, I introduced the resolution in the House of Representatives during the

early part of last year which would provide for the organization of an international trade-agreement congress the objects of which should be to eliminate by mutual agreement all possible methods of retaliation and discrimination in international trade'. See H. Hinton, *Cordell Hull: A Biography*, Doubleday, Doran, and Company, Inc., Garden City, NY, 1942, p. 112.

50. See Allen, op. cit., p. 107.
51. Quoted in Lockwood, op. cit., p. 17.
52. He continued: 'The second road is to rely upon our high degree of national self-containment, to increase our tariffs, to create quotas and discriminations of agricultural and other products and thus to secure a larger measure of economic isolation from world influences. It would be a long road of readjustments into unknown and uncertain fields. But it may be necessary if the first way is closed to us. Some measures may be necessary pending cooperative conclusions with other nations. The third road is that we inflate our currency, consequently abandon the gold standard, and with our depreciated currency attempt to enter a world economic war, with the certainty that it leads to complete destruction, both at home and abroad'. Quoted in Taylor, op. cit., pp. 6–7.
53. See Sayre, op. cit., p. 36.
54. See Lockwood, op. cit., p. 57.
55. In this respect, in Art. VII of the Mutual Aid Agreement of 28 February 1942, the two countries specifically agreed to work together towards 'the elimination of all forms of discriminatory treatment in international commerce, and … the reduction of tariffs and other trade barriers'.
56. In the Atlantic Charter, President Roosevelt and Prime Minister Churchill stated 'certain common principles in the national policies of their respective countries on which they base their hopes for a better future for the world. … Fourth, they will endeavor, with due respect for their existing obligations, to further the enjoyment by all States, great or small, victor or vanquished, of access, on equal terms, to the trade and to the raw materials of the world which are needed for their economic prosperity'. However, the reservation of the 'respect for their existing obligations' led Cordell Hull to consider that it 'deprived the article of virtually all significance since it meant that Britain would continue to retain her Empire tariff preferences against which I had been fighting for eight years'. See Hull, *The Memoirs*, op. cit., pp. 975–6.
57. A detailed, first-hand account of these debates is provided by E.F. Penrose, *Economic Planning for the Peace*, Princeton University Press, Princeton, NJ, 1953.
58. See R. Gardner, *Sterling–Dollar Diplomacy in Current Perspective*, Columbia University Press, New York, pp. 16–17.
59. See J. Culbert, 'War-time Anglo-American Talks and the Making of the GATT', *The World Economy*, December 1987, p. 384.
60. See Thomas Zeiler, *Free Trade Free World: The Advent of the GATT*, The University of North Carolina Press, Chapel Hill, 1999, p. 34.
61. Ibid., pp. 29–32.
62. Experts from outside government also made important contributions. For instance, Percy Bidwell from the Council on Foreign Relations already in 1944 proposed that the Allied countries entered into a comprehensive agreement on postwar commercial policy, pledging themselves to reduce tariffs, abolish quantitative restrictions, remove prohibitions and restrictions on exports and imports, eliminate all kinds of tariff discrimination and stem unfair competition in foreign trade. See P. Bidwell, 'A Postwar Commercial Policy for the United States', *American Economic Review*, 1944, no. 1, suppl., pp. 349–51.
63. See Department of State 'Proposals for Expansion of World Trade and Employment', publication 2411, Commercial Policy Series 79, 1945, reprinted in *Department of State Bulletin*, XIII, 1945, pp. 912–29. The British endorsement of the Trade Proposals, in principle, was part of the Anglo-American Financial and Commercial Agreements of December 1945. In the period 1943–45, most of the discussions had been carried out in the context of the implementation of Art. VII of the lend–lease agreement. On the British side, postwar planning had also evolved. The British plan included the establishment of an international trade organization (which came to be known as the Commercial Union),

linking countries that would agree to reduce trade barriers. The originator of this plan was James Meade, who at the time was a member of the Economic Section of the British War Cabinet secretariat. The text of the plan is reproduced in *The World Economy*, December 1987, pp. 400–407. For a detailed account of the British approach, see Jean-Christophe Graz, *Aux Sources de l'OMC: La Charte de la Havane*, Librairie Droz, Genève, pp. 131–58.

64. Quoted in S. Aaronson, *Trade and the American Dream: A Social History of Postwar Trade Policy*, 1996, The University Press of Kentucky, Lexington, p. 48.

65. Reproduced in UN, Economic and Social Council, *Report of the First Session of the Preparatory Committee of the United Nations Conference on Trade and Employment*, London, October 1946, Doc. E/PC/T/33, p. 42.

66. See US Department of State 'Suggested Charter for the International Trade Organization', publication 2598, Commercial Policy Series, 93, 1945. The text is also contained in United Nations, Economic and Social Council, *Report of the First Session of the Preparatory Committee*, op. cit., pp. 52–67.

67. See K. Knorr, 'The American Trade Proposals', mimeo, Yale Institute of International Studies, October 1946, p. 4.

68. See J.B. Condliffe, *Obstacles to Multilateral Trade*, National Planning Association, Washington, DC, April 1947, p. 12.

69. ' ... [V]ery frequently the world images that have been created by ideas, like a switchman, have determined the tracks along which action has been pushed by the dynamic of interest.' See M. Weber, *The Protestant Ethic and the Spirit of Capitalism*, Scribner, New York, 1958, p. 280.

70. '... [I]ntransigent American protectionism is at least as serious an obstacle to the successful realization of the American trade proposals as the protectionism of other countries. ...' See J. Viner, 'Conflicts of Principle in Drafting a Trade Charter', *Foreign Affairs*, July 1947, p. 613.

71. See Art. 24 (1).

72. This procedure was only adopted about 20 years later in the GATT Kennedy Round.

73. See Gardner, op. cit., pp. 271–80.

74. See S. Bailey, *Congress Makes a Law*, Vintage Books, New York, 1950.

75. Suggested Charter, Art. 4.

76. Havana Charter, Art. 23.

77. See W. Brown, Jr., *The United States and the Restoration of World Trade*, The Brookings Institution, Washington, DC, 1950, p. 311.

78. While not defined as such at the time, this more modern designation is used throughout the study.

79. The only reference to the issue in the Suggested Charter can be found in the introduction where the purpose of the trade organization is given, and it includes encouraging and assisting the industrial and general development of member countries, particularly those in the early stages of development. In the ECOSOC resolution that called for an international conference on trade and employment, the Preparatory Committee was asked 'to take into account the special conditions which prevailed in countries whose manufacturing industry is still in its initial stages of development, and the questions that arise in connection with commodities which are the subject to special problems of adjustment in international markets'. (UN Economic and Social Council, *Report of the First Session of the Preparatory Committee*, op. cit., p. 42). This language was not part of the original US draft resolution.

80. See UN Doc. EPCT/A/PV.22, 1947, pp. 16–17.

81. Id., pp. 19–24.

82. See UN doc. EPCT/C.II/37, 1947, p. 7.

83. See C. Wilcox, *A Charter for World Trade*, The Macmillan Company, New York, 1949, p. 126.

84. See UN Doc. E/Conf.2/C.3/SR.26, 1948.

85. See UN Doc. EPCT/A/PV.22, 1947, p. 41.

86. See Wilcox, op. cit., p. 126.

87. See Art. 28(1).
88. Art. 12 (*International Investment for Economic Development and Reconstruction*), para. 2 (a) (ii).
89. See D. Acheson, 'The ITO Charter: A Code of Fair Trade Practices', Statement by Secretary Acheson before the House Committee on Foreign Affairs made on 19 April 1950, US Department of State Publication 384, May 1950.
90. For instance, with regard to arbitrary customs valuation procedures (Art. VII), excessive fees and formalities (Art. VII and IX), protectionist exchange arrangements (Art. XV), and the abuse of trade monopolies (Art. XVII).
91. Tariff binding can also be effected on a unilateral basis, although such occurrence has remained extremely rare in the GATT/WTO history.
92. More specifically, in this regard the GATT provides that 'there should be some equivalence between the damage suffered because of the modification, and the compensation offered. Although Art. XXVIII GATT is not very precise on this point, the quest for equivalence finds support in two provisions. First, Art. XXVIII.2 GATT which reads: 'In such negotiations and agreement, which may include provision for compensatory adjustment with respect to other products, the contracting parties concerned shall endeavour to maintain a general level of reciprocal and mutually advantageous concessions not less favourable to trade than that provided for in this Agreement prior to such negotiations'. In this very limited sense, reciprocity is the legal foundation permitting this action. Second, the Interpretative Note referring to Art. XXVIII GATT reads in § 4.6: 'It is not intended that provision for participation in the negotiations of any contracting party with a principal supplying interest, and for consultation with any contracting party having a substantial interest in the concession which the applicant contracting party is seeking to modify or withdraw, should have the effect that it should have to pay compensation or suffer retaliation greater than the withdrawal or modification sought, judged in the light of the conditions of trade at the time of the proposed withdrawal or modification, making allowance for any discriminatory quantitative restrictions maintained by the applicant contracting party.' See P. Mavroidis, *A Commentary to the GATT*, Oxford University Press, forthcoming, 2005.
93. See J. Jackson, *World Trade and the Law of GATT*, The Michie Company, Charlottesville, Virginia, 1969, p. 170.
94. See E.-U. Petersmann, *Constitutional Functions and Constitutional Problems of International Economic Law*, University Press Fribourg, Fribourg, 1991, pp. 232–3. See also P. VerLoren van Themaat, *The Changing Structure of International Economic Law*, Martinus Nijhoff, The Hague, 1981, p. 87.
95. See G. Winham, *The Evolution of International Trade Agreements*, University of Toronto Press, Toronto, 1992, p. 51. On the interpretation of the meaning of 'commercial considerations', see Appellate Body Report, Canada – Measures Relating to Exports of Wheat and Treatment of Imported Grain, WT/DS276/AB/R, 30 August 2004, paras. 137–51. On this point, the Appelate Body took a somewhat less pro-market approach than the USA was requesting.
96. See Petersmann, op. cit., p. 233.
97. See H. Feis, 'The Conflict over Trade Ideologies', in *Foreign Affairs*, January 1947, p. 217. Feis, an influential State Department advisor, summarized the basic economic conceptions that underpinned the USA's negotiation objectives as follows: '(1) that governments should reduce all types of restrictions imposed on imports and exports; (2) that each should abstain from actions which would cause products produced within their territories to be offered in foreign markets at prices out of correspondence with domestic prices; (3) that each should permit products from every foreign land to compete within its markets on equal terms, and thereby leave the origin of imports to be settled by universal competition; (4) that each should accord all foreign buyers equal opportunity to secure its production the same terms; (5) that each should abstain from bilateral agreements for the exchange of goods that would or might lessen the opportunity for others to compete for the trade'.
98. See Gardner, op. cit., p. 379.
99. See Wilcox, op. cit., p. 112.

100. See, for instance, Paul Nitze, Deputy to the Assistant Secretary of State for Economic Affairs, who remarked that: 'one of the elements that a businessman wants to see included in a sound trade program is fair rules of trade. This is what the Charter for an International Trade Organization ... seeks to provide'. See P. Nitze, 'A Sound International Trade Program. Its Meaning for American Business', in US Department of State publication 3341, Commercial Policy Series 117, November 1948, p. 15.

101. A State Department press release reporting on the GATT tariff round taking place in Torquay, England announced that, based on the recommendation of the concerned federal agencies, the President had agreed that 'the proposed Charter for an International Trade Organization should not be resubmitted to Congress' for ratification. Department of State, *Bulletin*, 18 December 1950, p. 977.

102. See Statement by Secretary Acheson, op. cit., p. 11.

103. On the public response to the ITO, see Aaronson, *Trade and the American Dream*, op. cit.

104. Quoted in the American Tariff League, *The Story Behind the GATT*, publication no. 140, July 1955, p. 19.

105. See W. Diebold, *The End of the ITO*, Princeton University, Princeton, NJ, 1952, p. 14.

106. Ironically, it was the US business groups that had requested rules on foreign investment, against the advice of the State Department.

107. US Council of the International Chamber of Commerce, Executive Committee, *Position with respect to the Havana Charter for an International Trade Organization*, New York, 1950, p. 2. One of the most extreme opponents to the Charter was Philip Cortney, a businessman who launched a successful campaign claiming that the Charter condoned socialist planning and was biased towards harmful full employment and inflationary policies. See P. Cortney, *The Economic Munich*, Philosophical Library, New York, 1949.

108. See Wilcox, op. cit., p. 171 et seq.

109. The Chamber of Commerce of the USA made this point clearly by stating that it supported all objectives of the ITO as stated in Art. 1 of the Charter and that it 'appreciated the thorough and unceasing efforts of the Department of State to achieve a worthwhile economic agreement, but was convinced that [such objectives] could not be obtained by the Havana Charter'. See Chamber of Commerce of the USA, *The Chamber and the Charter*, Washington, DC, 1949, p. 4.

110. See Viner, 'Conflicts of Principle', op. cit., pp. 627–8.

111. See D. Tarullo, 'Beyond Normalcy in the Regulation of International Trade', *Harvard Law Review*, vol. 100, 1987, p. 550. 'Broadly conceived, the international trade regime divides traders and trade relations into the normal and the deviant ... As seen from the trade regime, normal trade is open, structured solely by comparative costs and pursued by private actors without governmental intervention. Normal traders are diversified, developed economies with stale currencies that free private enterprises to participate in trade without abnormal state support or regulation. Everything else – subsidies, dumping, cartels, dependence, instability, state trading, underdevelopment, undue vulnerability to imports, exchange rate instability, and international price supports – is abnormal.' See D. Kennedy, 'Turning to Market Democracy: A Tale of Two Architectures', *Harvard International Law Journal*, vol. 32, no. 2, Spring 1991, pp. 379–80.

112. The phrase was originally coined by John Williamson in 1990 to refer to the lowest common denominator of policy advice being addressed by the Washington-based financial institutions to Latin American countries. For a review of the debate, see, for instance, J. Williamson, 'What Should the World Bank Think About the Washington Consensus?', *World Bank Research Observer*, vol. 15, no. 2, August 2000, pp. 251–64.

113. In the presence of domestic economic distortions, such as inflexible or immobile production factors or external economies or diseconomies, a subsidy directly targeting them may be the most efficient policy response, see H. Johnson, 'Optimal Trade Intervention in the Presence of Domestic Distortions', in R. Baldwin et al., eds., *Trade, Growth and the Balance of Payments*, Rand McNally, Chicago, 1965. 'Strategic' trade theories have lent some intellectual underpinning to policies that target particular industries for support when oligopolistic market structures, economies of scale and product differentiation prevail.

114. It has been argued that 'unbridled and competing national subsidies can undermine world prosperity'. G. Hufbauer and J. Erb, *Subsidies in International Trade*, Institute for International Economics, Washington, DC, 1984, p. 6. See also V. Korah, *EC Competition Law and Practice*, Sweet and Maxwell, London, 1994, p. 34 where she states: 'Possibly the most important way for states to distort trade is by the grant of aid'.

115. The Australian Subsidy on Ammonium Sulphate, 30 April 1950, GATT, BISD II (1952) 188. The position was reiterated in EEC-Payments and Subsidies paid to Processors and Producers of Oilseeds and Related Animal Feed Proteins, 25 January 1990, GATT BISD (37th Supp.) 1991.

116. Agreement on the Interpretation and Application of Art. VI, XVI and XXIII of the General Agreement on Tariffs and Trade, GATT, BISD 26th Supp. 56 (1980).

117. Signatories to the Code were industrial countries and 12 among the most advanced developing countries.

118. See the Agreement on Subsidies and Countervailing Measures in *The Results of the Uruguay Round of Multilateral Trade Negotiations: The Legal Texts*, WTO, Geneva 1995. On the Agreement see, in general, M. Matsushita, T. Schoenbaum and P. Mavroidis, *The World Trade Organization: Law, Practice, and Policy*, Oxford University Press, Oxford, 2003, pp. 259–99.

119. Subsidies Agreement Art. 1 (Definition of a Subsidy). Subsidies are deemed to exist in two instances: First, when a benefit-conferring financial contribution is granted by government or any public body, including sub-national government entities. Such contribution may involve: i) transfer of funds (e.g. grants, loans, equity infusion, or potential transfers, such as loan guarantees); ii) forgone government revenue (such as tax credits or other fiscal incentives); iii) goods or services provided by a government (other than general infrastructure); iv) payments by or on behalf of a government to a funding mechanism, or the government direction to a private body to perform the same functions as outlined in the previous three categories. Second, when any form of benefit-conferring price or income support is provided for.

120. Art. 2 (Specificity). Some ambiguities obviously remain and the agreement makes allowance for them introducing the concept of *de facto* specificity.

121. If the granting authority, or the legislation under which it operates, establishes automatic eligibility criteria or conditions for access to a subsidy programme that 'are neutral, which do not favour certain enterprises over others, and which are economic in nature and horizontal in application, such as number of employees or size of enterprise' (Art. 2(b), note 2), then the programme will be deemed 'non-specific'. The reference to the number of employees and the size of enterprise seems to suggest that subsidies aimed at small- and medium-sized enterprises (SMEs) will be considered 'non-specific'. In some countries, SMEs tend to be concentrated in few sectors, so that the subsidies targeted at them may ultimately favour certain specific industries. Art. 2.1(c) provisions on *de facto* non-specificity should provide a safeguard against this possibility.

122. Art. 3 (Prohibition).

123. The Agreement on Agriculture does not prohibit export subsidies *per se*, but sets negotiated, quantitative limits.

124. Examples of export subsidies are detailed in the Annex 1 to the Agreement.

125. Art. 27 (Special and Differential Treatment of Developing Country Members) and 29 (Transformation into a Market Economy).

126. Art. 4 (Remedies).

127. Art. 5 (Adverse Effects). As for subsidies maintained on agricultural products, Art. 13 of the Agreement on Agriculture provides for limited and temporary exemptions.

128. Art. 6 (Serious Prejudice).

129. Producers accounting for less than 25 per cent of total production have no standing to initiate a countervailing duty investigation, according to Art. 11.4 (Initiation and Subsequent Investigation). Investigations must be terminated if the amount of the subsidy is *de minimis*, namely less than 1 per cent on an *ad valorem* basis, or if the volume of subsidized export, or the injury, is negligible, Art. 11.9. Less stringent thresholds apply to

developing countries (Art. 27.10 (Special and Differential Treatment of Developing Country Members)).

130. Art. 5(a) (Adverse Effects), note 11.
131. Art. 15.1 (Determination of Injury).
132. Art. 15.2 and 15.4. Moreover, injuries caused by factors unrelated to the subsidized imports shall not be attributed to them. Among such factors, mention is made of trade-restrictive practices between foreign and domestic producers, Art. 15.5.
133. Art. 18.1 (Undertakings).
134. Art. 21.1 (Duration and Review of Countervailing Duties and Undertakings).
135. Art. 21.3.
136. Contingent protection refers to those forms of protection that 'can be employed only if the behaviour or performance of a domestic industry or of foreign industries exporting to the domestic market meet certain pre-specified criteria. It contrasts with standard protection, for example a bound tariff, which once set, is independent of the performance or behaviour of either domestic or foreign industries. The primary forms of contingent protection authorised by the GATT are emergency safeguard actions to counter the effects of surges in imports (Art. XIX); AD actions (Art. VI); and duties to countervail the effects in the domestic market of foreign subsidies (Art. XVI)'. See B. Hindley, 'Contingent Protection After the Uruguay Round', 1994, mimeo, p. 1. On the notion of contingent protection, see R. de C. Grey, 'Contingent Protection, Managed Trade and the Decay of the Trade Relations System', in R. Snape, ed., *Issues in World Trade Policy: GATT at the Crossroads*, Macmillan Press, London, 1986, pp. 17–29.
137. The same divergence of objectives characterized the Tokyo Round Code. It has been noted that: 'to the United States, the Agreement is an instrument to control subsidies. To the rest of the world, it is an instrument to control US countervailing duties'. See P. Messerlin, 'Public Subsidies to Industry and Agriculture and Countervailing Duties', mimeo, 1986, p. 16.
138. An analysis of the issue, in the US countervailing duty context, is presented in the opinion in *Carbon Steel Wire Rod from Poland*, 49 Fed. Reg. 19 375 (Dep't Comm. 1984). 'In a market economy, scarce resources are channelled to their most profitable and efficient uses by the market forces of supply and demand. We [Int'l Trade Administration of the Dep't of Commerce] believe a subsidy ... is definitionally any action that distorts or subverts the market process and results in a misallocation of resources, encouraging inefficient production, and lessening world wealth. ... In the absence of government intervention, market economies are characterised by flexible prices determined through the interaction of supply and demand. In response to these prices, resources flow to their most profitable and efficient uses. To identify subsidies in this pure market economy, we would look to the treatment a firm or sector would receive absent government action. In the absence of the [subsidy], the firm would experience market-determined costs for its inputs and receive a market-determined price for its output. The subsidy received by the firm would be the difference between the special treatment and the market treatment'.
139. The notion of the competitive *process* is an important one. Trade practices that distort the process through which markets determine outcomes are considered unacceptable. See Bhagwati, *Protectionism*, op. cit.; id., 'Fair Trade, Reciprocity and Harmonisation', in A. Deardorf and R. Stern, *Analytical and Negotiating Issues in the Global Trading System*, University of Michigan Press, Ann Arbor, 1994. A quite similar notion of 'equitable competition' has been referred to by R. Cass and R. Boltuck, 'Antidumping and Countervailing Duty Law: The Mirage of Equitable International Competition', in J. Bhagwati and Robert Hudec, eds., *Fair Trade and Harmonization: Prerequisite for Free Trade*, vol. 2, The MIT Press, Cambridge, MA, Legal Analysis, 2nd edn., 1996, p. 351 et seq. See also John Jackson, *The World Trading System*, 1997, pp. 298–300.
140. Judge Hand so described the innocent sources of competitive strength that vigorous competitors may bring to bear in the marketplace. *United States v. Aluminum Co. of America*, 148 F.2nd 416 (2d Cir. 1945).
141. 'Natural advantages' are considered to 'derive from sources like historical specialisation, skills in the workforce, supply of laborers, natural resources endowments, and

technological developments'. In contrast, 'artificial advantages' include 'targeted favourable tax laws, interest-free loans from the government, subsidized export credits, high tariff walls preventing competitive imports, [and] state-conferred monopolies'. D. Wood, '"Unfair" Trade Injury: A Competition-Based Approach', *Stanford Law Review*, vol. 41, 1989, p. 1173. Other examples could be added, compounding the difficulty, which Wood points out, of separating out neatly the two categories. However, constructing an economic standard or model of competition for regulatory purposes is as difficult at the international level as it is at the level of domestic antitrust law.

142. See, for instance, United States – Taxes on Petroleum and Certain Imported Products, GATT BISD 34th Supp. 136 (1988); EEC-Payments and Subsidies Paid to Processors and Producers of Oilseeds and Related Animal-Feed Proteins, GATT BISD 37th Suppl. 86 (1991).

143. The same Article also calls for negotiations on the development of the 'necessary multilateral disciplines to avoid such tradedistortive effects'.

144. 'A subsidy is treated in the GATT framework as a "distortion" of international trade, that is, as creating a disparity between the actual costs incurred in producing a particular good and those which must be borne by the firm undertaking its production'. See W. Schwartz and E. Harper, 'The Regulation of Subsidies Affecting International Trade', *Michigan Law Review*, vol. 70, 1972, p. 831.

145. For a discussion of societal preferences that cannot be validated in private market transactions, including national security, the preservation of rural lifestyles, regional development, and the like, being referred to as 'private–public intersectorial economies', see Schwartz and Harper, 'The Regulation of Subsidies Affecting International Trade', op. cit., p. 844.

146. For a dismal view on the feasibility of this assessment in the domestic, countervailing duty context, see D. Tarullo, op. cit., p. 558 where he stated that '... [D]etermining whether a particular government intervention distorts or restores "true" costs is impossible in practice. The cumulative effects of government intervention are so complicated that one cannot disentangle these effects from some hypothetical underlying undistorted market.'

147. The *de facto/de jure* distinction has been elaborated in the administration of the US countervailing duty legislation. See, in particular the holding of *Cabot v. United States*, 620 F. Supp. 722 (Ct. Int'l Trade 1985), declining to accept nominal general availability as incompatible with the specificity requirement for countervailability.

148. A few 'specific' regional, research and environmental subsidies, provided that they met certain strict requirements, were considered, under now lapsed provisions, as non-actionable or, in a sense, permitted or *per se* legal, in light of the important social and economic goals they are designed to further. See Art. 8 (Identification of NonActionable Subsidies). Art. 11.1 of the Tokyo Round Code recognized that 'government assistance for various purposes is widely provided by Members and that the mere fact that such assistance may not qualify for nonactionable treatment ... does not in itself restrict the ability of Members to provide such assistance'.

149. Art. 5 (Adverse Effects).

150. In the European Community context, the European Court of Justice has adopted a low standard of evidence to determine whether competition and trade between member states is distorted. The Court considers that where inter-firm competition exists, any financial aid, by artificially strengthening the position of the recipient firm and conversely hampering the competitors' ability to increase exports and market shares, is capable of distorting competition. Case C-305/89, *Italy v. Commission*, 1991 E.C.R. I-1603, I-1642; Case 730/79, *Philip Morris v. Commission*, 1980 E.C.R. 2671, 2688.

151. The Australian Subsidy on Ammonium Sulphate, GATT II BISD 188 (1952); EEC-Payments and Subsidies Paid to Processors and Producers of Oilseeds and Related Animal-Feed Proteins, GATT BISD 37th Suppl. 86 (1991).

152. In 1955, the GATT Contracting Parties took a general decision that identifies a domestic subsidy as a measure whose introduction subsequent to the negotiation of a concession need not normally be expected: 'A contracting party which has negotiated a concession has a reasonable expectation, failing evidence to the contrary, that the value of the concession

will not be nullified or impaired by the contracting party which granted the concession by the subsequent introduction or increase of a domestic subsidy' (see BISD 3S/224).

153. The Agreement originally offered clearer guidance as it provided in Art. 6(1) that 'serious prejudice' was deemed to exist when the subsidy affected the cost and revenue structure of the targeted firm or industry relative to competitors and thus influenced its supply behaviour. Such presumption might be rebutted if no trade effect arose. However, such provision expired at the end of 1999 (Art. 31).

154. Art. 5(a) (Adverse Effects), note 11. It is not made clear, though, whether injury should be determined in the same manner both for the purpose of establishing adverse effects and for that of imposing a countervailing measure.

155. For instance, the provision of a regional development subsidy that only offsets the additional cost that the recipient firm incurs in locating in the targeted area would not create an 'artificial' cost advantage. However, the same firm may well be quite competitive and successful in export markets so as to displace sales by local competitors. For a discussion in the countervailing duty context, see C. Goetz, L. Granet and W. Schwartz, 'The Meaning of "Subsidy" and "Injury" in the Countervailing Duty Law', *International Review of Law and Economics*, vol. 6, 1986, p. 17 et seq.; R. Diamond, 'Economic Foundations of Countervailing Duty Law', *Virginia Journal of International Law*, vol. 29, 1989, p. 767 et seq. In addition, the alleged injury may be caused by imports from different countries and by a host of other elements. In Art. 15.5 (Determination of Injury) the Agreement requests the authorities administering countervailing duty laws to consider 'other factors' that may be responsible for the injury and not attributable to the subsidized imports.

156. The Agreement (Art 15.5) calls for the examination of 'any known factors other than the subsidized imports which at the same time are injuring the domestic industry, and the injuries caused by these other factors must not be attributed to the subsidized imports'. Interpreting 'injury' as requiring proof of this link seems to make this notion more consonant with the US-developed concept of 'antitrust injury', 'which is to say injury of the type the antitrust laws were intended to prevent ... reflect[ing] the anticompetitive effect either of the violation or of the anticompetitive acts made possible by the violation'. *Brunswick Corporation v. Pueblo Bowl-o-Mat, Inc.* 429 U.S. 477 (1977). On the contrary, in the *Outboard Marine I* case, the Court, perhaps too broadly, rejected any application of the antitrust laws to complaints of foreign subsidization: 'The antitrust laws were not intended as a sanctuary for those who cannot compete against lower prices be they the result of simple efficiency, economy of scale, cheap labor, technological expertise or anything other than commercially mischievous conduct. Thus, although plaintiff is injured by defendant's capability to offer lower prices as a result of foreign government subsidies to manufacturer Pezetel, the Court concludes that the antitrust laws do not provide a remedy for such loss'. *Outboard Marine Corp. v. Pezetel*, 461 F. Supp. 384 (D. Del. 1978). The Subsidies Agreement instead seems to suggest that members recognize the potential distortive and anticompetitive effects of subsidies and want to regulate them.

157. Countervailing duty laws' 'purpose is to offset the unfair competitive advantage that foreign producers would otherwise enjoy from export subsidies paid by their governments. While it would be wrong to condemn all export subsidies as bad government policy, many are by their nature market distortions; thus a programme of countervailing duties is not inconsistent with a competitive, market-oriented trade policy. Certainly, the countervailing duty laws can be subject to abuse, and it is not always easy to determine what constitutes an export subsidy. There may also be times, such as where the domestic industry is concentrated and enjoying oligopolistic pricing, where even subsidized competition should be welcomed. However, as a general matter there is no contradiction between a rational and well-administered countervailing duty law and the policy of antitrust'. See J. Atwood and K. Brewster, *Antitrust and American Business Abroad*, Shepard's/McGraw-Hill, Colorado Springs, 1981, p. 64.

158. Various GATT articles contain provisions permitting countries to withdraw or temporarily cease to apply obligations and in some cases to impose trade restrictions. They include Art. VI, XI, XII, XVIII, XX, XXI, XXV and XXVIII. The Arrangement Regarding

International Trade in Textiles (MFA) of 1973, as well as certain protocols of accession, also contain special safeguard provisions.

159. Opinions on Art. XIX are quite unanimous. See for instance J. Jackson, *World Trade*, op. cit., p. 557, who considered it 'extraordinarily oblique, even for GATT language'; G. Sampson, 'Safeguards', in J.M. Finger and A. Olechowski, eds., *The Uruguay Round: A Handbook on the Multilateral Trade Negotiations*, The World Bank, Washington, DC, 1987, p. 143, stated that 'Article XIX has rarely, if ever, been interpreted in a way that would appear to be consistent with the text'.

160. See Agreement on Safeguards in WTO, *The Results of the Uruguay Round of Multilateral Trade Negotiations: The Legal Texts*, WTO, Geneva 1995. On the Agreement see, in general, Matsushita et. al., op. cit., pp. 181–216.

161. See J. Perez-Lopez, 'GATT Safeguards: A Critical Review of Article XIX and its Implementation in Selected Countries', *Case Western Journal of International Law*, vol. 23, 1991, p. 528.

162. See GATT, Report on the Withdrawal by the United States of a Tariff Concession under Art. XIX of the GATT, 1951 (the so-called 'Hatter's Fur Case'). As a result of this case, the prerequisite cause of 'unforeseen developments' has been essentially 'read out' of the GATT agreement. 'One can almost conclude that an increase in imports can *itself* be an unforeseen development'. See Jackson, *World Trade*, op. cit., p. 561. In the same vein, Sampson, op. cit., states on p. 143 that 'any increase in imports, even if through normal changes in international competitiveness, could therefore be considered actionable under Art. XIX'.

163. See the Agreement Preamble where 'the importance of structural adjustment and the need to enhance rather than limit competition in international markets' are recognized.

164. See Atwood and Brewster, op. cit., p. 66; B. Cohen, 'Section 201 and 406 of the Trade Act of 1974, and their Relationship to Competition Law and Policy', *Antitrust Law Journal*, vol. 56, 1987, pp. 476–7.

165. 'It is tempting to argue that assistance for import-competition-affected adjustment is unreasonable and inefficient, that all changes require adjustment, and that assistance should be provided in a generic fashion for all kinds of changes rather than just for import-related changes. This viewpoint is valid in a cosmopolitan world that does not differentiate between foreign and domestic communities. However, in the real world the refusal to accept change – and hence the need to accommodate to it and facilitate it through adjustment assistance – is greater when the source of the disturbance is presumed to be foreign. ... The case for differential adjustment assistance rests on this asymmetry in communities' attitudes toward change from foreign and domestic sources. It is logical, therefore, to combine temporary protection (afforded under safeguards measures) with adjustment assistance (such as retraining programs for workers)'. See Bhagwati, *Protectionism*, op. cit., pp. 118–19.

166. Similarly, adjustment preoccupations are not completely foreign to competition policy. Mention could be made of the 'failing company' defence, which allows for a more lenient approach to mergers and joint ventures or the special treatment for recession, rationalization, and structural crisis cartels in a number of jurisdictions.

167. For a negative view on the adjustment rationale for safeguard measures, see A. Sykes, 'The Safeguard Mess: A Critique of WTO Jurisprudence', *World Trade Review*, vol. 2, no. 3, 2003, pp. 287–8.

168. Furthermore, in order to help stem the protectionist capture of safeguards, strengthened transparency and surveillance is provided for by the creation of the Committee on Safeguards. Consultation and dispute settlement mechanisms should work in the same direction. Transparency is also required in the investigation phase, when exporters and 'other interested parties', presumably including consumer groups and competition authorities, can voice their concerns and present evidence 'as to whether or not the application of a safeguard measure would be in the public interest', Art. 3 (Investigation).

169. Art. 5.1 (Application of Safeguard Measures) and 7.1 (Duration and Review of Safeguard Measures).

170. Art. 7.2.

171. '...[A]djustment assistance and safeguard against market disruption need to be considered as complementary and not substitute policies. Adjustment assistance is designed to increase the speed with which change can be absorbed and digested; safeguards against market disruption are designed to slow down the speed of the change that has to be absorbed and digested. Optimum policy with respect to change associated with shifting comparative advantage in response to the development and diffusion of technology requires joint optimization with respect to both types of policy, not prior choice of one line or other of policy and subsequent optimization with respect to it alone. Both policies also require drawing a fine line between optimal pacing of change and protectionist resistance to change, a line which is probably significantly easier to draw and maintain where the two policies are considered jointly than when the full weight of responsibility for controlling the rate of change and absorption of it is placed on one type of policy only'. See H. Johnson, 'Technological Change and Comparative Advantage: An Advanced Country's Viewpoint', *Journal of World Trade Law*, Jan.–Feb. 1975, p. 13.

172. Art. 4 (Determination of Serious Injury or Threat Thereof). It is generally understood that the 'serious injury' standard should be more difficult to meet than the 'material injury' standard foreseen in AD/CVD regulation, although the latter is also unclear. Several factors to be considered in the investigation are enumerated. They include: the rate and amount of the increase in import in absolute and relative terms, the share of the domestic market taken by increased imports, changes in the level of sales, production, productivity, capacity utilization, profits and losses, and employment.

173. Art. 2 (Conditions).

174. See the Hatter's Fur Case, op. cit. In this case it was decided that, when a country determines that its industry has suffered serious injury, it is entitled to the benefit of any 'reasonable doubt' on the matter in the event of a dispute on the applicability of Art. XIX. The consequence thus seems to be that the exporting country needs to disprove serious injury, more than the importing country has to prove it. See A. Sykes, 'GATT Safeguards Reform: The Injury Test' in M. Trebilcock and R. York, eds., *Fair Exchange: Reforming Trade Remedy Laws*, C.D. Howe Institute, Toronto, 1990, p. 204 et seq.

175. Some countries have defined these concepts in domestic legislation, and vast jurisprudence has ensued. See Perez-Lopez, op. cit.

176. Art. 5.2(b) (Application of Safeguard Measures). A country may depart from allocating quotas among suppliers on a non-discriminatory basis, as prescribed in Art. XIII (Non-discriminatory Administration of Quantitative Restrictions) of the GATT, provided that it can demonstrate to the Committee on Safeguards that imports from certain countries have increased disproportionately as compared to the total increase in the representative period, that the selective application is justified, and that the conditions of applications are equitable to all suppliers. A selective application is not permitted in cases of threat of serious injury, nor is it eligible for extension beyond the initial four years. The modalities of the departure from non-discrimination are not specified. Nor are the notions of disproportionate increase or equitable conditions.

177. Art. 11 (Prohibition and Elimination of Certain Measures), note 3.

178. Auctioned quotas share the same advantage. Thus, for instance, in the USA the President is authorized to sell import licences at public auctions. 19 U.S.C. § 2581.

179. See Art. XIII (Non-discriminatory Administration of Quantitative Restrictions) of the GATT.

180. Developing countries are excluded from the application of safeguard measures if their share of the safeguard-invoking country imports is *de minimis*, as defined in Art. 9.1 (Developing Country Members).

181. See J. Tumlir, 'A Revised Safeguard Clause for GATT?', *Journal of World Trade Law*, vol. 7, 1973, p. 408.

182. See the Agreement's Preamble.

183. See G. Curzon, 'Crisis in the International Trading System', in H. Corbet and R. Jackson, eds., *In Search of a New Economic Order*, Croom Helm, London, 1974, p. 36.

184. See Wilcox, op. cit., pp. 35–6.

185. See Viner, 'Conflicts of Principle', op. cit., pp. 627–8.

5. Rethinking fairness in the evolution of the international trade policy and rule-making discourse

In the trade policy discourse, the major structural deviation from the fairness approach championed by the USA and described in the previous chapters of the study is to be found in what goes under the name of 'special and differential treatment' afforded to developing countries. This principle has a long and troubled history, which largely coincides with the long-standing efforts of developing countries to modify the international trading system's rules, which generally are perceived to be slanted in favour of developed countries[1] to meet their own specific needs and interests. In particular, since the regime's birth, developing countries have argued that the GATT is quite stringent with regard to the types of restrictions (e.g., quotas) that they may want to use, while being more lenient with regard to the instruments that industrial countries generally employ (e.g. subsidies for primary products).

Hence, the arguments go beyond the simple consideration that, because of differences in bargaining assets (e.g. developed nations have more to offer in terms of trade opportunities in their markets) or relative power, the negotiations' results (i.e., those of the GATT itself and subsequent rounds) were unfair. The developing countries' objections often point out that, *because* of the way the system is set up and rules are designed, the resulting balance of benefits and burdens is unfair. This points to a more fundamental difference with regard to the respective understanding of what is 'fair'. Indeed, developing countries often seem to espouse a different notion of fairness.

From the US postwar planners' perspective, issues related to economic development and trade were not of primary concern, as it is evinced from their virtual absence in the Proposals and Suggested Charter. The position was that developing countries could benefit by participating fully in a multilateral, non-discriminatory system, with the lowest possible level of tariffs and no quantitative restrictions. This position, which Britain and other developed countries generally supported, gave rise to a bitter conflict, as seen during the parallel negotiations of the Havana Charter and the GATT. The position of developing countries was often antithetical to that of industrial ones. From his perspective, Wilcox described it as follows:

It was the basic policy of India ... to promote rapid and large-scale industrialization, and the effectuation of this policy required the imposition of direct controls on foreign trade. Such controls should not be judged by themselves but by the purposes for which they were employed. And the purpose of economic development was clearly justified. ... The position of many of the countries of Latin America was even more extreme. Wealth and income, they argued, should be redistributed between richer and poor states. Upon the rich, obligations should be imposed; upon the poor, privileges should be conferred.[2]

With this kind of rift with respect to the objectives and the benefits to be expected from international trade rule-making, it is not surprising that appreciation for the regime's fairness has diverged considerably since its early days.

5.1   THE GATT AND DEVELOPING COUNTRIES

Despite limited successes during the final phases of the Havana Charter negotiations, the GATT incorporated very little consideration of the developing countries' demands, even though 11 out of the 23 original signatories were developing countries. As a result, at the outset, developing country contracting parties participated in GATT disciplines on an essentially equal basis and had to justify recourse to any non-tariff barriers according to standard GATT principles and provisions. In particular, GATT Art. XVIII did allow exceptions in support of developing industries, but the provisions were not unique to developing countries and required prior approval. In part, for this reason, developing countries made more frequent recourse in the early 1950s to balance-of-payments-based exceptions under Art. XII, which did not require prior approval, but were also not specifically tailored to developing countries' needs.[3]

The idea of relaxing normal GATT rules and granting special and differential treatment gained prominence after the accession of a number of newly independent developing countries to the GATT in the 1950s. Most of these countries also challenged the GATT's basic fairness assumption, arguing that it was neither realistic nor fair to expect poor countries with fragile economies, mainly former colonies, to compete on equal terms with industrial countries. At the same time, economists started studying the trade relationships between richer and poorer states in depth, highlighting the particular risks and vulnerabilities that smaller and weaker economies face in international trade.[4]

The need for flexibility with regard to GATT obligations for developing countries was recognized at the 1954–55 GATT Review Session, when substantial revisions to Art. XVIII were decided and Art. XXVIII bis was introduced. Under Art. XVIII, as amended, 'a contracting party the economy of which can only support low standards of living and is in the early stages of development' is able to modify or withdraw concessions under Art. II 'in order to promote the establishment of a particular industry with a view to raising the general standard of living of its people' (Section A); to institute, maintain, or intensify quantitative restrictions 'to safeguard its external financial position and to ensure a level of reserves adequate for the implementation of its programme of economic development' (Section B); or to introduce other import restrictions 'required to promote the establishment of a particular industry with a view to raising the general standard of living of its people' (Section C). However, a 1955 GATT Working Party report stressed that the new text still meant that any future action permitted under it should be undertaken 'on condition that any other contracting party affected by such action would also be free to take such measures as may be necessary to restore the balance of benefits'.[5] Furthermore, Art. XXVIII bis, which was drafted to set out a framework for future GATT negotiations, recognized that such negotiations should take into account 'the needs of less-developed countries for a more flexible use of tariff protection to assist their economic development'.

The 1955 revision reflected the emphasis on import substitution that prevailed in many developing countries' policies in the 1950s. However, an interest in promoting exports was already being felt, and in 1958 the GATT-commissioned Haberler Report[6] confirmed the view that developing countries' export earnings were insufficient to meet their development needs and stressed the responsibility of industrial countries' protectionist policies in the predicament of developing countries. As a result of such increased awareness, developing countries were exempted from the prohibition on export subsidies, when the provisions regarding such a ban (Art. XIV:4) were finally given effect in 1960.[7] More broadly, in 1964, the GATT Contracting Parties adopted three articles on 'Trade and Development', as the new Part IV of the Agreement was entitled.[8] While designed to promote development and developing countries' interests in the trading system, Part IV was never more than a set of 'best-endeavour' undertakings, with no legal force. Art. XXXVI:3, for instance, states that: 'there is a need for positive efforts designed to ensure that less-developed contracting parties secure a share in the growth in international trade commensurate with the needs of their economic development'. One particularly significant feature of Part IV, however, was the assertion of the principle of non-reciprocity in Art. XXXVI:8. Non-reciprocity meant that, in the course of trade negotiations, developing countries would not be expected to make contributions inconsistent with their individual development and financial and trade needs. While recognizing the principle is important, as one analyst put it: 'less-developed countries obtained a great deal of verbiage and very few precise commitments'.[9]

Meanwhile, the debate over the need to increase preferential access to developed country markets continued in both the GATT and the UN. In the context of the 1st United Nations Development Decade, 1961, Resolution 1707 called for a 'prompt undertaking to facilitate the expansion of trade of the developing countries ... and [to achieve] the extension by economically developed countries to the less developed countries of advantages not necessarily requiring full reciprocity' of commitments.[10] Further action took place, as of 1964, in the newly established UN Conference on Trade and Development (UNCTAD). Progress on establishing a preferential tariff scheme for developing countries was made at the second UNCTAD meeting in New Delhi in 1968, when the USA reversed its previous hostile stance, in line with its traditional antagonism towards preferential treatment. Resolution 21(ii) at UNCTAD II called for the establishment of a 'generalized, non-reciprocal, non-discriminatory system of preferences in favour of the developing countries, including special measures in favour of the least advanced among the developing countries'. It further stated that such preferences had three objectives: to increase the export earnings of developing countries, to promote their industrialization, and to accelerate their rates of economic growth.

However, it was not until 1971 that legal authority for a preferential tariff programme was agreed upon within the GATT. This took the form of a 10-year waiver to the MFN principle. The waiver authorized each industrial country to establish a Generalized System of Preference (GSP) scheme, as it was termed, provided that the programmes' benefits were (potentially) extended to all developing countries. The shape of the individual GSP schemes remained for each country to decide, and there was no international law obligation to establish them in the first place. The various national GSP schemes have remained quite different in terms of eligibility requirements, product coverage, and margin of preference. The USA only introduced a GSP scheme in 1974 and implemented it with effect from 1 January 1976.[11] Another waiver gave permission to developing countries to exchange trade concessions among themselves.

Subsequently, in 1979, as part of the Tokyo Round negotiations, the GATT contracting parties adopted the Decision on Differential and More Favourable Treatment, known as the 'Enabling Clause'.[12] The Enabling Clause became the framework document for trade and development issues in the GATT and firmly established the legal basis for the GSP. The Enabling Clause restated the principle of non-reciprocity[13] and stipulated that 'notwithstanding the provisions of Article I of the General Agreement, contracting parties may accord differential and more favourable treatment to developing countries, without according such treatment to other contracting parties' in the following areas:

a) Preferential tariff treatment accorded by developed contracting parties to products originating in developing countries in accordance with the Generalized System of Preferences; b) Differential and more favourable treatment with respect to the provisions of the General Agreement concerning non-tariff measures governed by the provisions of instruments multilaterally negotiated under the auspices of the GATT; c) Regional or global arrangements entered into amongst less-developed contracting parties …; d) Special treatment on the least developed among the developing countries in the context of any general or specific measures in favour of developing countries.

However, the clause also states that

less-developed contracting parties expect that their capacity to make contributions or negotiated concessions or take other mutually agreed action under the provisions and procedures of the General Agreement would improve with the progressive development of their economies and improvement in their trade situation …

The more favourable treatment is thus temporary, and the USA has withdrawn eligibility for several countries over time.[14]

Beyond the value of preferential access, which is still quite controversial to this day,[15] the principles of non-reciprocity and differential treatment allowed developing countries to make only limited market-access commitments and relatively few tariff bindings in the Tokyo Round. Moreover, in respect of the new agreements in the area of non-tariff measures (the 'codes') reached in the Tokyo Round,[16] the so-called 'code approach' was adopted, whereby such agreements only applied to signatories.[17] While the codes contained various special and differential treatment provisions, most developing countries refrained from signing them. The reasons for their reluctance to accede to the codes varied, but they largely revolved around the view that they neither addressed nor were relevant to their concerns.

Also in the light of these disappointing results, the effectiveness of the special and differential provisions remained contested. In 1985, the Leutwiler Report, commissioned by the then GATT Director-General Dunkel stressed that: 'special treatment is of limited value. Far greater emphasis should be placed on permitting and encouraging developing countries to take advantage of their competitive strengths and on incorporating them more fully into the trading system, with all the appropriate rights and responsibilities that this entails'.[18] This recommendation dovetails with the renewed emphasis on the markets' role and distrust for government intervention that characterized the 1980s in some major economies, especially the USA. This position seemed to be vindicated in the developing world, where protectionist, import-substitution policies had not obtained the expected results. Furthermore, especially the most advanced and open among the developing countries were disenchanted with the notion of special and differential treatment and with preference schemes, as they recognized that the logic of reciprocity still existed and that countries that were not required to reciprocate often found few concessions were accorded to them.[19] Consequently, they were ready to bargain for more market access in the sectors of their interest, such as agriculture and textiles, where industrial country protectionism still held sway, against a curtailment of non-reciprocity of obligations. While more emphasis was placed on additional transitional time to adjust to the burdens of fully implementing new obligations, developing countries gave up the code approach in favour of the 'single undertaking'. Under this approach, prospective members of the new World Trade Organization (WTO) had to agree to virtually all its disciplines as a package deal of sorts.[20] The WTO was not to continue the practice of *de facto* application of GATT treatment to many developing countries (31 in 1986), which enjoyed the benefits of membership without taking up any enforceable obligations.[21] Furthermore, the stricter and more effective dispute settlement system of the WTO ensures to a much greater degree that commitments are taken and rules applied even in cases when the interests of developing countries were sidestepped or compromised.[22]

The Uruguay Round negotiations yielded a large number of special and differential treatment provisions. The majority of them can be characterized as 'best-endeavour' clauses. As summarized by the WTO Secretariat, by the year 2000:

> the universe of special and differential treatment consists of 145 provisions spread across the different Multilateral Agreements on Trade in Goods; the General Agreement on Trade in Services; The Agreement on Trade-Related Aspects of Intellectual Property; the Understanding on Rules and Procedures Governing the Settlement of Disputes; and various Ministerial Decisions. Of the 145 provisions, 107 were adopted at the conclusion of the Uruguay Round, and 22 apply to least-developed country Members only.[23]

This vast array of provisions can be divided into three main types. First, developing countries are granted longer time frames for implementing WTO Agreements than developed countries. These vary considerably from two years (in the case of the Agreements on Sanitary and Phytosanitary Measures (SPS) and on Import Licensing) to ten years (in the case of the Agreement on Agriculture). Second, developing countries are accorded greater flexibility in the application of many WTO Agreements provisions. Such flexibility is generally in the form of exemptions from commitments otherwise generally applying to members or of a reduced level of commitments. Third, developing countries are promised technical assistance in several areas, including SPS, technical barriers to trade, customs valuation, services, and intellectual property. For all these categories, several specific provisions are addressed to the least-developed countries.

The end result of the Uruguay Round was a considerable erosion of special and differential treatment, mainly because it was addressed piecemeal in each of the negotiating groups in which the Round was conducted, without an underlying consensus as to the trade measures required by developing countries as essential elements of their development process. In the decade that has almost elapsed since the Uruguay Round agreements came into force, the controversy regarding the effectiveness of special and differential provisions has not subsided; if anything, it has intensified. Preferential tariff treatment continued to be eroded as a result of further MFN liberalization, while preference utilization on the part of the vast majority of potential beneficiary remained limited at best. As late as 2001, WTO Ministers agreed that: 'all special and differential treatment provisions shall be reviewed with a view to strengthening them and making them more precise, effective and operational'.[24]

5.2   THE CONCEPT OF SPECIAL AND DIFFERENTIAL TREATMENT

From the days of the Havana Charter negotiations, developing countries have advanced the view that a system predicated on equal treatment and reciprocity was not fair. As one member of the US delegation put it, they sought 'unequal and more onerous obligations' from industrialized countries.[25] Furthermore, they considered that the allowed exceptions were mainly in the industrial countries' interest. A fair regime needed to adopt a different approach, which would recognize their substantive difference in terms of economic development. Until 1955, all contracting parties were considered equal under GATT law. The fairness approach based on equal treatment and reciprocity applied both in formal legal terms and with regard to the economic substance of the rules. This was quite in line with the traditional view prevailing in international law and well accepted in the USA that all independent states are equal.[26] And, of course, developing nations did not contest this, as they were actually quite jealous of their newly acquired independence. But very early on, they stressed that their political independence and equality was not matched by economic independence and equality. In particular, what they disputed was the notion that without specific efforts, free competition and free markets would almost automatically promote their industrialization and development, bringing about the desired economic and social advancement.

This difference of views, as seen in the previous section, yielded some results after years of controversy, both in terms of the developing countries' ability to protect their own markets (in particular under Art. XII and XVIII of GATT,[27] relating to balance of payments) and their capacity to enhance their trade opportunities in their developed partners' markets (through the various GSP schemes). However, even with respect to these advances, views continued to differ. From the perspective of many developed countries, particularly the USA, special and differential treatment should be seen as an exception to the equal application of rules. This is why non-reciprocal concessions and provisions are generally voluntary (as the GSP preferences) and temporary. Hence, this also explains the US emphasis on the eventual 'graduation' of beneficiary countries from its GSP scheme.[28]

Market-based competition, as the reference model for the trade regime, has not been modified by the special and differential treatment notion. Market-based competition is expected to yield trade opportunities on a fair basis when all participants follow the same rules. If there are specific problems, such as in the case of developing countries, specific, but transitory, exceptions can be provided for. However, developing countries are also to 'make contributions or negotiated concessions' (in the words of the Enabling Clause) in due course. The reference model, despite all the protectionist backslidings, remains anchored to reciprocity and the contribution-based distribution of benefits and burdens prevailing in market transactions. Once the temporary adjustment problems are solved, the system should return to full reciprocity. The quicker, the better, as the system's market-inspired behavioural rules are deemed of equal benefit to developed and developing countries alike.[29] Hence, there is the provision of technical assistance to facilitate and speed up the process.

In contrast, from the developing countries' perspective, differential treatment was considered to be an instrument in achieving a more 'equitable' trading system. For them, the trading system could be considered as fair only if it was also equitable, allowing developing countries to move from formal equality towards substantive equality. This preoccupation was not entirely new. In 1935, the Permanent Court of International Justice considered this issue when it said that: 'equality in law precludes discrimination of any kind; whereas equality in fact may involve the necessity of different treatment in order to attain a result which establishes an equilibrium between different situations'.[30] Similarly, in the 1966 *South West Africa* case, Judge Tanaka opined that 'to treat matters differently according to their inequality is not only permitted but required'.[31] This approach has a long tradition in Western thought, dating back to when Aristotle made this point in the *Nicomachean Ethics*.[32]

Developing countries' representatives espoused this line of thinking and argued it forcefully. In the 1954–55 GATT Contracting Parties session, the Indian delegate stated: 'equality of treatment is equitable only among equals. A weakling cannot carry the same load as a giant'.[33] In the same vein, the Uruguayan representative noted that the MFN was 'not the proper means to combat underdevelopment because economic inequality among states can only be put right through unequal treatment favoring some in order to obtain effective equalization in the end'.[34] In 1964, Prebisch stressed that 'the free play [of market forces] is admissible in relations between countries that are structurally similar, but not between those whose structures are altogether different', which means that the 'rules of reciprocity in trade negotiations must be changed because of the economic inequality between countries'.[35]

Hence, from a developing country's perspective, fairness cannot be based on reciprocity and commutative justice, but needs to be based on equity and distributive justice. In this vein, International Court of Justice Judge Bedjaoui argued:

> This international law of participation, genuinely all-embracing and funded on solidarity and co-operation, must give great prominence to the principle of equity (which corrects inequalities) rather than to the principle of equality. In doing so, it must keep the objective in view, which consist of reducing and, if possible, even of eradicating the gap that exists between a minority of rich nations and a majority of poor nations.[36]

Hence, the principle of equity aims at correcting existing distributions of wealth and meeting developing countries' needs. Need is considered to be the distributively just criterion.[37]

This approach was not only argued within the GATT, but also gave rise to a broader movement in various fora, principally within the UN, to establish a new system of economic relations – which came to be known as the New International Economic Order (NIEO) – informed by the principle of equity and by the request of differential and more favorable treatment for developing countries.[38] Hundreds of provisions, generally of a non-binding nature, were adopted by UN organs in many areas, from trade to debt issues, and from environmental protection to technology transfer. Their philosophy is well expressed in the preamble to the 1974 Declaration Concerning the Establishment of a NIEO, which identifies the principles of equity, the interdependence of all peoples, and cooperation among states as the bases of the NIEO.[39] For the first time, the General Assembly called for eliminating inequality and correcting injustices. The purpose of cooperation was declared to be the elimination of disparities among states and the preferential treatment of, and active assistance to, the less-developed countries. The same year, the Charter on Economic Rights and Duties of States called for the establishment of an NIEO based on equity, sovereign equality, interdependence, common interests, and cooperation among states. It referred to 'mutual and equitable benefit' as an essential element of the NIEO, and to 'promotion of international social justice and 'international cooperation for development'.[40] Article 6 of the Charter underlined the states' duty to contribute to the development of international trade by taking into account the interests of producers and consumers. According to that article: 'All States share the responsibility to promote the regular flow and access of all commercial goods traded at stable, remunerative and equitable prices, thus contributing to the equitable development of the world economy, taking into account, in particular, the interests of developing countries'. The USA and the overwhelming majority of western industrial countries voted against, or abstained from voting on the Charter.[41]

The 1979 Enabling Clause and the introduction of GSP schemes in several developed countries probably constituted the high mark of the implementation of equity within the GATT regime. It was so perceived at the time of its introduction. Yusuf then could write that: 'the application of differential treatment to the economic relations of developed and developing states implies notions of equity and justice. It reflects a trend towards the internationalization of the welfare state principles, by introducing at the international level such legal concepts as the collective responsibility of the community for the social and economic well-being of its members'.[42] In a sense, these initiatives could be seen as an attempt to globalize the 'embedded liberalism compromise'. However, the developed and developing country visions of the economic order, and the trade regime in particular, remained in many respects incompatible. Developed countries, particularly the USA, have continued 'to strongly resist the "welfare system" rhetoric and insist on *their* sovereignty, *their* freedom to contract, *their* right to continue to run an economic system on traditional principles and terms. ... They think trade is a two-way street based on reciprocal agreements and arrangements, not on preference for the Third World'.[43] Preferences – reluctantly agreed upon – are seen as a strategy towards the fuller integration of developing countries into the trade regime, once the expected benefits of trade have 'trickled down' to the preference beneficiaries.[44]

In contrast, equity seeks to influence market outcomes, as opportunities to trade can be considered equitable only among competitors having equal trading abilities. 'Rules which treat all partners in the same way ... are suitable as long as the partners have the same capacity to benefit from the standards in place'.[45] The competitive market, with its distributive norm based on contributions as the reference model for the fairness of the trade regime, remains irreconcilable with the need-based, equitable-trading system consistently advocated by developing countries, at least until the early 1980s.[46]

But the NIEO efforts in general, and the attempts to achieve a new order in trade in particular, have remained largely unsuccessful.[47] The limited special and differential treatment provisions won by developing countries amount, at best, to adjustments, certainly not structural changes, of the existing trade regime. While developed countries resisted quite consistently any recognition, let alone imposition, of significant legal obligations, by the time of the special session of the General Assembly in 1990, a shift had occurred in the debate's focus. Indeed, the resulting Declaration of International Economic Cooperation did not mention any of the crucial terms used earlier, and even the phrase 'new international economic order' was absent.[48] This resolution adopted a different approach to North–South relations, focusing on human rights and protecting the environment. On trade and developing countries' specific needs, it only stated that, in the context of the then ongoing Uruguay Round of negotiations, it was vitally important that these 'result[ed] in a balanced outcome, preserving and strengthening the multilateral trading system, enabling trade liberalization and increased market access for the exports of developing countries'.

Reflecting the new thinking in parts of the developing world, the Uruguay Round brought about a partial modification and a relative weakening of the approach to the special and differential treatment for developing countries. As seen, much more emphasis was put on transitional adjustment. Longer time periods are allowed for developing countries, at the end of which rules are scheduled to 'phase in' automatically. A number of exceptions are provided, but as in the case of developed countries, these are considered the necessary adaptations to special circumstances that in no way undermine the general approach of the system. Essentially, the model remains that of the competitive market, which is ultimately deemed to ensure fairness. The quest for equity had receded. A new consensus, which gave pride of place to market forces in the development process (sometimes referred to as the 'Washington Consensus', also to stress its US roots), appeared to be emerging. At the conclusion of the Uruguay Round, such consensus seemed to spread to the trade regime.[49] But the convergence of views, if such convergence ever existed, did not last long, as the failure of the 1999 WTO ministerial meeting in Seattle clearly showed. Equity preoccupations were back on the forefront of the debate and have continued to fuel the ongoing controversy surrounding 'globalization'.

5.3   BOTTOM-UP FAIRNESS: THE FAIR TRADE MOVEMENT

By the late 1940s, another strand of thought, and especially of action, had started to emerge in the developed world, challenging even more fundamentally the traditional, market-based notion of fairness prevailing in the capitals of many industrial countries and certainly the USA. This was based on the recognition that existing trading relations with the Third World were not producing the expected benefits for the people participating in such trade. Trade was 'unfair' to them. What counted were not so much the relations between countries; instead, fairness was judged on the results that international trade produced, or failed to, on people in the South and their well-being.

As early as the London Economic Conference in 1933, the importance of increasing the primary commodity producers' purchasing power by keeping the export prices of raw materials at a fair remunerative level was recognized, together with the problems created by protectionist practices that often led to overproduction and downward pressure on prices. After much controversy, the Havana Charter incorporated provisions on international commodity agreements, which were not carried over into the GATT. The latter never took any role in this area, mainly because the USA and other industrial countries considered that these types of agreements were not compatible with the GATT system.[50] Nevertheless, a number of them were concluded in the following years, without much success.

And yet, the predicament of commodity producers, the people mainly affected by international trade at the time in the majority of developing countries, continued, providing ample proof that the way trade was organized and the price they received for their produce did not translate into commensurate benefits and 'raising standards living', in the words of the GATT Preamble.[51] Grass roots initiatives thus started to emerge to modify such market-inspired trading arrangements, with the aim of increasing the income of poor producers in the South. The basic idea was that out of the price paid to producers in developing countries, a much higher share of the value of the product must be transferred to them than what is usually the case and that production should be conducted under certain minimum conditions (for instance with regard to labour and environmental standards).[52] Fair-trade initiatives thus essentially sought and still seek to redress power imbalances (which can also be viewed as competition distortions) between large businesses and distributors and small producers, trying to ensure a decent quality of life and standard of living for workers. Fair-trade operations ensure that producers are paid a decent premium price that covers the costs of production and allows for a living wage in the local context, despite often serious fluctuations in world commodity prices. Already in 1946, Keynes had stressed this concept, when he stated that: 'proper economic prices should be fixed not at the lowest possible level, but at a level sufficient to provide producers with proper nutritional and other standards'.[53] Beyond this, 'fair traders seek to incorporate ethics, environmental issues, human rights, and other concerns into international trade policy. ... Fair differs significantly from normal for-profit trade: it is ultimately concerned with the welfare of the producer and sees success for all parties as contingent upon eliminating exploitation'.[54]

The first 'fair-trade' activities started in the USA with Ten Thousand Villages and SERRV,[55] which began trading with poor communities in the late

1940s.[56] In Europe, Oxfam begun importing and selling crafts made by Chinese refugees in Hong Kong in the late 1950s. In 1964, Oxfam created the first Alternative Trading Organization (ATO) in Britain. Parallel initiatives were taking place in the Netherlands with the establishment of the importing organization S.O.S. Wereldhandel (now Fair Trade Organisatie) in 1967. ATOs were subsequently set up in several other European countries. A new impulse to develop fair trade came in the late 1980s with the introduction of fair-trade labels, starting with the Max Havelaar one in the Netherlands, and it has not stopped growing since.

'Fair trade' is a particular trade arrangement whereby products, which have been produced in developing countries respecting a series of social and environmental criteria, are sold in industrialized countries at a premium price, thus shielding the producers against the high volatility of market prices for their products. The fair-trade organization achieves this goal by reducing the intermediation chain through direct import and distribution of products by non-profit retailers.[57] In this way, local producers' revenues are up to 3–4 times greater than those earned through traditional trade channels, thus ensuring that their basic needs are met. Consumers receive assurances that the premium price thay pay is justified by the actual respect of fair-trade criteria through the use of labels that, in some cases, fair-trade organizations license on the basis of compliance verification.

Fair-trade initiatives also aim to ensure that producers are provided with opportunities for advancement, on an equal basis for all people, particularly the most disadvantaged, that production is carried out in an environmentally sustainable fashion, and that working conditions are healthy and safe. Furthermore, other important features of the fair-trade relationship may be seen as attempts to solve recurrent market failures in developing countries. These include the anticipated financing of investment that can remedy the chronic lack of financing for poor producers; the destination of part of the higher price paid by 'rich' consumers to projects that reinforce the provision of deficient public goods (e.g., health, education) to local communities; and the long-run partnership between fair traders and producers in the South, which leads to the building up of social capital there.

The notion of fairness that inspires the fair-trade movement is obviously very different from that which underpins the existing trade regime. 'Fair trade ... represents not a challenge to the existence of the market itself, but rather to how markets are constructed and administered, how they deliver and apportion economic benefit to participants'.[58] It shares with the equity-based approaches to international trade the importance attached to providing a more favourable treatment, albeit not to poor countries but directly to poor producers. Both approaches aim at redistributing income, either through lower, preferential tariffs (such as through the GSP scheme) or through premium (fair-trade) prices.[59] But while special and differential treatment remains in the general fold of traditional GATT and now WTO law, with its focus on the (legal) treatment of products, fair-trade initiatives are aimed at directly modifying the 'treatment' poor producers, men and women, receive. There lies an important difference between these conceptions of fairness. The first advocates *international* (i.e., interstate) equity to redress the inequalities that separate the North from the South. The second focuses on human justice and the needs and rights of individual people in the South. Starting in the 1960s, such a needs-based notion of socio-economic justice has been recognized in a number of international human rights instruments[60] and was beginning to have a broader heed in international fora.[61] However, as in the case of the NIEO-inspired demands of regime change, not much impact can be detected in the trade policy area, beyond the GSP and the limited special and differential treatment provisions of the GATT and then the WTO Agreements. But surely this kind of bottom-up fairness has contributed to the ongoing debate on the ethical questions surrounding globalization.

The enduring fairness notion that has inspired much of the US approach, in its trade policy and in the construction of the trade regime, is based, as seen, on the putative justice of the market exchange, whereby each of the two parties, absent any free-riding, obtains benefits commensurate to its respective contributions. 'Fair trade' challenges this basic assumption and aims to ensure that international exchanges of commodities and other products provide tangible benefits to each individual producer involved in such trade, even beyond income to include an effective respect of her or his human rights. In this sense, it provides a much needed reminder of who the ultimate beneficiaries of trade are and what the true fairness benchmark is.

NOTES

1. 'The General Agreement was drafted primarily with the interests of the developed countries in view, and adequate consideration was not given to the needs of developing countries'. See K.R. Gupta, *A Study of General Agreement on Tariffs and Trade*, S. Chand and Co., New Delhi, 1967, p. 185. See also *Proceedings of the United Nations Conference on Trade and Development*, E/CONF.46/141, New York, 1964, p. 5 et seq.
2. See Wilcox, op. cit., pp. 31–2.
3. See R.E. Hudec, 'GATT and the Developing Countries', *Columbia Business Law Review*, no. 1, 1992, p. 67 et seq.; Jackson, *World Trade*, op. cit., p. 638 et seq.
4. See J. Viner, *International Trade and Economic Development*, Free Press, Glencoe, IL, 1952, pp. 120–50; G. Myrdal, *An International Economy: Problems and Prospects*, Harper, New York, 1956; and A.O. Hirschman, *The Strategy of Economic Development*, Yale University Press, New Haven, CT, 1958.
5. See Working Party Report of the 1954–55 Review Session, GATT, Basic Instruments and Selected Documents, 3rd Supp. 1955 Geneva, p. 79.
6. GATT, *Trends in International Trade* (the Haberler Report), Geneva, 1958.
7. See Declaration Giving Effect to the Provision of Art. XVI:4 of GATT, GATT Doc. L/1864, 1960.

8. Art. XXXVI (Principles and Objectives), Art. XXXVII (Commitments), and Art. XXXVIII (Joint Action).
9. See K. Dam, *The GATT: Law and International Economic Organization*, University of Chicago Press, Chicago, IL, 1970, p. 237.
10. Resolution 1707 (XVI) 'International trade as the primary instrument for economic development' of 19 December 1961 reproduced in U Thant, *United Nations Development Decade: Proposals for Action. Report of the Secretary General*, United Nations, New York, 1962, p. 76. Resolution 1710 (XVI) 'United Nations Development Decade. A Programme for international economic co-operation' of 19 December 1961 also called on UN members to pursue policies designed to ensure the developing countries an equitable share of the earnings from the extraction and marketing of their natural resources.
11. The US GSP scheme (periodically re-authorized by act of Congress) has evolved over the years but has always included various conditionalities that limit its non-reciprocal character. Regarding the designation of beneficiary countries (see 19 U.S.C. §2462), the statute lists a few of developed countries that are ineligible. It next forecloses beneficiary status to eight other categories of nations: (1) 'communist' countries (with exceptions): (2) countries that are parties to an 'arrangement' which withholds 'supplies of vital commodity resources from international trade' (aimed at OPEC); (3) countries that injure US commerce by affording preferences to other developed countries; (4) countries that expropriate the property of US citizens, including intellectual property, without just compensation; (5) countries that fail to enforce binding arbitral awards in favour of US citizens; (6) countries that aid or abet terrorism or fail to take 'steps to support the efforts of the United States to combat terrorism'; (7) countries that have not taken steps 'to afford internationally recognized worker rights'; and (8) countries that fail to fulfil their 'commitments to eliminate the worst forms of child labor'. The last five exclusions can be waived by the President in the 'national economic interest'. The President has the discretion to confer beneficiary status on any country not excluded by the above criteria, and the statute provides additional factors that the President must consider in exercising this discretion. Along with the prospective beneficiary's interest in the programme and its level of development, the President must consider whether the country provides 'equitable and reasonable access to [its] markets and basic commodity resources' and 'adequate and effective protection of intellectual property rights', whether it has taken steps to reduce investment-distorting practices and barriers to trade in services, and whether it takes steps to afford internationally recognized worker rights. The statute also provides for 'mandatory graduation' of 'high-income' countries, without defining the term 'high income'.
12. Decision on Differential and More Favourable Treatment, Reciprocity and Fuller Participation of Developing Countries, 28 November 1979, GATT B.I.S.D., 26th Supp., 1980, p. 203.
13. Paragraph 5 of the Enabling Clause states that 'developed countries do not expect the developing countries, in the course of trade negotiations, to make contributions which are inconsistent with their individual development, financial and trade needs. Developed contracting parties shall therefore not seek, neither shall less-developed contracting parties be required to make, concessions that are inconsistent with the latter's development, financial and trade needs'.
14. Hong Kong, Korea, Singapore and Taiwan were 'graduated', as the procedure is generally referred to, in 1989, Mexico in 1994 (upon entry into force of the NAFTA), and Malaysia in 1997.
15. See UNCTAD, 'Quantifying the benefits obtained by developing countries from the Generalized System of Preferences', Note by the UNCTAD secretariat, UNCTAD/ITCD/TSB/Misc.52, Geneva, 1999.
16. The codes covered technical barriers to trade, customs valuation, import licensing, subsidies and countervailing measures, antidumping, and government procurement. The texts are collected in GATT, *The Texts of the Tokyo Round Agreements*, Geneva, 1986.
17. The codes signatories could extend the trade treatment under any code to GATT parties that had not agreed to that code. Furthermore, the broad GATT MFN obligation was deemed to require that at least some of the code benefits apply to all GATT members. However, the

USA, in line with its long-standing concern for 'free-riding' in its Tokyo Round implementing legislation did not extend code treatment of three agreements (the subsidies CVD code, the government procurement code, and the technical standards code) to all other GATT contracting parties. Entitlement to each of the code's treatment for other parties was conditional upon their application of the respective code.

18. See GATT, *Trade Policies for a Better Future* (the Leutwiler Report), Geneva, 1985, p. 44.
19. See C. Michalopoulos, 'Developing Country Strategies for the Millennium Round', *Journal of World Trade*, October 1999, p. 25.
20. 'At the very last minute, the terms of the [developed–developing country] bargain have further been altered by a radical new demand by the developed countries [i.e., the single undertaking] ... Under this approach, governments would have to decide between accepting everything or leaving the GATT.' See Hudec, op. cit., p. 76.
21. These countries were given this status on a provisional basis, since they, as former colonies, had been previously part of a GATT customs territory through the country responsible for their foreign and economic relations.
22. Poor countries may also find themselves caught in the middle of other (rich) countries' disputes, as it happened in the banana controversies pitting the EC against various other WTO Members but in particular the USA. In that instance, 'the greatest damage caused by the banana dispute and the consequent enforced change in the EU trade regime has been, and will be, experienced by third parties to the dispute – the previously preferred ACP exporting countries', see R. Read, 'The Banana Split: The EU–US Banana Trade Dispute and the Effects of EU Market Liberalisation', in N. Perdikis and R. Read, eds., *The WTO and the Regulation of International Trade: Recent Trade Disputes Between the EU and the United States*, Edward Elgar: Cheltenham, UK and Northampton, MA, USA, 2005, p. 130.
23. Implementation of Special and Differential Treatment Provisions in WTO Agreements and Decisions, Note by the Secretariat, WTO doc. WT/COMTD/W/77, 25 October 2000, p. 3.
24. See Doha Ministerial Declaration, WTO doc. WT/MIN(01)/DEC/1, 20 November 2001, paragraph 44. On the situation of developing countries in the WTO, see J. Trachtman, 'Legal Aspects of a Poverty Agenda at the WTO: Trade Law and "Global Apartheid"', *Journal of International Economic Law*, vol. 6, no. 1, March 2003, pp. 3–21.
25. J.R. Schaetzel as quoted in Zeiler, op. cit., p. 139.
26. In *The Antelope* case, the Supreme Court, in an opinion written by Chief Justice John Marshall, held that: 'No principle of general law is more universally acknowledged, than the perfect equality of nations', *The Antelope* case, United States, Supreme Court, 1825, 10 Wheaton, 66.
27. See C. Thomas, 'Balance-of-Payments Crises in the Developing World: Balancing Trade, Finance and Development in the New Economic Order', *American University International Law Review*, vol. 15, 2000, p. 1249 et seq.
28. See Jackson, *The World Trading System*, op. cit., pp. 322–5.
29. This was also based on orthodox economic theory, particularly prevalent at the time, which saw international trade as a powerful means for developing countries to 'catch up' with developed ones. See G. Meier, *The Inetrnational Economics of Development*, Harper and Row, New York, 1968, Chapter 8.
30. Quoted in S.S. Goodspeed, *The Nature and Function of International Organization*, Oxford University Press, New York, 1959, p. 12.
31. See ICJ Reports, 1966, p. 6.
32. 'If the persons are not equal, their [just] shares will not be equal; but this is the source of quarrels and recriminations, when equals have and are awarded unequal shares or unequal equal shares'. See Aristotle, *Nicomachean Ethics*, Book 5, Chapter 3, 118–19 (translated by Martin Ostwald, Macmillan Publishing, New York, 1962).
33. Quoted in K. Kock, *International Trade Policy and the GATT 1947–67*, Almqvist and Wiksell, Stockholm, 1969, p. 289.
34. Quoted in H. Gros Espiell, 'The Most-Favoured-Nation Clause: Its Present Significance in GATT', *Journal of World Trade Law*, 1971, p. 29.
35. See Report by the Secretary General of the UN Conference on Trade and Development, *Towards a New Trade Policy for Development*, reproduced in *Proceedings of the United*

Nations Conference on Trade and Development, vol. II: Policy Statements, UN doc. E/CONF.46/141, New York, 1964, pp. 18–19.

36. See M. Bedjaoui, *Towards a New International Economic Order*, Holmes and Meier, New York, 1979, p. 119

37. See, for instance, I. Haq, 'From Charity to Obligation: A Third World Perspective on Concessional Resource Transfers', *Texas International Law Journal*, vol. 14, no. 3, 1979, p. 406.

38. See W. Verwey, 'The Principle of Preferential Treatment for Developing Countries', *Indian Journal of International Law*, July–Dec., 1983, pp. 343–500.

39. Declaration of 1 May 1974 Concerning the Establishment of a New International Economic Order, G.A. Res. 3201, UN GAOR, 6th Spec. Sess., Supp. no. 1, U.N. doc. A/9559, 1974.

40. UN Charter of Economic Rights and Duties of States, G.A. Res. 3281 (XXIX), UN doc. A/3281, 1974.

41. The Declaration and the NIEO Programme for Action were adopted by consensus, but the USA clearly expressed its opposition.

42. See A. Yusuf, '"Differential and More Favourable Treatment": The GATT Enabling Clause', *Journal of World Trade Law*, vol. 14, no. 6, 1980, p. 492.

43. See L. Henkin, *International Law: Politics and Values*, Martinus Nijhoff, Dordrecht, 1995, pp. 165–6.

44. In the minds of many economists in the North, and the USA in particular, the relaxing of reciprocity could actually be detrimental to developing countries. 'The rich may have done a great disservice to the poor by giving up the principle of reciprocity so that the poor can enjoy the benefits of tariff reductions in the rich countries without having to "give up" anything in return'. See R. Cooper, 'Third World Tariff Tangle', *Foreign Policy*, no. 4, Fall, 1971, p. 48.

45. See P. Cullet, 'Differential Treatment in International Law: Towards a New Paradigm of Inter-state Relations', *European Journal of International Law*, vol. 10, no. 3, 1999, p. 557.

46. In an interesting recent Report dealing with the legality of some aspects of the GSP of the European Communities the WTO Appellate Body stressed the obligation for developed WTO members to provide preferential treatment under a GSP scheme to respond positively to the needs of developing countries. And, at the same time, it showed sensitivity to the differing needs of developing countries that may even authorize preference-granting countries in responding to such needs to treat 'different developing-country beneficiaries differently'. See Report of the Appellate Body, European Communities – Conditions for the granting of tariff preferences to developing countries, WT/DS246/AB/R, 7 April 2004, para. 162.

47. 'In view of the very limited profits derived by the vast majority of developing countries so far from such important legal steps as the adoption of the GSP Waiver, the Enabling Clause, or the principle of standstill [i.e. Art. XXXVII:1(b)], it seems justified to think that in this respect the GATT efforts do not essentially differ from NIEO-oriented efforts made in other fora'. See W. Verwey, 'The Principles of a New International Economic Order and the Law of the General Agreement on Tariffs and Trade (GATT)', *Leiden Journal of International Law*, vol. 3, no. 2, October 1990, pp. 140–41.

48. UN Declaration of International Economic Cooperation, UN GAOR 18th Spec. Sess., Supp. 2, UN doc. A/S.18/15, 1990.

49. See A. Narlikar, *International Trade and Developing Countries: Bargaining and Coalitions in the GATT and WTO*, Routledge, New York, 2003.

50. See Dam, op. cit., p. 245.

51. This state of affairs was also the focus of the 'dependency theory', which denounced the 'unequal exchange' terms between Nothern centres and Southern peripheries; see for instance, I. Roxborough, *Theories of Underdevelopment*, Macmillan, London, 1979.

52. Fair trade is not necessarily antagonistic to traditional market-based efficiency maximization. From a theoretical perspective 'the bilateral definition of a price different from the market one has sound microeconomic grounds. We must consider in fact that, traditionally, trade in primary products occurs between a monopolistic/oligopolistic transnational company which buys from a large number of atomistic LDC producers at a

price which is affected by the relative bargaining power of the two counterparts. The fair trade price may therefore be ideally considered as the market price which would prevail if the two counterparts would have equal bargaining power and may therefore be viewed as a non governmental minimum wage measure taken by private citizens in developed countries. Using prices as a policy instrument to transfer resources to the South cannot be considered a market distortion also because the fair trade opens in the North a new market where 'contingent ethical' products are sold (fair trade coffee is a different product from traditional coffee exactly as an umbrella when it rains is not the same product as an umbrella when it does not rain). In this sense we may argue that fair trade is a step forward market completeness when consumers' preferences include social responsibility'. See L. Becchetti and F. Adriani, 'Fair Trade: A "Third Generation Welfare" Mechanism to Make Globalisation Sustainable', CEIS Working Paper no. 170, Rome, 2002. On the economics of fair trade see also M. Leclair, 'Fighting the Tide: Alternative Trade Organizations in the Era of Global Free Trade', *World Development*, vol. 30, no. 6, 2002, pp. 949–58 and R. Maseland and A. De Vaal, 'How Fair is Fair Trade?', *De Economist*, vol. 150, 2002, pp. 251–72.

53. J.M. Keynes, 'The international control of raw material prices', *The Collective Writings of John Maynard Keynes*, vol. XXVII, Macmillan, London, 1980.

54. See A. Morris Groos, 'International Trade and Development: Exploring the Impact of Fair Trade Organizations in the Global Economy and the Law', *Texas International Law Journal*, vol. 34, 1999, p. 387. For a more critical view, see T. Mutersbaugh, 'Ethical Trade and Certified Organic Coffee: Implications of Rules-Based Agricultural Product Certification for Mexican Producer Households and Villages', *Transnational Law and Contemporary Problem*, Spring 2002, pp. 89–107. The generally accepted definition of fair trade reads: 'Fair Trade is a trading partnership, based on dialogue, transparency and respect, that seeks greater equity in international trade. It contributes to sustainable development by offering better trading conditions to, and securing the rights of, marginalised producers and workers – especially in the South.' See *Fair Trade Yearbook: Challenges of Fair Trade 2001–2003*, European Fair Trade Association, Brussels, p. 24. See also G. Moore, 'The Fair Trade Movement: Parameters, Issues and Future Research', *Journal of Business Ethics*, vol. 53, 2004, pp. 73–86.

55. SERRV (Sales Exchange for Refugee Rehabilitation and Vocation) International was started in 1949 to help refugees in Europe to recover economically and socially from World War II. Its first initiative was to import wooden cuckoo clocks from Germany to Maryland and sell them in the USA.

56. See M. Littrell and M. Dickson, *Social Responsibility in the Global Market: Fair Trade of Cultural Products*, Sage Publications, Thousand Oaks, CA, 1999; M. Barrat-Brown, *Fair Trade: Reform and Realities in the International Trading System*, ZED Books, London, 1993; L. Raynolds, 'Re-embedding Global Agriculture: The International Organic and Fair Trade Movements', *Agriculture and Human Values*, vol. 17, no. 3, 2000, pp. 297–309.

57. The volume of goods sold through 'fair trade' is increasing, though it is still a very small proportion of international trade. The fair-trade market is estimated at about US$400–500 million in retail sales each year, as compared to a total world merchandise trade of $8.8 billion in 2004. Sales of fair-trade products through alternative channels and supermarkets are estimated in Europe at about US$230 million and at $100 million in the USA. The fair-trade product with the highest market share is banana in Switzerland with 15 per cent, while the market share for other fair-trade products, such as tea and coffee, is generally around 2–3 per cent.

58. D. Jaffee et al., 'Bringing the "Moral Charge" Home: Fair Trade within the North and within the South', *Rural Sociology*, vol. 69, no. 2, June 2004, p. 192.

59. Another major but ultimately unsuccessful initiative aimed at altering the terms of trade faced by poor producers was the EC STABEX scheme first established in the 1970s under the Lomé Convention. This was a stabilization system offering the ACP States substantial funds to finance their agricultural sectors when they encountered serious difficulties because of falls in export earnings.

60. See 1948 Universal Declaration of Human Rights, Art. 2 and 1966 International Covenant on Economic, Social and Cultural Rights, Art. 11.
61. 'The solution of these [economic and social maldistribution and misuse of resources] problems cannot be left to the automatic operation of market mechanisms. ... In the international system the powerful nations have secured the poor countries' raw materials at low prices ... have engrossed all the value-added from processing the materials and sold the manufactures back, often at monopoly prices. ... Our first concern is to redefine the whole purpose of development. This should not be to develop things but to develop man. Human beings have basic needs: food, shelter, clothing, health, education. Any process of growth that does not lead to their fulfilment – or, even worse, disrupts them – is a travesty of the idea of development. ... We believe that 30 years of experience with the hope that rapid economic growth benefiting the few will "trickle down" to the mass of the people has proved to be illusory. We therefore reject the idea of "growth first, justice in the distribution of benefits later"'. Cocoyoc Declaration, adopted by the United Nations Environment Programme/United Nations Conference on Trade and Development Symposium on Patterns of Resource Use, Environment and Development Strategies, 12 October 1974.

6. Conclusion

The fairness idea has strongly influenced the US trade policy discourse, as well as the adoption and implementation of specific trade policies, and it has had a distinctive effect on the construction of the multilateral trading system and its evolution. While the object of continued controversy, and often used instrumentally and rhetorically to cover other, sometime conflicting, policy objectives, and while encircled – some would say supported, others undermined – by exceptions in rule design and application, fairness has played and continues to play a key role in policy- and rule-making.

The notion of fairness prevailing in the USA has been an important guiding principle in its trade policy action since the inception of the Republic. It has been based on equality of treatment, reciprocity, and no free-riding, and ultimately on market competition as its reference model. In the light of the impact it has had on the formation and subsequent development of the multilateral trade regime, fairness can be considered one of the regime's constitutive rules.[1] Indeed, it seems possible to argue that there is no trade or exchange (of goods and services) as a social practice without synallagmatic consideration, and there is no trade agreement without a reciprocal and mutually advantageous exchange of concessions and favours between the parties. In this sense, equality of treatment, reciprocity, and no free-riding make up the regime itself.[2] In addition, fairness needs to be afforded to domestic groups that may lose out as a result of international trade and trade agreements (the 'no-injury to domestic producers' principle). The various types of safeguards, which operationalize the 'embedded liberalism compromise', are again an integral part of the regime and the shared under-standing of it. However, fairness appears to have influenced the US trade policy discourse and its contribution to the establishment of the trade regime more deeply than the liberal (free-trade) idea, as corrected by New Deal-inspired interventionism.

If anything, the rejection of the ITO project pointed in the direction of an entrenched appeal of the *laissez-faire* version of capitalism in the USA, at least in the realm of foreign economic relations. In the trade field, the projection of the New Deal regulatory state into the international arena could have been a plausible explanation, at least the institutional form of the regime, perhaps not its policy content, had the ITO come into being.[3] However, the final impossibility to bring about a shared understanding of the proper balance between fair market rules and state intervention led to the demise of the proposed ITO regime. The enduring use of the market model and private enterprise competition as the benchmark for the conduct of 'fair'-trade relations within the GATT helps put the 'embedded liberalism' claim into perspective. Surely, the important safeguards included in the regime to ensure economic stability and promote adjustment were influenced by the New Deal approach, but they also had a longer tradition in the 'no-injury to domestic producers' principle, which has always characterized the domestic side of fairness in the USA. As a result, fairness certainly helps in understanding why the trade regime got to be *so* and not *otherwise*, even though other important ideational factors, certainly including protection as well as liberal ideas (as more or less socially 'embedded'), interacted with it and played important roles.

However, this narrative could tell a convincing story only if one were to fully disregard the expectations of developing countries and, nowadays, large sections of transnational civil society; and, as a consequence, if one were to consider the trade regime as the industrial countries' own regime. But a regime is legitimate and effective solely if it is characterized by a large congruence or convergence among participants of what Ruggie called 'social purpose'. Hence, from this broader perspective, fairness can be considered as a trade regime's constitutive rule only in its role as a 'minimum' benchmark or 'default' behavioural standard connected to the imperative of commutative justice. But, when the situation is characterized by significant, substantive inequality and the distribution of burden and benefits among the regime's participants is skewed, equity considerations are invoked, at least, as a necessary complement to this understanding of fairness. This is why developing countries have strongly argued, *inter alia*, for the relaxing of the reciprocity principle. Furthermore, the notion that (adjustment) assistance, through both special rules and transfers, is only conceivable and due in a domestic context to fulfil the no-injury requirement of domestic fairness, remains to these days controversial. The NIEO expectations and aspiration that there could be forms and means to extend the 'welfare state' approach to the global level have remained unfulfilled. The 'fair-trade' movement objective to channel a higher portion of trade benefits to poor producers is still largely unsatisfied. At least from the perspective of many developing countries and civil society groups, fairness without equity is partial, truncated justice.

As a result, fairness has never won full consensus among all participants in the trade regime. And if disagreements on the design of rules (also partly reflecting different conceptions on the role of government intervention in international trade) bedevilled the relations even in the industrial country camp during the gestation phase of the regime (during and after World War II), the even stronger disagreements that separated developed and developing countries from the time of the negotiations to these days are a testimony of an enduring tension with regard to the appropriate meaning of fairness in the international trading system.

6.1 FAIRNESS OR EQUITY?

The key question thus remains whether commutative and distributive justice, fairness and equity, can be jointly sought or whether their respective meanings are intrinsically different – or worse, incompatible – thus preventing any common pursuit. In the face of growing inequality across nations, many developing countries and emerging transnational civil society groups have been increasingly assigning part of the blame for this predicament to the free-market approach under which the trade regime mainly operates. The recurrent failures in the current round of WTO trade negotiations (as well as its arduous preparatory phase) can be partly ascribed to this lack of consensus on what a 'fair' *and* 'equitable' regime is, and how it should operate. Indeed, a modicum of consensus on these notions remains a key factor in the continuing legitimacy of the trade (and virtually any) regime and its satisfactory working.

Encouragingly, the entire international community seems to grow in its awareness that a world in which 15.6 per cent of humankind living in 'high-income economies' have 81 per cent of global income, while the other 84.4 per cent of humankind share the remaining 19 per cent is unjust and unsustainable.[4] And, importantly, it seems to become conscious of 'the role that the design of the *global* institutional order plays in the persistence of severe poverty'.[5] Such collective responsibility has been recognized in the clearest terms in the 2000 UN Millennium Declaration, which states that 'the central challenge we [the UN member states] face today is to ensure that globalization becomes a positive force for all the world's people. For while globalization offers great opportunities, at present its benefits are very unevenly shared, while its costs are unevenly distributed'. In this respect, the value of 'solidarity' is recognized as 'essential to international relations in the twenty-first century'. Solidarity requires that 'global challenges must be managed in a way that distributes the costs and burdens fairly in accordance with basic principles of equity and social justice. Those who suffer or who benefit least deserve help from those who benefit most'.[6]

The fairness approach, which has characterized the GATT and subsequently the WTO regime, remains important, since, with all its backslidings and protectionist reflexes, it has promoted significant gains for (many of) its participants and the advancement of multilateral cooperation. The US postwar planners' (including first and foremost Cordell Hull's) relentless determination to pursue equality of treatment and reciprocal and mutually advantageous trade arrangements and to reject bilateralism, preferential treatment, and free-riding, fully in line with the country's trade policy tradition, had the great merit of inspiring and finally bringing about a system that had the requirements of fairness at its core. This was a great, historical advancement over the power-based trade arrangements and escalating protectionism that had prevailed before World War II and a key step in the process of international cooperation in commercial matters. But that system could be a truly fair one only for industrial countries sharing a comparable level of development, and even among those, the ravages of war had to be addressed before the benefits of trade could materialize.

However, as designed and as it has developed since, the trade regime, with its enduring focus on reciprocal bargaining, does not seem able to guarantee equity and true solidarity. The system clearly needs to promote both fairness (as commutative market-based justice), thus contributing to economic efficiency (and enlarging the proverbial pie), and distributive justice (through an equitable sharing of such a pie), by electing to foster equitable development as one of its key objectives. Reciprocity needs to be considered a second-order value and be subjected to equity and solidarity.[7] Solidarity cannot be extended only, through safeguards measures, to domestic producers that may be injured because of liberalization measures. Solidarity needs to straddle borders in pursuit of development, which is deontologically imperative[8] as well as an interest shared by the entire international community.[9] Indeed, 'by asserting the common good ... the majority of States have set in train a process in which the emphasis is placed on whatever may be expected to contribute to reducing the de facto inequalities between States and to promote greater heed for the long-term interests of the globe'.[10]

The multilateral trade regime is fully part of the global economic governance system and as such cannot escape from the 'requirements of justice'.[11] The regime can no longer simply aim at ensuring non-discrimination and reciprocity as a way of eliminating trade barriers, which distort the functioning of markets, and hope that this 'fair' approach will also produce 'equitable' results. A full rethinking and reordering of priorities is required if an 'equitable' trading system, as called for by the Millennium Declaration, is to be achieved.

A useful and (hopefully) consensual avenue may be to adopt a rights-based approach to distributive justice, building upon the wide acceptance that human rights have received in the post-World War II period. Justice can be understood as 'the system of entitlements on the basis of which people can demand social recognition of their legitimate claims (e.g. for resources, freedoms, etc.)',[12] and human rights can be considered minimum, necessary expressions of these entitlements. Indeed, most human needs have been framed in modern times as legitimate rights to which people can aspire, and which governments have an obligation to respect and provide for.[13] Hence, in the trade area, generally recognized economic and social rights, from the right to food to the right to health, could provide a benchmark of what people can claim as a matter of justice. Steps in the direction of fulfilling such rights for all would mean moving closer to the realization of distributive justice. However, despite the growing attention paid in the North to the issues of inequality and poverty, pursuing a justice discourse in the WTO continues to be a challenge. The trade regime still remains solidly steeped in its traditional, narrow fairness approach, notwithstanding the (limited) concessions to the notion of special and differential treatment for developing countries. One possible gateway for introducing the discourse could be the concept of sustainable development, which entails – in its wider understanding – a commitment to both human development and the fulfilment of basic human rights.

Human development embodies a concept of development that goes beyond economic growth to include the development of the human person as a main outcome. In this context, equity needs to be considered with respect to well-being, a significantly broadened concept with respect to 'welfare', as generally understood in the utilitarian and welfare economics tradition. 'The idea of human development focuses directly on the progress of human lives and wellbeing. Since wellbeing includes living with substantial freedoms, human development is also integrally connected with enhancing certain capabilities – the range of things a person can do and be in leading a life'.[14]

Hence, development is not only the acquisition of more goods and services, but also the enhanced freedom to choose, or the capability to lead the kind of life one values.[15] On the other side, poverty is the deprivation of basic capabilities, not just lowness of income.[16] Although income inequality is of crucial importance, it does not exhaust all deprivations that lead to poverty, including unemployment, ill health, lack of education, and social exclusion. Hence, the emphasis needs to be placed on the broader notion of social and economic (not just income) equality and freedom. Indeed, not always and automatically does income growth translate into individual achievements ('capabilities to function' or 'functionings') in terms of well-being and substantive freedoms.

The approach focused on capabilities thus broadens the understanding of development to include both human well-being and freedom, which means widening the choices people enjoy in the political, civil, social, economic, and cultural spheres. As such,

> human development shares a common vision with human rights. The goal is human freedom. And in pursuing capabilities and realizing rights, this freedom is vital. People must be free to exercise their choices and to participate in decision-making that affects their lives. Human development and human rights are mutually

reinforcing, helping to secure the well-being and dignity of all people, building self-respect and the respect of others.[17]

Furthermore, 'if human development focuses on the enhancement of the capabilities and freedoms that the members of a community enjoy, human rights represent the claims that individuals have on the conduct of individual and collective agents and on the design of social arrangements to facilitate or secure these capabilities and freedoms'.[18]

The body of rules that govern international trade represents one important example of such social arrangements. These rules need to be designed and interpreted with the ultimate goal of enhancing human development and human rights. Indeed, 'economic growth, increased international trade and investment, technological advance – all are very important. But they are means, not ends. Whether they contribute to human development in the 21st century will depend on whether they expand people's choices, whether they help create an environment for people to develop their full potential and lead productive, creative lives'.[19]

While human rights as such are not mentioned anywhere in WTO law,[20] the notion of development has acquired a certain pre-eminence. The Preamble of the Marrakesh Agreement establishing the WTO, in its opening paragraph, recognizes that international economic and trade relations should have among their objectives both the 'raising of standards of living' and 'sustainable development'. And the preamble contributes to delineating the context within which the interpretation of specific provisions must be conducted, in the light of the instrument's objectives.[21] In this way, these references establish a textual bridge between the pursuit of both human development – which needs to be inclusive of human rights – and WTO law. The reference to standards of living, which was already present in the 1947 Preamble of the GATT, stresses one of the key capabilities necessary for human development.[22] The inclusion of the objective of sustainable development, which was added at the inception of the WTO in 1994, aligns this organization with the goals that the international community has set for itself on numerous occasions and restated, most recently, in the Millennium Declaration.

Sustainable development and human development are by no means incompatible or alternative concepts. On the contrary, the two are mutually supportive and are sometimes made to converge in the notion of 'sustainable human development'.[23] Furthermore, with the adoption of the Declaration on the Right to Development, 'development' itself has been characterized as a human right.[24] This Declaration advances a number of important normative claims. First, it defines development as 'a comprehensive economic, social, cultural and political process, which aims at the constant improvement of the wellbeing of the entire population and of all individuals on the basis of their active, free and meaningful participation in development and in the fair

distribution of benefits resulting therefrom'.[25] Second, it declares that the right
to development is a human right 'by virtue of which every human person and
all peoples are entitled to participate in, contribute to, and enjoy economic,
social, cultural and political development, in which all human rights and
fundamental freedoms can be fully realized'.

The Declaration, as confirmed by the 1993 Vienna Declaration,[26] and again
most recently by the Millennium Declaration, thus represents the shared
appreciation within the internationally community that the realization of
human rights is an integral part of the process of development.[27] This fuller
understanding of development also binds (or at least ought to bind) states in
their international economic and trade relations. The reference to the pursuit
of the objective of development in the Preamble of the Marrakesh Agreement
seems to point in the same direction. While the link with human rights norms
has never been tested in WTO dispute settlement proceedings, the Appellate
Body 'has shown itself as sensitive to the range of normative sources in
international law and policy relevant to the elaboration of meanings of trade
rules ...[and] is *in principle* open to interconnectedness in the interpretation of
"development"'.[28]

Moreover, as a human right, the right to development

> confers unequivocal obligation on duty-holders: individuals in the community,
> states at the national level, and states at the international level. National states have
> the responsibility to help realize the process of development through appropriate
> development policies. Other states and international agencies have the obligation to
> cooperate with the national states to facilitate the realization of the process of
> development.[29]

The duty to cooperate, to assist developing countries as a matter of solidarity,
and the commitment to promote human development and the realization of
human rights for all, from poor farmers in Africa, to women garment
producers in Asia, to mine workers in Latin America, constitutes the real
'fairness' challenge for the trading system of the 21st century. However, the
enduring debate over the balancing of freedom rights linked to the efficient
operation of the market system and the social rights required to ensure an
acceptable degree of equity remains unresolved. A better understanding of
how the fairness idea underpins the existing trading system can help transcend
it.

NOTES

1. See Chapter 1, sections 1.2 and 1.3 above.
2. 'Notions, such as reciprocity in the trade regime are *neither* its ends *nor* its means: in a
   quintessential way, they *are* the regime – they *are* the principled and shared understanding
   the regime comprises'. See Ruggie, *Constructing the World Polity*, op. cit., p. 99.

3. This explanation is advanced by A.-M. Burley, 'Regulating the World: Multilateralism, International Law, and the Projection of the New Deal Regulatory State', in J.G. Ruggie, ed., *Multilateralism Matters: The Theory and Praxis of an Institutional Form*, Columbia University Press, New York, 1993, p. 125 et seq. See also M.J. Hogan, 'Revival and Reform: America's Twentieth-Century Search for a New Economic Order Abroad', *Diplomatic History*, vol. 8, no. 4, pp. 287–310. E. Kapstain's communitarian reading of the 'embedded liberalism bargain' appears quite convincing; see E. Kapstain, 'Models of International Justice', *Ethics and International Affairs*, vol. 18, no. 2, 2004, p. 83.

4. See World Bank, *World Development Report 2003*, Oxford University Press, New York, 2002, p. 235. Inequalities in wealth are significantly greater than inequalities in income. 'The additional cost of achieving and maintaining universal access to basic education for all, basic health care for all, reproductive health care for all women, adequate food for all and safe water and sanitation for all is … less than 4% of the combined wealth of the 225 richest people in the world'. See UNDP, *Human Development Report 1998*, Oxford University Press, New York, 1998, p. 30.

5. See T. Pogge, 'World Poverty and Human Rights', *Ethics and International Affairs*, vol. 19, no. 1, 2005, pp. 5–6.

6. United Nations Millennium Declaration, UN General Assembly Resolution, A/RES/55/2, 18 September 2000.

7. 'Solidarity is neither charity nor welfare; it is an agreement among formal equals that will all refrain from actions that would significantly interfere with the realization of common goals and fundamental interests. Solidarity requires an understanding that every member of the community must consciously and constantly conceive of its own interests as being inextricable from the interests of the whole'. See R. St. J. Macdonald, 'The Principle of Solidarity in Public International Law', in C. Dominicé et al., eds., *Études de Droit International en l'honneur de Pierre Lalive*, Helbing and Lichtenhahn, Basle, 1993, p. 293.

8. See F. Garcia, *Trade, Inequality, and Justice: Toward a Liberal Theory of Just Trade*, Transnational Publishers, Ardsley, NY, 2003.

9. On the notion of community interest, see B. Simma, 'From Bilateralism to Community Interest in International Law', *Collected Courses of the Hague Academy of International Law*, 1994, p. 229 et seq.

10. M. Bedjaoui, 'General Introduction', in M. Bedjaoui, ed., *International Law: Achievements and Prospects*, Martinus Nijhoff Publishers, Dordrecht, 1991, p. 14.

11. 'The requirements of justice apply to institutions and practices (whether or not they are genuinely cooperative) in which social activity produces relative or absolute benefits or burdens that would not exist if the social activity did not take place'. See C. Beitz, *Political Theory and International Relations*, Princeton University Press, Princeton, NJ, 1979, p. 131. For a different perspective see T. Nagel, 'The Problem of Global Justice', *Philosophy and Public Affairs*, vol. 33, no. 2, Spring 2005, pp. 113–47.

12. See W. Kymlicka, *Liberalism, Community, and Culture*, Clarendon Press, Oxford, 1989, p. 234.

13. See J. Galtung, *Human Rights in Another Key*, Polity Press, Oxford, 1994.

14. See UNDP, *Human Development Report*, New York, 2000, p. 19.

15. Capabilities are thus the substantive freedom to achieve alternative 'functionings' combinations. Indeed, 'living may be seen as consisting of a set of interrelated "functionings", consisting of beings and doings. A person's achievement in this respect can be seen as the vector of her functionings. The relevant functionings can vary from such elementary things as being adequately nourished, being in good health, avoiding escapable morbidity, and premature mortality, etc. to more complex achievements, such as being happy, having self-respect, taking part in the life of the community and so on'. See A. Sen, *Inequality Reexamined*, Oxford University Press, Oxford, 1992.

16. See A. Sen, *Development as Freedom*, Alfred A. Knopf, New York, 2001, in particular Chapter 4.

17. See *Human Development Report*, New York, 2000, p. 9.

18. Id., p. 20.

19. See *Human Development Report*, New York, 2002, p. 13.

20. However, there seems to be little doubt that, as a matter of treaty interpretation, WTO law needs to be read and applied consistently with the human rights obligations of WTO Members. This is obviously particularly important when interpreting the existing exceptions in WTO agreements. See, for instance, S. Charnovitz, 'The Moral Exception in Trade Policy', *Virginia Journal of International Law*, vol. 38, 1998, pp. 689–745; R. Howse and M. Matua, *Protecting Human Rights in a Global Economy: Challenges for the World Trade Organization*, Rights and Democracy, Montreal, 2000; G. Marceau, 'WTO Dispute Settlement and Human Rights', *European Journal of International Law*, vol. 13, no. 4, 2002, pp. 753–814; E.-U. Petersmann, 'Human Rights and the Law of the World Trade Organization', *Journal of World Trade*, April 2003, pp. 241–81.

21. In this respect, the Vienna Convention on the Law of Treaties, 1969, United Nations Doc. A/CONF.39/27, Art. 31, states that a treaty 'shall be interpreted in good faith in accordance with the ordinary meaning to be given to the terms of the treaty in their context and in the light of its object and purpose.' The text of the treaty itself, 'including its preamble and annexes' constitutes an important 'context' for treaty interpretation as well as an expression of the treaty's objectives.

22. For instance, the UNDP Human Development Index measures the average achievements in a country on three basic dimensions of human development: a long and healthy life, knowledge, and a decent standard of living.

23. 'Sustainable human development seeks to expand choices for all people – women, men and children, current and future generations – while protecting the natural systems on which all life depends. Moving away from a narrow, economy-centred approach to development, sustainable human development places people at the core, and views humans as both a means and an end of development. Thus sustainable human development aims to eliminate poverty, promote human dignity and rights, and provide equitable opportunities for all through good governance, thereby promoting the realization of all human rights – economic, social, cultural, civil and political'. See 'Integrating human rights with sustainable human development. A UNDP policy document', UNDP, mimeo, New York, 1998, p. 5. Furthermore, the 1995 Beijing Declaration stresses that: 'Eradication of poverty based on sustained economic growth, social development, environmental protection and social justice requires the involvement of women in economic and social development, equal opportunities and the full and equal participation of women and men as agents and beneficiaries of people-centred sustainable development'.

24. Declaration on the Right to Development, General Assembly Resolution 4/128, 4 December 1986.

25. Ibid., Preamble. See also Art. 2.

26. Vienna Declaration and Programme of Action, adopted by consensus at the World Conference on Human Rights on June 25, 1993.

27. In spite of the Declaration, the characterization of the 'right to development' as a human right remains controversial. See, for instance, Henkin, *International Law: Politics and Values*, op. cit., p. 181.

28. See UN Economic and Social Council, Commission on Human Rights, 'Mainstreaming the right to development into international trade law and policy at the WTO' (report prepared by R. Howse), UN doc. E/CN.4/Sub.2/2004/17, para. 21.

29. See A. Sengupta, 'The Right to Development as a Human Right', François-Xavier Bagnoud Center for Health and Human Rights, Harvard School of Public Health, mimeo, 2000, p. 5.

Bibliography

Aaronson, S., *Trade and the American Dream: A Social History of Postwar Trade Policy*, The University Press of Kentucky, Lexington, KY, 1996.

Abbott, K., 'Defensive Unfairness: The Normative Structure of Section 301', in J. Bhagwati and R. Hudec, eds., *Fair Trade and Harmonization: Prerequisites for Free Trade*, The MIT Press, Cambridge, MA, 1996.

Abramson, V. and L. Lyon, *Government and Economic Life*, The Brookings Institution, Washington, DC, 1940.

Acheson, D., 'The ITO Charter: A Code of Fair Trade Practices', Statement by Secretary Acheson before the House Committee on Foreign Affairs made on 19 April 1950, Department of State Publication 384, May 1950.

Adams, J.S., 'Inequity in Social Exchange', in L. Berkowitz, ed., *Advances in Experimental Social Psychology*, vol. 2, Academic Press, New York, 1965.

Adler, E., 'Seizing the Middle Ground: Constructivism in World Politics', *European Journal of International Relations*, vol. 3, no. 3, 1997, pp. 319–59.

Adler E. and P. Haas, 'Epistemic Communities, World Order, and the Creation of a Reflective Research Program', *International Organization*, vol. 46, no. 1, 1992, pp. 367–90.

Allen, W., 'The International Trade Philosophy of Cordell Hull, 1907–1933', *The American Economic Review*, vol. XLII, 1953, pp. 101–16.

Allen, W., 'Issues in Congressional Tariff Debates, 1890–1930', *Southern Economic Journal*, vol. XX, no. 4, April 1954, pp. 340–55.

American Tariff League, *The Story Behind the GATT*, 140, July 1955.

Aristotle, *Nicomachean Ethics*, translated by M. Ostwald, Macmillan, New York, 1962.

Arndt, H., *The Economic Lessons of the Nineteen-Thirties*, Oxford University Press, Oxford, 1944.

Arneson, R., 'The Principle of Fairness and Free-Rider Problems', *Ethics*, vol. 92, 1982, pp. 616–33.

Atiyah, P.S., *An Introduction to the Law of Contract*, Clarendon Press, Oxford, 1995.

Atwood J. and K. Brewster, *Antitrust and American Business Abroad*, Shepard's/McGraw-Hill, Colorado Springs, Colo., 1981.

Bailey, S., *Congress Makes a Law*, Vintage Books, New York, 1950.

Bailyn, B., *The Ideological Origins of the American Revolution*, Belknap Press of Harvard University Press, Cambridge, MA, 1992.

Barrat Brown, M., *Fair Trade: Reform and Realities in the International Trading System*, ZED Books, London, 1993.

Barrie, R., *Congress and the Executive: The Making of the United States Foreign Trade Policy, 1789–1968*, Garland, New York, 1987.

Bauer, R., I. de Sola Pool and L. Dexter, *American Business and Public Policy: The Politics of Foreign Trade*, Atherton, New York, 1963.

Baumol, W., *Superfairness*, The MIT Press, Cambridge, MA and London, UK, 1986.

Bayard T. and K. Elliott, *Reciprocity and Retaliation in US Trade Policy*, Institute for International Economics, Washington, DC, 1994.

Beard, C. and M., *The Rise of the American Civilization*, Macmillan, New York, 1930.

Becchetti, L. and F. Adriani, 'Fair Trade: A "Third Generation Welfare" Mechanism to Make Globalisation Sustainable', CEIS Working Paper no. 170, Rome, 2002.

Becker, L., *Reciprocity*, University of Chicago Press, Chicago, IL, 1990.

Bedjaoui, M., *Towards a New International Economic Order*, Holmes and Meier, New York, 1979.

Bedjaoui, M., 'General Introduction', in M. Bedjaoui, ed., *International Law: Achievements and Prospects*, Martinus Nijhoff, Dordrecht, 1991.

Beitz, C., *Political Theory and International Relations*, Princeton University Press, Princeton, NJ, 1979.

Bellah, R. et al., *Habits of the Heart: Individualism and Commitment in American Life*, University of California Press, Berkeley, CA, 1996.

Bemis, S., *A Diplomatic History of the United States*, H. Holt and Company, New York, 1938.

Benn, S., 'Justice', in P. Edwards, ed., *The Encyclopaedia of Philosophy*, Macmillan, New York, 1972.

Berlin, I., 'Equality as an Ideal', in F. Olafson, ed., *Justice and Social Policy*, Prentice-Hall, Englewood Cliffs, NJ, 1961.

Berry, B., 'Justice as Reciprocity', in B. Berry, *Liberty and Justice*, Clarendon Press, Oxford, 1991.

Bhagwati, J., *Protectionism*, The MIT Press, Cambridge, MA, 1988.

Bhagwati, J., *The World Trading System at Risk*, Harvester Wheatsheaf, New York, 1991.

Bhagwati, J., 'Fair Trade, Reciprocity and Harmonisation', in A. Deardorf and R. Stern, eds., *Analytical and Negotiating Issues in the Global Trading System*, The University of Michigan Press, Ann Arbor, MI, 1994.

Bhagwati, J., 'Trade Liberalisation and "Fair Trade" Demands: Addressing the Environmental and Labour Standards Issues', *The World Economy*, November 1995, pp. 745–59.

Bidwell, P., 'A Postwar Commercial Policy for the United States', *American Economic Review*, no. 1, suppl., 1944, pp. 340–53.

Billet, L., 'The Just Economy: The Moral Basis of *The Wealth of Nations*', *Review of Social Economy*, December 1976, pp. 295–315.

Blyth, M., *Great Transformations: Economic Ideas and Institutional Change in the Twentieth Century*, Cambridge University Press, Cambridge, 2002.

Bovard, J. 'The Fair Trade Fraud', St. Martin's Press, New York, 1991.

Brittan, L., 'How to Make Trade Liberalisation Popular', *The World Economy*, November 1995, pp. 761–67.

Broad, C.D., 'On the Function of False Hypotheses in Ethics', *International Journal of Ethics*, vol. 26, 1916, pp. 384–90.

Bronz, G., 'The International Trade Organization Charter', *Harvard Law Review*, vol. 62, no. 7, 1949, pp. 1087–125.

Brown, Jr., W., *The United States and the Restoration of World Trade*, The Brookings Institution, Washington, DC, 1950.

Bull, H., *The Anarchical Society: A Study of Order in World Politics*, Macmillan, London, 1977.

Burley, A.-M., 'Regulating the World: Multilateralism, International Law, and the Projection of the New Deal Regulatory State', in J.G. Ruggie, ed., *Multilateralism Matters: The Theory and Praxis of an Institutional Form*, Columbia University Press, New York, 1993.

Camerer, C. and R. Thaler, 'Ultimatums, Dictators and Manners', *Journal of Economic Perspectives*, vol. 9, 1995, pp. 209–19.

Campbell, T.D., *Adam Smith: The Science of Morals*, Rowman and Littlefield, Totowa, NJ, 1971.

Cantril, H., *Public Opinion, 1935–1946*, Princeton University Press, Princeton, NJ, 1951.

Cass, R. and R. Boltuck, 'Antidumping and Countervailing Duty Law: The Mirage of Equitable International Competition', in J. Bhagwati and R. Hudec, eds., *Fair Trade and Harmonization: Prerequisite for Free Trade*, vol. 2, Legal Analysis, The MIT Press, Cambridge, MA, 1996.

Chamber of Commerce of the United States, *The Chamber and the Charter*, Washington, DC, 1949.

Chapman, J., 'Justice and Fairness', in C. Friedrich and J. Chapman, eds., *Justice*, Atherton Press, New York, 1963.

Charnovitz, S., 'The Moral Exception in Trade Policy', *Virginia Journal of International Law*, vol. 38, 1998, pp. 689–745.

Chipman J. and J. Moore, 'The New Welfare Economics, 1939–1974', *International Economic Review*, October 1978, pp. 547–84.

Clark, J.B., *The Distribution of Wealth*, Macmillan, New York, 1902.

Cohen, B., 'Section 201 and 406 of the Trade Act of 1974, and their Relationship to Competition Law and Policy', *Antitrust Law Journal,* vol. 56, 1987, pp. 467–83.

Condliffe, J.B., *Obstacles to Multilateral Trade*, National Planning Association, Washington, DC, April 1947.

Conti, D., *Reconciling Free Trade, Fair Trade, and Interdependence: The Rhetoric of Presidential Economic Leadership*, Praeger, Westport, CT, 1998.

Cooper, R., 'Third World Tariff Tangle', *Foreign Policy*, no. 4, Fall, 1971.

Cortney, P., *The Economic Munich*, Philosophical Library, New York, 1949.

Crandall, S. 'The American Construction of the Most-Favored-Nation Clause', *The American Journal of International Law*, vol. 7, 1913, pp. 708–23.

Croly, H., *The Promise of American Life*, Bobbs-Merrill, Indianapolis, IN, 1965.

Culbert, J., 'War-time Anglo-American Talks and the Making of the GATT', *The World Economy*, December 1987, pp. 381–99.

Culbertson, W., *Commercial Policy in War Time and After*, Appleton, New York, 1919.

Culbertson, W., *Reciprocity: A National Policy for Foreign Trade*, McGraw-Hill, New York, 1937.

Cullet, P., 'Differential Treatment in International Law: Towards a New Paradigm of Inter-State Relations', *European Journal of International Law*, vol. 10, no. 3, 1999, pp. 549–82.

Curzon, G., *Multilateral Commercial Diplomacy*, Michael Joseph, London, 1965.

Curzon, G., 'Crisis in the International Trading System', in H. Corbet and R. Jackson, eds., *In Search of a New Economic Order*, Croom Helm, London, 1974.

Dagan, H., *Unjust Enrichment*, Cambridge University Press, Cambridge, 1997.

Dam, K., *The GATT: Law and International Economic Organization*, The University of Chicago Press, Chicago, IL, 1970.

Das, D., *International Trade Policy: A Developing-Country Perspective*, Macmillan, London, 1990.

Davidson, J., *A Crossroads of Freedom: 1912 Campaign Speeches of Woodrow Wilson*, Yale University Press, New Haven, CT, 1956.

Davis, H., *America's Trade Equality Policy*, American Council on Public Affairs, Washington, DC, 1942.

de C. Grey, R., 'Contingent Protection, Managed Trade and the Decay of the Trade Relations System', in R. Snape, ed., *Issues in World Trade Policy: GATT at the Crossroads*, Macmillan, Houndmills, Basingstoke, Hampshire, 1986.

de Roover, R., 'Monopoly Theory Prior to Adam Smith: A Revision', *Quarterly Journal of Economics*, vol. LXV, no. 3, 1951, pp. 492–524.

de Roover, R., 'The Concept of Just Price: Theory and Economic Policy', *The Journal of Economic History*, vol. XVIII, no. 4, December 1958, pp. 418–34.

Destler, I.M., *American Trade Politics*, second edn., Institute for International Economic, Washington, DC, 1992.

Destler I.M., and J. Odell, *Anti-Protection: Changing Forces in United States Trade Politics*, Policy Analyses in International Economics 21, Institute for International Economics, Washington, DC, 1987.

Deutsch, M. *Distributive Justice: A Social-Psychological Perspective*, Yale University Press, New Haven, CT, 1985.

Diamond, M., 'Ethics and Politics: The American Way', in R. Horwitz, ed., *The Moral Foundations of the American Republic*, University Press of Virginia, Charlottesville, VA, 1986.

Diamond, R., 'Economic Foundations of Countervailing Duty Law', *Virginia Journal of International Law*, vol. 29, 1989, pp. 767–812.

Diebold, W., *New Directions in our Trade Policy*, Council on Foreign Relations, New York, 1941.

Diebold, W., *The End of the ITO*, Princeton University, Princeton, NJ, 1952.

Dietrich, E., 'French Import Quotas', *American Economic Review*, vol. XXIII, December 1933, pp. 661–74.

Eckes, A., *Opening America's Market: United States Foreign Policy Since 1776*, The University of North Carolina Press, Chapel Hill, NC, 1995.

Eckes, A., 'United States Trade History', in W. Lovett, A. Eckes and R. Brinkman, *United States Trade Policy: History, Theory and the WTO*, Armonk, New York and London, 1999.

Edwards, R., 'Economic Sophistication in Nineteenth Century Congressional Tariff Debates', *Journal of Economic History*, vol. 30, 1970, pp. 802–38.

Eichengreen, B., 'Hegemonic Stability Theories of the International Monetary System', in R. Cooper et al., eds., *Can Nations Agree?*, The Brookings Institution, Washington, DC, 1989.

Eiser, J.R., 'Cooperation and Conflict Between Individuals', in H. Tajfel and C. Fraser, eds., *Introducing Social Psychology*, Penguin Books, Harmondsworth, 1978.

Elster, J., *The Cement of Society: A Study of Social Order*, Cambridge University Press, Cambridge, 1989.

European Fair Trade Association, *Fair Trade Yearbook: Challenges of Fair Trade 2001–2003*, Brussels, 2003.

Evans, P., H. Jacobson and R. Putnam, *Double-Edged Diplomacy: International Bargaining and Domestic Politics*, University of California Press, Berkeley and Los Angeles, CA, 1993.

Fanfani, A., *Le origini dello spirito capitalistico in Italia*, Vita e Pensiero, Milan, 1933.

Feher E. and S. Gächter, 'Fairness and Retaliation: The Economics of Reciprocity', *Journal of Economic Perspectives*, vol. 14, no. 3, Summer 2000, pp. 159–81.

Fehr E., and J.R. Tyran, 'Institutions and Reciprocal Fairness', *Nordic Journal of Political Economy*, vol. 23, no. 2, 1996, pp. 133–44.

Fehr, E., S. Gächter and G. Kirchsteiger, 'Reciprocity as a Contract Enforcement Device: Experimental Evidence', *Econometrica*, vol. 65, no. 4, 1997, pp. 833–60.

Fehr, E., G. Kirchsteiger and A. Reidl, 'Gift Exchange and Reciprocity in Competitive Experimental Markets', *European Economic Review*, vol. 42, no. 1, 1998, pp. 1–34.

Feis, H., 'The Conflict over Trade Ideologies', *Foreign Affairs*, January 1947, pp. 217–28.

Fetter, F., 'Congressional Tariff Theory', *American Economic Review*, vol. XXIII, September 1933, pp. 413–27.

Finnis, J., *Natural Law and Natural Rights*, Clarendon Press, Oxford, 1980.

Foley, M., *American Political Ideas: Traditions and Usages*, Manchester University Press, Manchester and New York, 1991.

Ford, J., *A Social Theory of the WTO: Trading Cultures*, Palgrave Macmillan, Houndmills, Basingstoke, Hampshire, 2003.

Franck, T., *The Power of Legitimacy among Nations*, Oxford University Press, New York, 1990.

Franck, T., *Fairness in International Law and Institutions*, Clarendon Press, Oxford, 1995.

Frank, C., *Foreign Trade and Domestic Aid*, The Brookings Institution, Washington, DC, 1977.

Frank, R., *Passions Within Reason: The Strategic Role of Emotions*, Norton, New York, 1988.

Fuller, L., *The Morality of Law*, Yale University Press, New Haven, CT, and London, UK, 1964.

Galtung, J., *Human Rights in Another Key*, Polity Press, Oxford, 1994.

Garcia, F., *Trade, Inequality, and Justice: Toward a Liberal Theory of Just Trade*, Transnational Publishers, Ardsley, NY, 2003.

Gardner, R., *Sterling–Dollar Diplomacy in Current Perspective*, Columbia University Press, New York, 1980.

Garten, J., 'New Challenges in the World Economy: The Antidumping Law and the United States Trade Policy', *World Competition*, vol. 17, no. 4, 1993, pp. 128–57.

General Agreement on Tariffs and Trade (GATT), *Trends in International Trade* (the Haberler Report), Geneva, 1958.

GATT, *Trade Policies for a Better Future* (the Leutwiler Report), Geneva, 1985.

GATT, *The Texts of the Tokyo Round Agreements*, Geneva, 1986.

Gill, E., 'Justice in Smith: The Right and the Good', *Review of Social Economy*, December 1976, pp. 275–94.

Gilpin, R., *The Political Economy of International Relations*, Princeton University Press, Princeton, NJ, 1987.

Goetz, C., L. Granet and W. Schwartz, 'The Meaning of "Subsidy" and "Injury" in the Countervailing Duty Law', *International Review of Law and Economics*, vol. 6, 1986, pp. 17–32.

Goldstein, J., 'Ideas, institutions, and American Trade Policy', *International Organization*, Winter 1988, pp. 179–217.

Goldstein, J., *Ideas, Interests, and American Trade Policy*, Cornell University Press, Ithaca, NY, 1993.

Goldstein J. and R. Keohane, eds., *Ideas and Foreign Policy: Beliefs, Institutions, and Political Change*, Cornell University Press, Ithaca, NY, 1993.

Goldwin, R., 'Of Man and Angels: A Search for Morality in the Constitution', in R. Horwitz, ed., *The Moral Foundations of the American Republic*, University of Virginia Press, Charlottesville, VA, 1986.

Golecki, M., 'Synallagma and Freedom of Contract: The Concept of Reciprocity and Fairness in Contracts from Historical and Law and Economics Perspective', *German Working Papers in Law and Economics*, vol. 2003, no. 18.

Gordley, J., 'Equality in Exchange', *California Law Review*, vol. 69, no. 6, December 1981, pp. 1587–656.

Gouldner, A., 'The Norm of Reciprocity', *American Sociological Review*, vol. 25, no. 2, April 1960, pp. 161–78.

Gowa, J., 'An Epitaph for Hegemonic Stability Theory? Rational Hegemons, Excludable Goods, and Small Groups', in J. Odell and T. Willett, eds., *International Trade Policies: Gains from the Exchange Between Economics and Political Science*, The University of Michigan Press, Ann Arbor, MI, 1990.

Graz, J.-C., *Aux Sources de l'OMC. La Charte de la Havane*, Librairie Droz, Geneva.

Greenberg, J., 'Approaching Equity and Avoiding Inequity in Groups and Organisations', in J. Greenberg and R.L. Choen, eds., *Equity and Justice in Social Behaviour*, New York, Academic Press, 1982.

Greenberg, J., 'Organizational Justice: Yesterday, Today and Tomorrow', *Journal of Management*, vol. 16, 1990, pp. 399–432.

Gros Espiell, H., 'The Most-Favored-Nation Clause: Its Present Significance in GATT', *Journal of World Trade Law*, 1971, pp. 29–44.

Gupta, K.R., *A Study of General Agreement on Tariffs and Trade*, S. Chand and Co., New Delhi, 1967.

Guth, W., R. Schmittberger and B. Schwarze, 'An Experimental Analysis of Ultimatum Bargaining', *Journal of Economic Behaviour*, vol. 3, 1982, pp. 367–88.

Haas, P., 'Introduction: Epistemic Communities and International Policy Coordination', *International Organization*, vol. 46, no. 1, 1992, pp. 1–35.

Haq, I., 'From Charity to Obligation: A Third World Perspective on Concessional Resource Transfers', *Texas International Law Journal*, vol. 14, no. 3, Summer 1979, pp. 389–424.

Hart, H.M., 'Processing Taxes and Protective Tariffs', *Harvard Law Review*, vol. 49, 1936, pp. 610–18.

Hart, H.L.A., 'Are There Any Natural Rights?', *Philosophical Review*, vol. 64, 1955, pp. 175–91.

Hartz, L., *The Liberal Tradition in America: An Interpretation of American Political Thought since the Revolution*, Harcourt Brace Jovanovich, San Diego, CA, 1955 [1991].

Hasenclever, A., P. Mayer and V. Rittberger, *Theories of International Regimes*, Cambridge University Press, Cambridge, 1997.

Henkin, L., *How Nations Behave: Law and Foreign Policy*, Praeger, New York, 1968.

Henkin, L., *International Law: Politics and Values*, Martinus Nijhoff, Dordrecht, 1995.

Hill, W., *The First Stages of the Tariff Policy of the United States*, American Economic Association, Baltimore, MD, 1893.

Hinton, H., *Cordell Hull: A Biography*, Doubleday, Doran, and Company, Inc., Garden City, New York, 1942.

Hirschman, A., *The Strategy of Economic Development*, Yale University Press, New Haven, CT, 1958.

Hobbes, T., *Leviathan*, edited by R. Tuck, Cambridge, Cambridge University Press, 1651 [1991].

Hody, C., *The Politics of Trade*, The University Press of New England, Hanover, NH, 1996.

Hofstadter, R., *The American Political Tradition*, Knopf, New York, 1957 [1973].

Hogan, M.J., 'Revival and Reform: America's Twentieth-Century Search for a New Economic Order Abroad', *Diplomatic History*, vol. 8, no. 4, Fall 1984, pp. 287–310.

Homans, G., *Social Behaviour: Its Elementary Forms*, Harcourt, Brace & World, New York, 1961.

Howse, R. and M. Matua, *Protecting Human Rights in a Global Economy: Challenges for the World Trade Organization*, Rights and Democracy, Montreal, 2000.

Hudec, R., '"Mirror, Mirror on the Wall": The Concept of Fairness in United States Foreign Trade Policy', in D. Fleming, ed., *Canada Japan and International Law*, 1990 Proceedings, Canadian Council of International Law, Ottawa, 1990.

Hudec, R., 'GATT and the Developing Countries', *Columbia Business Law Review*, no. 1, 1992, pp. 67–77.

Hufbauer G. and J. Erb, *Subsidies in International Trade*, Institute for International Economics, Washington, DC, 1984.

Hull, C., *The Memoirs of Cordell Hull*, Macmillan, New York, 1948.

Hume, D., *A Treatise of Human Nature*, Dolphin Books, Garden City, NJ, 1739 [1961].

Humphrey, D., *American Imports*, Twentieth Century Fund, New York, 1955.

Hunt, G., ed., *The Writings of James Madison*, G.P. Putnam's Sons, New York, 1900.

Hurrell, A., 'International Society and the Study of Regimes: A Reflective Approach', in V. Rittberger (with the assistance of P. Mayer), ed., *Regime Theory and International Relations*, Clarendon Press, Oxford, 1993.

Ikenberry, J., 'Creating Yesterday's New World Order: Keynesian 'New Thinking' and the Anglo-American Postwar Settlement', in J. Goldstein and R. Keohane, eds., *Ideas and Foreign Policy: Beliefs, Institutions, and Political Change*, Cornell University Press, Ithaca, NY, 1993.

Ikenberry, J., D. Lake and M. Mastanduno, eds., *The State and American Foreign Policy*, Cornell University Press, Ithaca, NY, 1988.

Isaacs, A., *International Trade: Tariffs and Commercial Policies*, R.D. Irwin, Chicago, IL, 1948.

Jackson, J., *World Trade and the Law of GATT*, The Michie Company, Charlottesville, Virginia, VA, 1969.

Jackson, J., *The World Trading System*, second edn., The MIT Press, Cambridge, MA, 1997.

Jacobsen, J., 'Much Ado about Ideas: The Cognitive Factor in Economic Policy', *World Politics*, vol. 47, no. 2, 1995, pp. 283–310.

Jefferson, T., *Summary View of the Rights of British America*, Philadelphia, B. Franklin, New York, 1774 [1971].

Johnson, D. and K. Porter, *National Party Platforms, 1840–1972*, University of Illinois Press, Urbana, IL, 1973.

Johnson, H., 'An Economic Theory of Protectionism, Tariff Bargaining, and the Formation of Customs Unions', *Journal of Political Economy*, vol. LXXIII, 1965, pp. 256–83.

Johnson, H., 'Optimal Trade Intervention in the Presence of Domestic Distortions', in R. Baldwin et al., eds., *Trade, Growth and the Balance of Payments*, Rand McNally, Chicago, IL, 1965.

Kahnemann, D., J.L. Knetsch and R. Thaler, 'Fairness as a Constraint on Profit Seeking: Entitlements in the Market', *American Economic Review*, vol. 76, no. 4, 1986, pp. 728–41.

Kaldor, N., 'Welfare Propositions of Economics and Interpersonal Comparisons of Utility', *Economic Journal*, vol. 49, September 1939, pp. 549–52.

Kaplan, E., *American Trade Policy, 1923–1995*, Greenwood Press, Westport, Conn., 1996.

Karol, D., 'Divided Government and Trade Policy: Much Ado About Nothing', *International Organization*, vol. 54, no. 4, Autumn 2000, pp. 825–44.

Kelly, W., ed., *Studies in United States Commercial Policy*, University of North Carolina Press, Chapel Hill, NC, 1963.

Keohane, R., *After Hegemony: Cooperation and Discord in the World Political Economy*, Princeton University Press, Princeton, NJ, 1984.

Keohane, R., 'Reciprocity in International Relations', *International Organization*, vol. 40, no. 1, 1986, pp. 1–28.

Keohane, R., 'Neoliberal Institutionalism: A Perspective on World Politics', in R. Keohane, ed., *International Institutions and State Power: Essays in International Relations Theory*, Westview Press, Boulder, CO, 1989.

Keynes, J.M., *The General Theory of Employment Interest and Money*, Macmillan, London, 1936.

Kindleberger, C., *The World in Depression, 1929–1939*, University of California Press, Berkeley, CA, 1973.

Knorr, K., 'The American Trade Proposals', mimeo, Yale Institute of International Studies, New Haven, October 1946.

Koch, A. and W. Paden, *The Life and Selected Writings of Thomas Jefferson*, The Modern Library, New York, 1944.

Kock, K., *International Trade Policy and the GATT 1947–67*, Almqvist and Wiksell, Stockholm, 1969.

Konow, J., 'Which Is the Fairest of All? A Positive Analysis of Justice Theories', *Journal of Economic Literature*, vol. XLI, December 2003, pp. 1188–239.

Koskenniemi, M., *From Apology to Utopia: The Structure of the International Legal Argument*, Finnish Lawyers' Publishing Company, Helsinki, 1989.

Krasner, S., 'State Power and the Structure of International Trade', *World Politics*, vol. 28, 1976, pp. 317–47.

Krasner S., ed., *International Regimes*, Cornell University Press, Ithaca, NY, 1983.

Kratochwil, F., *Rules, Norms and Decisions: On the Conditions of Practical and Legal Reasoning in International Relations and Domestic Affairs*, Cambridge University Press, Cambridge, 1989.

Kratochwil F. and J.G. Ruggie, 'International Organization: A State of the Art on an Art of the State', *International Organization*, vol. 40, 1986, pp. 753–75.

Kronman, A., 'Contract Law and Distributive Justice', *Yale Law Journal*, vol. 89, no. 3, January 1980, pp. 472–511.

Kymlicka, W., *Liberalism, Community, and Culture*, Clarendon Press, Oxford, 1989.

Lake, D., *Power, Protection, and Free Trade. International Sources of United States Commercial Strategy, 1887–1939*, Cornell University Press, Ithaca, NY, 1988.

Larkin, J.D., *President's Control of the Tariff*, Harvard University Press, Cambridge, MA, 1936.

Larkin, J.D., *Trade Agreements: A Study in Democratic Methods*, Columbia University Press, New York, 1940.

League of Nations, *International Convention Relating to the Simplification of Customs Formalities*, 3 November 1923, Geneva, 1923.

League of Nations, International Conference on the Abolition of Import and Export Restrictions, Geneva, 17 October to 8 November 1927, *Proceedings of the Conference*, Geneva, 1928.

League of Nations, *Equality of Treatment in the Present State of International Commercial Relations: The Most-Favoured-Nation Clause*, Official No. C.376.M.250.1936.II.B., Geneva, 1936.

League of Nations, *Commercial Policy in the Interwar Period: Proposals and National Policies*, Geneva, 1942.

League of Nations, *Quantitative Trade Controls: Their Causes and Nature*, prepared by G. Haberler (in collaboration with M. Hill), Princeton University Press, Princeton, NJ, 1943.

League of Nations, *Trade Relations Between Free-Market and Controlled Economies*, prepared by J. Viner, Princeton University Press, Princeton, NJ, 1943.

Leddy, J., 'United States Commercial Policy and the Domestic Farm Program', in W. Kelly, ed., *Studies in United States Commercial Policy*, The University of North Carolina Press, Chapel Hill, NC, 1963.

Leddy J. and J. Norwood, 'The Escape Clause and Peril Points Under the Trade-Agreements Program', in W. Kelly, ed., *Studies in United States*

Commercial Policy, University of North Carolina Press, Chapel Hill, NC, 1963.

Lerner, M.J., *The Belief in a Just World: A Fundamental Delusion*, Plenum Press, New York, 1980.

Letiche, J., *Reciprocal Trade Agreements in the World Economy*, King's Crown Press, New York, 1948.

Letwin, W., 'The English Common Law Concerning Monopolies', *The University of Chicago Law Review*, vol. XXI, 1953–54, pp. 355–85.

Leventhal, G.S., 'The Distribution of Rewards and Resources in Groups and Organizations', in E. Walster and L. Berkowitz, eds., *Advances in Experimental Social Psychology*, Academic Press, New York, 1976.

Levy, M., O. Young and M. Zürn, 'The Study of International Regimes', *European Journal of International Relations*, vol. 1, 1995, pp. 267–330.

Lewis, E., *A History of the American Tariff 1789–1860*, Charles H. Kerr and Company, Chicago, IL, 1896.

Lewis, T.J., 'Adam Smith: The Labor Market as the Basis of Natural Rights', *Journal of Economic Issues*, vol. 11, 1977, pp. 21–50.

Lindgren, J.R., *The Social Philosophy of Adam Smith*, Martinus Nijhoff, The Hague, 1973.

Littrell, M. and M. Dickson, *Social Responsibility in the Global Market: Fair Trade of Cultural Products*, Sage Publications, Thousand Oaks, CA, 1999.

Locke, J., *The First Treatise on Government* [1690], in J. Locke, *Two Treatises on Government*, I. Shapiro, ed., Yale University Press, New Haven, CT, 2003.

Lockwood, W., *The Foreign Trade Policy of the United States*, American Council of Pacific Relations, New York, 1936.

Low, P., *Trading Free: The GATT and US Trade Policy*, The Twentieth Century Fund Press, New York, 1993.

Lowi, T., 'American Business, Public Policy, Case-Studies, and Political Theory', *World Politics*, vol. 16, 1963, pp. 682–3.

Macdonald, R. St. J., 'The Principle of Solidarity in Public International Law', in C. Dominicé et al., eds, *Études de Droit International en l'honneur de Pierre Lalive*, Helbing and Lichtenhahn, Basle, 1993.

MacFie, A.L., *The Individual in Society*, George Allen & Unwin, London, 1967.

Madison, J., *The Federalist*, no. 10, in A. Hamilton, J. Madison and J. Jay, eds., *The Federalist Papers* [1788], edited by C. Rossiter, Mentor, New York, 1999.

Marceau, G., 'WTO Dispute Settlement and Human Rights', *European Journal of International Law*, vol. 13, no. 4, 2002, pp. 753–814.

Matsushita, M., T. Schoenbaum and P. Mavroidis, *The World Trade Organization: Law, Practice, and Policy*, Oxford University Press, Oxford, 2003.

Mayer, W., 'Endogenous Tariff Formation', *American Economic Review*, vol. 74, no. 5, 1984, pp. 970–85.

McClosky, H. and J. Zaller, *The American Ethos: Public Attitudes toward Capitalism and Democracy*, Harvard University Press, Cambridge, MA, 1984.

Meltzer, A., 'Monetary and Other Explanations of the Start of the Great Depression', *Journal of Monetary Economics*, vol. 2, 1976, pp. 75–93.

Michalopoulos, C., 'Developing Country Strategies for the Millennium Round', *Journal of World Trade*, October 1999, pp. 1–30.

Mikesell, R., *United States Economic Policy and International Relations*, McGraw-Hill, New York, 1952.

Miller, D., 'Distributive Justice: What the People Think', *Ethics*, vol. 102, April 1992, pp. 555–93.

Miller, H., *Treaties and Other International Acts of the United States of America*, US Government Printing Office, Washington, DC, 1931–1948.

Morris Groos, A., 'International Trade and Development: Exploring the Impact of Fair Trade Organizations in the Global Economy and the Law', *Texas International Law Journal*, vol. 34, 1999, pp. 379–411.

Mutersbaugh, T., 'Ethical Trade and Certified Organic Coffee: Implications of Rules-Based Agricultural Product Certification for Mexican Producer Households and Villages', *Transnational Law and Contemporary Problem*, Spring 2002, pp. 89–107.

Myrdal, G., *An International Economy: Problems and Prospects*, Harper, New York, 1956.

Nagel, T., 'The Problem of Global Justice', *Philosophy and Public Affairs*, vol. 33, no. 2, Spring 2005, pp. 113–47.

Neufield, M., 'Interpretation and the "Science" of International Relations', *Review of International Studies*, vol. 19, no. 1, 1993, pp. 39–61.

Nicolaides, P., 'How Fair is Fair Trade?', *Journal of World Trade Law*, no. 4, 1987, pp. 147–62.

Nitze, P., 'A Sound International Trade Program: Its Meaning for American Business', US Department of State publication 3341, Commercial Policy Series 117, November 1948.

Noonan, T., *The Scholastic Analysis of Usury*, Harvard University Press, Cambridge, MA, 1957.

Notter, H., *Postwar Foreign Policy Preparation, 1939–1945*, Dept. of State, Washington, DC, Publication 3580, General foreign policy series 15, 1949.

Okun, A., *Equality and Efficiency: The Big Tradeoff*, Washington, DC, The Brookings Institution, 1975.

Pareto, V., *Manual of Political Economy*, A.M. Kelley, New York, 1971.

Pastor, R., *Congress and the Politics of United States Foreign Economic Policy, 1929–1976,* University of California Press, Berkeley, CA, 1980.

Pearson, C., 'Free Trade, Fair Trade? The Reagan Record', in C. Pearson and J. Riedel, eds., *The Direction of Trade Policy*, Basil Blackwell, Cambridge, MA, 1990.

Penrose, E.F., *Economic Planning for the Peace*, Princeton University Press, Princeton, NJ, 1953.

Perez-Lopez, J., 'GATT Safeguards: A Critical Review of Article XIX and its Implementation in Selected Countries', *Case Western Journal of International Law*, vol. 23, 1991, pp. 517–79.

Petersmann, E.-U., *Constitutional Functions and Constitutional Problems of International Economic Law*, University Press Fribourg, Fribourg, 1991.

Petersmann, E.-U., 'Human Rights and the Law of the World Trade Organization', *Journal of World Trade*, April 2003, pp. 241–81.

Philpott, D., *Revolutions in Sovereignty: How Ideas Shaped Modern International Relations*, Princeton University Press, Princeton, NJ, 2001.

Pigman, G., 'Hegemony and Trade Liberalization Policy: Britain and the Brussels Sugar Convention of 1902', *Review of International Studies*, vol. 23, no. 2, 1997, pp. 185–210.

Pogge, T., 'World Poverty and Human Rights', *Ethics and International Affairs*, vol. 19, no. 1, 2005, pp. 1–7.

Polanyi, K., 'Aristotle Discovers the Economy', in K. Polanyi, C.M. Arensberg and H. Pearson, *Trade and the Market in the Early Empires*, Free Press, Glencoe, IL, 1957.

Price R. and C. Reus-Smit, 'Dangerous Liaisons? Critical International Theory and Constructivism', *European Journal of International Relations*, vol. 4, no. 3, 1998, pp. 259–94.

Rabin, M., 'Incorporating Fairness into Game Theory and Economics', *American Economic Review*, vol. 83, no. 5, 1993, pp. 1281–302.

Rabin, M., 'Psychology and Economics', *Journal of Economic Literature*, vol. 36, no. 1, 1998, pp. 11–46.

Rawls, J., 'Justice as Fairness', *The Philosophical Review*, vol. LXVII, 1958, pp. 164–94.

Rawls, J., 'Legal Obligation and the Duty of Fair Play', in S. Hook, ed., *Law and Philosophy*, New York University Press, New York, 1964.

Rawls, J., 'Justice as Reciprocity', in S. Gorovitz, ed., *Utilitarianism*, Bobbs-Merrill, Indianapolis and New York, 1971.

Rawls, J., *A Theory of Justice*, Cambridge University Press, Cambridge, MA, 1971.

Reis, H.T., 'The Multidimentionality of Justice', in R. Folger, ed., *The Sense of Injustice: Social Psychological Perspectives*, Plenum Press, New York, 1984.

Rhodes, C., *Reciprocity, U.S. Trade Policy, and the GATT Regime*, Cornell University Press, Ithaca, 1993.

Richardson, J.D., ed., *A Compilation of the Messages and Papers of the Presidents, 1789–1907*, Bureau of National Literature and Art, New York, 1908.

Röhl, K.F. and S. Machura, *Procedural Justice*, Dartmouth Publishing, Aldershot, UK, 1997.

Roseman, S., ed., *Papers and Addresses of Franklin D. Roosevelt 1940/45*, Harper and Brothers, New York, vol. 1944–1945.

Roth, A.E., 'Bargaining Experiments', in A.E. Roth and J.H. Kagel, eds., *Handbook of Experimental Economics*, Princeton University Press, Princeton, NJ, 1995.

Ruggie, J.G., 'Embedded Liberalism Revisited: Institutions and Progress in International Economic Relations', in E. Adler and B. Crawford, eds., *Progress in Postwar Economic Relations*, Columbia University Press, New York, 1991.

Ruggie, J.G., 'At Home Abroad, Abroad at Home: International Liberalization and Domestic Stability in the New World Economy', *Millennium*, vol. 24, no. 3, 1995, pp. 507–26.

Ruggie, J.G., *Constructing the World Polity*, Routledge, London and New York, 1998.

Runciman, W.C., 'Processes, End-States, and Social Justice', *Philosophical Quarterly*, vol. 28, 1978, pp. 37–45.

Sampson, E.E., *Justice and the Critique of Pure Psychology*, Plenum Press, New York, 1983.

Sapir, A., 'Who's Afraid of Globalization? Domestic Adjustment in Europe and America', in R. Porter et al., *Efficiency, Equity and Legitimacy: The Multilateral Trading System at the Millennium*, The Brookings Institution, Washington, DC, 2001.

Sapori, A., 'Il giusto prezzo nella dottrina di San Tommaso e nella pratica del suo tempo', *Studi di storia economica (secoli XIII-XIV-XV)*, Sansoni, Florence, 1955.

Sayre, F., *America Must Act*, World Peace Foundation, Boston and New York, 1936.

Sayre, F., *The Way Forward: The American Trade Agreements Program*, Macmillan, New York, 1939.

Schattschneider, E.E., *Politics, Pressure and the Tariff*, Prentice Hall, New York, 1935.

Schumpeter, J., *History of Economic Analysis*, Allen & Unwin, Boston, MA, 1954.

Schwartz W. and E. Harper, 'The Regulation of Subsidies Affecting International Trade', *Michigan Law Review*, vol. 70, 1972, pp. 831–58.

Sen, A., *On Income Inequality*, Clarendon Press, Oxford, 1972.

Sen, A., *Inequality Reexamined*, Oxford University Press, Oxford, 1992.

Sen, A., *Development as Freedom*, Knopf, New York, 2001.

Sengupta, A., 'The Right to Development as a Human Right', François-Xavier Bagnoud Center for Health and Human Rights, mimeo, Harvard School of Public Health, 2000.

Setser, V., 'Did Americans Originate the Conditional Most-Favored-Nation Clause?', *Journal of Modern History*, September 1933, pp. 319–23.

Siegan, B., 'The Constitution and the Protection of Capitalism', in R. Goldwin and W. Schambra, eds., *How Capitalistic is the Constitution?*, American Enterprise Institute for Public Policy Research, Washington, DC, 1982.

Sikkink, K., *Ideas and Institutions: Developmentalism in Brazil and Argentina*, Cornell University Press, Ithaca, New York, 1991.

Simma, B., 'From Bilateralism to Community Interest in International Law', *Collected Courses of the Hague Academy of International Law*, Martinus Nijhoff, The Hague, 1994.

Simmons, A.J., *Moral Principles and Political Obligations*, Princeton University Press, Princeton, NJ, 1979.

Smith, A., *The Theory of Moral Sentiments*, Liberty Fund, Indianapolis, 1759 [1976].

Smith, A., *The Wealth of Nations*, Random House, New York, 1776 [1937].

Smith, S., 'In Defence of Substantive Fairness', *The Law Quarterly Review*, vol. 112, January 1996, pp. 138–58.

Snidal, D., 'Coordination versus Prisoner's Dilemma: Implications for International Cooperation and Regimes', *American Political Science Review*, December 1985, pp. 923–42.

Stanwood, E., *American Tariff Controversies in the Nineteenth Century*, Houghton Mifflin, Boston, MA, 1903.

Strackbein, O., *American Enterprise and Foreign Trade*, Public Affairs Press, Washington, DC, 1965.

Sudgen, R., 'Reciprocity: The Supply of Public Goods through Voluntary Contributions', *Economic Journal*, vol. 94, 1984, pp. 772–87.

Sykes, A., 'GATT Safeguards Reform: The Injury Test', in M. Trebilcock and R. York, eds., *Fair Exchange: Reforming Trade Remedy Laws*, Toronto, 1990.

Sykes, A., 'The Safeguard Mess: A Critique of WTO Jurisprudence', *World Trade Review*, vol. 2, no. 3, 2003, pp. 287–8.

Syrett, H., ed., *The Papers of Alexander Hamilton*, Columbia University Press, New York, 1961.

Tarullo, D., 'Beyond Normalcy in the Regulation of International Trade', *Harvard Law Review*, vol. 100, 1987, pp. 546–628.

Tasca, H., *The Reciprocal Trade Policy of the United States: A Study in Trade Philosophy*, University of Pennsylvania Press, Philadelphia, PA, 1938.

Tasca, H., *World Trading Systems: A Study of American and British Commercial Policies*, International Institute of Intellectual Cooperation, Paris, 1938.

Taussig, F.W., ed., *State Papers and Speeches on the Tariff*, Harvard University, Cambridge, MA, 1892.

Taussig, F.W., 'The Tariff Act of 1913', *Quarterly Journal of Economics*, vol. 28, 1914, pp. 1–30.

Taussig, F.W., *The Tariff History of the United States*, G.P. Putnam's Sons, New York, 1923.

Taylor, A., *The New Deal and Foreign Trade*, Macmillan, New York, 1935.

Thibout J. and L. Walker, *Procedural Justice: A Psychological Analysis*, Lawrence Erlbaum, Hillsdale, NJ, 1975.

Thomas, C., 'Balance-of-Payments Crises in the Developing World: Balancing Trade, Finance and Development in the New Economic Order', *American Univ. International Law Review*, vol. 15, 2000, pp. 1249–77.

Thomas, H., 'Adam Smith's Philosophy of Science', *Quarterly Journal of Economics*, Winter 1965, pp. 212–33.

Thomson, W., 'Equity in Exchange Economies', *Journal of Economic Theory*, vol. 29, 1983, pp. 217–44.

Trachtman, J., 'Legal Aspects of a Poverty Agenda at the WTO: Trade Law and "Global Apartheid"', *Journal of International Economic Law*, vol. 6, no. 1, March 2003, pp. 3–21.

Tumlir, J., 'A Revised Safeguard Clause for GATT?', *Journal of World Trade Law*, vol. 7, no. 4, July–August 1973, pp. 404–20.

United Nations (UN), Declaration Concerning the Establishment of a New International Economic Order, 1 May 1974, G.A. Res. 3201, U.N. GAOR, 6th Spec. Sess., Supp. no. 1, UN Doc. A/9559, 1974.

UN, Charter of Economic Rights and Duties of States, G.A. Res. 3281 (XXIX), UN Doc. A/3281, 1974.

UN, Declaration on the Right to Development, G.A. Resolution 4/128, 4 December 1986.

UN, Declaration of International Economic Cooperation, U.N. GAOR 18th Spec. Sess., Supp. 2, UN Doc. A/S.18/15, 1990.

UN, United Nations Millennium Declaration, UN General Assembly Resolution, A/RES/55/2, 18 September 2000.

United Nations Conference on Trade and Development (UNCTAD), *Proceedings of the United Nations Conference on Trade and Development*, UN Doc. E/CONF.46/141, New York, 1964.

UNCTAD, Report by the Secretary General, *Towards a New Trade Policy for Development*, reproduced in *Proceedings of the United Nations Conference on Trade and Development*, vol. II: Policy Statements, UN Doc. E/CONF.46/141, New York, 1964.

UN Development Programme (UNDP), *Human Development Report 1998*, Oxford University Press, New York, 1998.

UNDP, *Human Development Report 2000*, Oxford University Press, New York, 2000.

UNDP, *Human Development Report 2002*, Oxford University Press, New York, 2002.

UN Economic and Social Council, *Report of the First Session of the Preparatory Committee of the United Nations Conference on Trade and Employment*, UN Doc. E/PC/T/33, London, October 1946.

UN Economic and Social Council, Commission on Human Rights, 'Mainstreaming the Right to Development into International Trade Law and Policy at the WTO' (report prepared by R. Howse), UN Doc. E/CN.4/Sub.2/2004/17.

United States, Department of State, 'Proposals for Expansion of World Trade and Employment', publication 2411, Commercial Policy Series 79, 1945, reprinted in *Department of State Bulletin*, XIII, 1945, pp. 912–29.

United States, Department of State, 'Suggested Charter for the International Trade Organization', publication 2598, Commercial Policy Series, 93, 1945.

United States, Tariff Commission, *Annual Report of the United States Tariff Commission*, Washington, DC, 1919.

United States, Tariff Commission, *Information Concerning Dumping and Unfair Foreign Competition in the United States and Canada's Antidumping Laws*, Washington, DC, 1919.

United States, Tariff Commission, *Reciprocity and Commercial Treaties*, Washington, DC, 1919.

United States, Tariff Commission, *Thirteenth Annual Report*, Washington, DC, 1929.

United States, Tariff Commission, *Tariff Bargaining Under Most-Favored-Nations Treaties*, Washington, DC, 1933.

United States Council of the International Chamber of Commerce, Executive Committee, *Position with respect to the Havana Charter for an International Trade Organization*, New York, 1950.

Varga, D., 'Amending United States Antidumping Laws to Create a Viable Private Right of Action: Must Fair Trade be Free?', *Vanderbilt Journal of Transnational Law*, vol. 21, 1988, pp. 1023–67.

VerLoren van Themaat, P., *The Changing Structure of International Economic Law*, Martinus Nijhoff, The Hague, 1981.

Verwey, W., 'The Principle of Preferential Treatment for Developing Countries', *Indian Journal of International Law*, July–December, 1983, pp. 343–500.

Verwey, W., 'The Principles of a New International Economic Order and the Law of the General Agreement on Tariffs and Trade (GATT)', *Leiden Journal of International Law*, vol. 3, no. 2, October 1990, pp. 117–42.

Victor, P., 'Antidumping and Antitrust: Can the Inconsistencies be Resolved?', *New York University Journal of International Law and Policy*, vol. 15, no. 2, 1983, pp. 339–50.

Viner, J., *Dumping: A Problem in International Trade*, A.M. Kelley, New York, 1923 [1966].

Viner, J., 'The Most-Favored-Nation Clause in American Commercial Treaties', *The Journal of Political Economy*, February 1924, pp. 101–29.

Viner, J., 'The Most-Favored-Nation Clause', in *Index* (Svenska Handelsbanken, Stockholm), vol. VI, January 1931, reprinted in J. Viner, *International Economics*, Free Press, Glencoe, IL, 1951.

Viner, J., 'Conflicts of Principle in Drafting a Trade Charter', *Foreign Affairs*, July 1947, pp. 612–28.

Viner, J., *International Trade and Economic Development*, Free Press, Glencoe, IL, 1952.

Wallace, H., 'American Agriculture and World Markets', *Foreign Affairs*, vol. 12, no. 2, January 1934, pp. 216–30.

Wallace, H., *New Frontiers*, Reynal and Hitchcock, New York, 1934.

Walster, E., G.W. Walster and E. Berscheid, *Equity: Theory and Research*, Allyn & Bacon, Boston, MA, 1978.

Walzer, M., *Spheres of Justice*, Martin Roberston, Oxford, 1983.

Weber, M., *The Methodology of the Social Sciences*, translated by E. Shils and H. Finch, Free Press, Glencoe, IL, 1949.

Wendt, A., 'Collective Identity Formation and the International State', *American Political Science Review*, vol. 88, no. 2, 1994, pp. 384–96.

Wilcox, C., *A Charter for World Trade*, The Macmillan Company, New York, 1949.

Wilkinson, J., *Politics and Trade Policy*, Public Affairs Press, Washington, DC, 1960.

Willett, C., *Aspects of Fairness in Contract*, Blackstone Press, London, 1996.

Winham, G., *The Evolution of International Trade Agreements*, University of Toronto Press, Toronto, 1992.

Wood, D., '"Unfair" Trade Injury: A CompetitionBased Approach', *Stanford Law Review*, vol. 41, 1989, pp. 1153–2000.

Woods, N., 'Economic Ideas and International Relations: Beyond Rational Neglect', *International Studies Quarterly*, vol. 39, 1995, pp. 161–80.

Worland, S., 'Adam Smith: Economic Justice and the Founding Fathers', in R. Skurski, ed., *New Directions in Economic Justice*, University of Notre Dame Press, Notre Dame and London, 1983.

Worland, S., 'Economics and Justice', in R. Cohen, ed., *Justice: Views from the Social Sciences*, Plenum Press, New York and London, 1986.

World Bank, *World Development Report 2003*, Oxford University Press, New York, 2002.

World Commission on the Social Dimension of Globalization, *A Fair Globalization: Creating Opportunities for All*, International Labour Office, Geneva, 2004.

World Trade Organization, *The Results of the Uruguay Round of Multilateral Trade Negotiations: The Legal Texts*, Geneva, 1995.

Wright, P., 'The Bearing of Recent Tariff Legislation on International Relations', *American Economic Review*, vol. XXIII, September 1933, pp. 16–26.

Yee, A., 'The Casual Effects of Ideas on Policies', *International Organization*, vol. 50, no. 1, Winter 1996, pp. 69–108.

Yusuf, A., '"Differential and More Favourable Treatment": The GATT Enabling Clause', *Journal of World Trade Law*, vol. 14, no. 6, November–December 1980, pp. 488–507.

Zajac, E., *Political Economy of Fairness*, The MIT Press, Cambridge, MA, 1995.

Zeiler, T., *Free Trade Free World: The Advent of the GATT*, The University of North Carolina Press, Chapel Hill, NC, 1999.

Index

AAA (Agricultural Adjustment Act) 99,
105
Adams, John 51, 52, 73, 74, 76
Agricultural Adjustment Act 1933
109–10
agriculture
and commercial treaties 78
commodity price fall 59–60
developing countries 167
exports 63, 78, 106, 109
Fordney–McCumber Act 1922 60
and GATT 129, 135
imports 61, 109
incomes 61, 109, 110, 134
overproduction 59–60
protection for 3, 60, 116, 118, 126,
131, 148
and tariffs 55, 59–60, 61, 63, 112
analytical framework 9–25
Antidumping Act
1916 68, 69–70
1921 60, 70–71
see also dumping
antitrust 28, 38, 71, 140
Clayton Antitrust Act 49, 68, 69
Sherman Antitrust Act 68, 70
Aquinas, Thomas 29, 30, 35
argol agreements 79–80, 83, 84
Aristotle 29, 30, 31, 37, 169
Atlantic Charter 114–15, 118
Australia
economic development 121–2
MFN treatment 105
safeguard clauses 121
tariffs 64, 119

balance-of-payments problems 20, 116,
121, 126, 130, 163, 168
Belgium, MFN pledge 77, 107
beliefs 13–14, 18
Bernardino of Siena, San 30, 31

Brazil
economic development 121–2
and subsidies 123
trade agreements 68, 79
Britain
Alternative Trading Organization 174
Atlantic Charter 114, 118
balance-of-payments difficulties 116
British Navigation Acts 52
Cobden–Chevalier Treaty 1860 77
and Commonwealth countries 120
domestic market monopoly 10–11, 53,
56, 73, 114
employment 115, 116, 122, 129
government intervention 115
Imperial Preferences 119, 120, 125–6,
129
lend-lease agreement 114
London Economic Conference 112,
173
MFN pledge 77, 83
Oxfam 174
preferential system 64
tariff reduction policy 119
trade with US 52, 53–4, 73
Brussels Financial Conference 1920 65
burdens and benefits distribution
and fairness 27, 39, 51, 61, 63, 98,
162
GATT and 132–3
and international trade 32, 53, 64, 127,
139, 147–8
safeguard rules and 142
business practices, restrictive 129

Canada
reciprocal agreements with 78, 81, 83,
84
tariffs 64
capitalism 16, 33–4, 38, 47, 50, 55
and democracy, tensions between 47

and desert-based principles 50
    dominance of 32, 33, 46
    and fairness 3, 50, 118
    importance of, in US 46–7, 65
    laissez-faire 19, 20, 46, 49, 104, 108
cartels 68, 130, 132
Chile, economic development 121–2
Churchill, Winston 114
Clark, J.B. 38
Clay, Henry 54, 55
Clayton Antitrust Act 49, 68, 69
Clayton, William 116, 118, 119, 120
Cleveland, Grover 56, 57
Cobden–Chevalier Treaty 1860 77
collective action 13, 14, 18, 39
Colombia, penalty duties 79
commercial treaties, equality of
    treatment through 73–85, 128, 131
competition 2–3, 46
    anticompetitive behaviour 68, 111,
        140, 144
    benchmark 138, 144, 169
    and fairness 27–8, 35, 49, 54, 64, 73,
        99, 110, 127–8
    and free-riding *see* free-riding
    import 51, 57, 64, 102, 103, 109, 128,
        141, 143–4
    origins of, historical 31
    and subsidies *see* subsidies
    unfair 39–40, 53, 63, 64, 68–71, 123,
        129–30, 133
complaint mechanism 127, 129, 136,
    140, 167, 187
Congress 58, 69, 70, 71, 75, 79, 81
    Acts passed *see under* USA
    commerce regulation powers 52–3
    Continental Congress 52, 73–4
    employment bill 120
    Plan 1776 74
    protectionist members 55–6, 66,
        115–16
    and tariffs 55, 60–63, 66–7, 82, 83,
        85, 100–102, 110, 112, 119
    and trade policy 54, 55, 75, 114, 124
    see also Democrats; Republicans
constructivism 15, 18, 20
consumers 11, 32, 51, 100
    and production priority 32, 33, 51
    and subsidies 134
    and tariffs 58, 64, 99

welfare losses 144–5
contract law 28, 32
contribution rule *see* equity
Coolidge, Calvin 98
countervailing duty laws (CVD) 2, 123,
    128, 135–8, 141
Cuba
    and subsidies 123
    tariffs 64
    trade agreements 79, 80–81, 83, 84,
        98
customs unions 79, 126

defence, national, and protection 53, 63,
    64, 65, 66, 78
democracy 29, 46, 118
    and capitalism, tensions between 47
    and desert-based principles 50
    and inequality 48
Democrats 49, 58–9, 68, 69, 78, 79, 81,
    99, 112, 116
    on dumping 69
    and fairness 59, 78
    and tariffs 55, 56, 59, 60, 61, 85, 100,
        101
    see also Congress
Depression 55–6, 61, 98, 114
developing countries
    agriculture 167
    balance-of-payments problems 121,
        163, 168
    code approach 166, 167
    economic development 121–2, 124,
        126, 129, 130, 164–5, 174
    fair trade movement 172–5
    fairness in 20, 81
    and GATT 162–8
    import quotas 122
    non-reciprocity in 164–5, 166–7
    preferential systems 67, 113, 122, 123,
        165–6, 170
    protectionism 167
    quantitative restrictions 122, 126, 130,
        162
    special and differential treatment 162,
        163, 166, 167–72, 175
    and subsidies 135, 136
    tariff setting 122, 130, 162, 165–7,
        168
    and WTO 167, 168

Dingley Act 1897 57, 79, 80
dispute settlement 127, 129, 136, 140,
   167, 187
distribution principles 38, 46
   and cultural values 36–7
   of desert 48, 50
distributive justice 3, 4, 29, 31, 35–9, 48,
   184–5
   see also equality; fairness; non-
      discrimination
domestic producers
   burdens and benefits distribution *see*
      burdens and benefits distribution
   no-injury principle *see* no-injury
      principle
   protection of 62, 63, 65
   see also exports; imports; production
dumping 2, 54, 60, 64, 66, 68–72, 98
   antidumping duty 70, 128, 138
   competitor protection 71, 111
   see also Antidumping Act

economic
   efficiency 39, 139, 141
   growth 19, 35, 110, 114, 119, 120
   nationalism 108
   theory, and fairness 38–40
   warfare 111
EEC, Treaty of Rome 140
Egypt, trade agreements 81
employment 114, 116–17, 119, 134
   Britain 115, 116, 122, 129
   difficulties in other countries 121
   escape clause 121
   full 120–21, 130
   and ITO Charter 120
   and protectionism 64, 79, 99, 100
   unemployment compensation 20
   see also labour
environmental standards 2, 4, 14, 16,
   139, 172
epistemic communities 14–15, 118
equal opportunity 48–9, 63, 64, 68, 70
equality 26, 31, 32, 35, 36–7, 46
   commercial treaties treatment 73–85,
      128, 131
   and fairness 50, 107, 108, 110, 117,
      126, 132–3, 169–70
   social and economic inequality,
      acceptance of 48–9

and trade policy 104, 105, 113–14,
   115, 117, 119
of treatment through commercial
   treaties 73–85
see also distributive justice; fairness;
   non-discrimination; tariffs
equity 17, 26, 36–7, 38, 171
Europe 57, 60, 67–9, 78, 174
   argol agreements 79–80, 83, 84
   and MFN pledge 75, 77, 83
   protectionism 67
   quantitative restrictions 65, 83
   trade agreements 79–80
   see also individual countries
exchange controls 118, 126
exports 65, 79, 83, 104, 105, 110
   agricultural 63, 78, 106, 109
   bounties 63, 66–8
   commodity agreements 55, 63, 66–8,
      130
   fair trade movement 172–5
   licences 104
   McKinley Act 1890 56, 57, 59
   preferential treatment 67, 119
   quotas 109
   subsidies 109, 123, 128, 135, 136
   VERs (voluntary export restraints)
      145
   see also imports; MFN; multilateral
      trade regime development;
      reciprocity; tariffs

fair trade movement 172–5
fairness 1–5, 12, 27–30, 39, 54, 78, 144
   burdens and benefits distribution
      see burdens and benefits
      distribution
   and competition *see* competition
   defining 26–45
   desert-based 48, 50
   in developing countries 20
   and economic theory 38–40
   in exchange (commutative justice)
      29–30, 34–6, 38, 48, 50, 133
   fair play principle 26–7, 28, 29, 31,
      35–6, 38, 40, 50
   in GATT 3, 111–24, 182, 183–4
   moral basis of 36
   multilateral trade regime development
      98–161, 184

Fairness in the world economy

and non-discrimination 2, 3, 50, 66,
    82, 84
and political philosophy 26–36
and reciprocity 26, 27–8, 36, 39, 50,
    57, 126–8
social psychology dimension 36–7
socio-economic ethos, US 46–50, 65,
    118, 120, 125, 126, 128, 130
study approach to 18–20
and tariffs *see* tariffs
see also equality; international trade
    policy; justice; protectionism
Federal Trade Commission Act 1914 71
Fordney–McCumber Act 1922 60, 71–2,
    82
foreign nations
exclusion for discriminatory practices
    105
and export bounties 63, 66–8
penalty duties for discriminatory
    practices 64, 72, 76, 79, 81, 98
unfair practices of 53, 58, 64, 66, 70,
    104–5, 114, 129–30, 144
France
Cobden–Chevalier Treaty 1860 77
commercial agreements with 74, 76,
    104
Germany, reciprocity treaty with 84
MFN pledge 77, 83, 84
quantitative restrictions 65
tariffs 64
Treaty of Amity and Commerce 74,
    76
Franklin, Benjamin 51, 52, 73–4
free-riding 18, 27, 38–9, 40
and international agreements 16, 115,
    117, 127, 133
and MFN policy 76, 82–3, 105, 106,
    114

GATT (General Agreement on Tariffs
    and Trade) 20, 66, 122, 186
adverse effects test 140–41
agriculture 129, 135
code approach 166, 167
commercial consideration principle
    128, 131
and developing countries 162–8
Emergency Action on Imports of
    Particular Products 142–3

Enabling Clause 165, 169, 171
evolution of 132–47
fairness in 3, 111–24, 182, 183–4
'grandfather clause' 125–6
GSP (Generalized System of
    Preference) scheme 165, 168–9,
    171, 174, 175
Haberler Report 1958 164
Leutwiler Report 166
negotiation results 124–32
safeguard rules 142–7
Schedules of Concessions 127
specificity test 139–40
and subsidies *see* subsidies
Subsidies Code 67–8, 135–6
Trade and Development articles 164
see also WTO
Genoa Conference 1922 65
Germany
barter agreement with 105
France, reciprocity treaty with 84
World War I, recovery after 68–9
globalization 4, 9–10, 17
goods 30, 31
discrimination against abroad 57
maximization of net 32, 35
misrepresentation of 72
primary and nonprimary 135
public, failure to provide 38–9
tariffs for specific 101–2
see also price; production
government
intervention 49, 119, 120, 128, 131,
    133, 134, 138–9
procurement rules 126
see also Congress; individual
    countries; state cooperation

Haberler Report 1958 164
Haiti, penalty duties 79
Hamilton, Alexander 53, 66
Harding, Warren 59, 82, 98
Harrison, Henry 56
Havana Charter 118, 120, 121, 122–3,
    124, 162, 163, 168, 173
Commercial Policy chapter 125, 129
negotiation results 129–32
Hawaii, reciprocal agreements with 78,
    83, 84
Hawkins, Harry 114

Hawley–Smoot Tariff 1930 11, 61, 62, 63–4, 99, 101, 120
health and safety 2, 65, 139
hegemonic stability theory 9–10
Holland *see* Netherlands
Hong Kong, fair trade 174
Hoover, Herbert 61, 62, 98, 112
Hull, Cordell 59, 64, 84–5, 99, 101–6, 109, 110–11
   and GATT 111, 114, 116, 118, 131, 183–4
human rights 16, 172, 185–7

ideas, and international relations 12–18, 117, 129
imports 2, 11, 50, 52, 58, 59, 60, 79
   at price below fair value in exporting country 69, 70
   blocking 105
   commodity agreements 130
   competition 51, 56–7, 64, 78, 102–3, 109, 128, 137, 141, 143–4
   entry exclusion 72
   fees 109
   licences 65, 104
   monopolies 108
   Payne–Aldrich Tariff 1909 58, 81
   penalty duty 79
   quotas 65, 66, 107–8, 109, 122, 132, 133, 146–7
   reimportation protection 59
   safeguard measures 2, 104, 128
   subsidies 67, 137
   surges 143, 144, 145
   trade legislation, unfair 50
   see also exports; MFN; quantitative restrictions; tariffs
income distribution 3, 4, 38, 39, 59, 185
   agriculture 61, 109, 110
India, economic development 122, 163
industries 20, 59, 109
   'war babies' 60
   see also production
infant industries, support for 53–6, 63–4, 66, 130, 134, 138
intellectual property rights 28, 71, 77
interest groups 2, 63
International Justice, Permanent Court of 169
international law 2, 16–17

international relations, role of ideas in 12–18
international trade policy 1–4, 9–13, 19, 63, 99
   Acts *see under* trade
   agreements programme, reciprocal 50, 98–111
   agriculture *see* agriculture
   collective action problems 13, 14, 18, 39
   deflationary pressures 121
   and Depression 55–6, 61, 98, 114
   development in US till 1930s 50–85
   and economic growth 114, 119, 120
   escape clauses 102, 119, 121
   evolution of 162–80
   fairness in *see* fairness
   and free-riding 16, 115, 117, 127, 133
   GATT *see* GATT
   and ideas 12–18, 117, 129
   legislation, unfair 50, 52, 66–73
   multilateral trade regime development 98–161
   representative period 65, 107–8, 109
   safeguard rules *see* safeguard rules
   specific covenants 82
   theoretical perspectives 9–15, 18–20
   trade bans 53
   trade barriers *see* trade barriers
   trade distortions 65
   trade remedies laws *see* antidumping; countervailing duty laws; safeguard rules
   'trade remedy' rules 20
   trade wars 81
   transparency in 126, 127, 135
investment 123–4, 130
Italy, tariff revisions against US 64
ITO (International Trade Organization) 116–18, 120, 123, 124, 129
   commercial policy chapter 125, 131
   commodity agreements 130
   rejection of 118, 130–31, 181–2

Jackson, Andrew 54, 55
Japan, cheap labour 105
Jay, John 75
Jefferson, Thomas 48, 51, 53, 73
justice 26, 36, 171
   and acquisitiveness 47–8

commutative 29–30, 34–6, 38, 48, 50,
    133
distributive 3, 4, 29, 31, 35–9, 48,
    184–5
see also equality; fairness; non-
    discrimination

Keynes, J.M. 12, 173
Kongo, trade agreements 81
Korean War 131

labour 4, 10, 32
    cheap 64, 105
    conditions 139
    protection 62, 63, 64
    slave 55
    see also employment
LaFollette, Robert 58, 61
Latin America, trade agreements with
    US 79
League of Nations 59, 82
legitimacy 3, 16–18, 20, 27
Leutwiler Report 166
liberalism 4, 11–12, 51
    embedded 19, 20, 111, 182
    laissez-faire 19, 20, 46, 49, 108
    see also international trade policy

McClure, Wallace 84
McKinley Act 1890 56, 57, 79
McKinley, William 79, 80, 85
Madison, James 49, 51, 53
marginalism 38
Marrakesh Agreement 186, 187
Marshall Plan 121, 131
mercantilism 2, 33, 46, 52
Mexico
    tariffs 64
    trade agreements with 78, 102, 128
MFN (most-favoured-nation) pledge 2,
    86–7, 105, 107, 108, 132, 168,
    169
    conditional 75–6, 77
    exception to 77, 80–81, 105
    and free-rider behaviour 76, 82–3,
        105, 106, 114
    and GATT 116, 119, 126, 128, 147,
        165
    unconditional form 66, 82–3, 84, 99,
        104, 109

Millennium Declaration 183, 184, 186,
    187
monopolistic practices 38, 52, 68, 104
    Britain 10–11, 53, 56, 73, 114
    and equal opportunity 49, 63, 64, 68,
        70
    and high tariffs 111
    and imports 59, 108
    and price 31, 35
Monroe, James 54
morality 31, 32, 65
    and self-interest 32–3, 34, 48
multilateral trade regime development
    fairness in 98–161, 184
    see also international trade policy

Napoleonic Wars 53, 64
national security 53, 63, 64, 65, 66,
    78
need principle 36–7
Netherlands 10, 174
    S.O.S. Wereldhandel 174
    Treaty with (1782) 75
New Deal programme 49–50, 56, 99,
    109, 181
New Welfare Economics 39
New Zealand, tariffs 64
NIEO (New International Economic
    Order) 170, 171, 175, 182
no-injury principle
    countervailing provision 67, 123
    and fairness 70, 71, 107, 110, 112–13,
        117–18, 147
    and reciprocity 57, 58, 68
    safeguards and 114, 145–6
    subsidies and 136, 137, 140, 141
    and tariffs 106, 111, 119, 128–9, 143
    US commitment to 101–4
non-discrimination
    and Atlantic Charter 114–15, 118
    exceptions to 110, 119
    fairness and 2, 3, 50, 66, 82, 84, 87,
        105, 112–13, 117
    and safeguard rules 111, 143, 146–7
    see also MFN
NRA (National Recovery Act) 99, 105,
    109

Ottawa Agreements 64
Oxfam 174

Pan–American conference 79, 80
Pareto improvement criterion 10, 39–40
Pasvolsky, Leo 114
Payne–Aldrich Tariff 1909 58, 81
Peek, George 105
political philosophy, and fairness 26–36
Portorose Conference 1921 65
preferential treatment 67, 113, 122, 123,
    165–6, 170
  GSP (Generalized System of
    Preference) scheme 165, 168–9,
    171, 174, 175
price 3, 35, 40, 56
  commodity agreements 59–60, 130
  and comparative advantage 57, 64,
    127
  discrimination 31, 58, 68, 69
  distortion 38, 128
  just 30–31, 34, 35, 64
  market 30–31, 32, 35, 118
  and monopolistic practices 31, 35
  undercutting 137
  see also goods; production; subsidies;
    tariffs
private sector 10, 11, 46, 47
private self-interest, constraints on 32–3
production 4, 11, 38, 46, 63, 67
  commodity agreements 130
  equalized costs of 2, 38, 56, 59, 60,
    62, 63, 72
  favouring specific groups 64
  priority over consumers 32, 33, 51
  private ownership of the means of 46
  subsidies 123, 128
  see also exports; goods; imports;
    industries; price; tariffs
profits 2, 32, 46
prohibition 52, 57, 65–6
property rights 32, 47, 48–9
protectionism 2, 20, 50, 53, 54, 63, 133
  agriculture 3, 60, 116, 118, 126, 131,
    148
  Articles of Confederation 52
  developing countries 167
  and employment 64, 79, 99, 100
  Europe 67
  excise taxes 109
  and fairness, built-in 55, 84, 112–13
  Hawley–Smoot Tariff 11, 61, 62,
    63–4, 99, 101

infant industries 53–6, 63–4, 66, 130,
    134, 138
  of labour 62, 63, 64
  Pennsylvania system of 53
  reduction in 98, 110, 112, 118
  rent-seeking 11, 147
  special interest 10, 11
  and subsidies *see* subsidies
  and taxation 55, 109
  and unfair trade legislation 71, 72–3
  and wage levels 54, 57
  see also reciprocity; rent-seeking;
    safeguard rules; tariffs

quantitative restrictions 64–6, 104, 108,
    111, 118, 121, 123, 128, 143, 147
  developing countries 118, 121, 122,
    123, 126, 128, 130, 143, 147, 162
  see also imports, quotas

rational choice theory 15
Rawls, J. 26, 27, 28, 37
reciprocity 2, 3, 11, 39, 52, 53, 110, 112,
    170
  advantages 53, 113
  bilateral treaties 79, 105, 113, 115,
    116, 117, 119, 127
  and collective action 39
  commercial treaties, through 73–85
  Dingley Act 1897 57, 79, 80
  and fairness 26, 27–8, 36, 39, 50, 57,
    126–8
  and legitimacy 17–18, 27
  McKinley Act 1890 56, 57, 79
  MFN clause *see* MFN
  no-injury principle *see* no-injury
    principle
  positive 39
  and retaliation 57, 61, 72, 82
  RTAA (Reciprocal Trade Agreements
    Act) *see* RTAA
  trade agreements programme 50,
    98–111
  Underwood–Simmons Act 59, 60, 68,
    120
  see also multilateral trade regime
    development; protectionism,
    safeguard rules; tariffs
rent-seeking 11, 147
  see also protectionism

Republicans 49, 57, 61, 81, 82, 98, 112, 119
  on dumping 69
  and fairness 78
  National Republican Progressive League 58, 61
  progressives 58, 61
  and reciprocity 80
  standpatters 58
  and tariffs 55–6, 58, 59, 60, 61, 63, 102, 106
  see also Congress
restitution law 28–9
Revenue Act 1916 69
Roman law, and price of goods 30
Roosevelt, Franklin D. 98–9, 101, 111, 112, 114
Roosevelt, Theodore 57, 58, 80, 81
RTAA (Reciprocal Trade Agreements Act) 99–100, 102–5, 108, 111, 113, 124, 128, 131
  and GATT 114, 116
  objections to 100
  'peril-point' procedure 103
Ruggie, J.G. 15, 18, 19, 20, 121, 182
Russia, MFN pledge 77

safeguard rules 3, 20, 121, 142–7
  and fairness 144
sanctions 53, 58
Scholastic Doctors 31, 35
self-interest principle 32–4
  and pursuit of profit 46, 47–8, 49
Sherman Antitrust Act 68, 70
Smith, Adam 10, 31–2, 33–5, 51
smuggling 55
social inequality, acceptance of 48
social-contract theory 32
S.O.S. Wereldhandel 174
South West Africa case 169
Spain
  MFN pledge 83
  tariffs 64
  trade agreements 79
special and differential treatment 162, 163, 166, 167–72, 175
state cooperation 15–16, 17–18, 20, 26–7, 37
  see also government intervention
study, purpose of 18–20

subsidies 53, 66, 67, 133, 138, 144
  actionable 136, 140
  export 109, 123, 128, 135, 136
  GATT Subsidies Code 67–8
  and primary commodities 123
  production 123, 128
  prohibited 136, 137
  rules 134–42
  specific and non-specific 136, 137
sugar 63, 66, 67, 79, 80
Sumner, W.G. 38, 49
supply-side theories 11
Switzerland
  MFN pledge 77
  USA–Switzerland treaty 77

Taft, William H. 58, 81
Tariff of Abominations 1828 55
Tariff Act
  1789 53
  1864 56
  1890 99
  1897 67, 99
  1909 67, 72
  1913 67
  1921, Emergency 70
  1922 62, 99, 103, 113
  1930 61–2, 67, 72, 99, 103, 113
Tariff Board 58, 59
Tariff Commission 60, 62, 70, 72, 77, 81, 86, 102, 103
tariffs 11, 20, 54, 55, 59, 63
  Articles of Confederation 52
  bill 1824 54–5
  bill 1832 55
  chief supplier principle 114
  concessions 101–3, 106–7, 114, 118–19, 125–9, 133, 137, 143
  countervailing duty laws 2, 66–8, 123, 128, 135–8, 141
  Dingley Act 1897 57, 79, 80
  discrimination 56, 58, 72, 83
  dual schedule 57–8, 81
  Fordney–McCumber Act 1922 60, 71–2, 82
  Hawley–Smoot Tariff 1930 11, 61, 62, 63–4, 99, 101, 120
  high 53–6, 58, 61–3, 80, 98–9, 103, 113, 119
  low 53, 59, 63

no-injury principle *see* no-injury
   principle
Payne–Aldrich Tariff 1909 58, 81
penalty duties 64, 72, 76, 79, 81
and price *see* price
principal supplier doctrine 106
product-specific 101
protective 50–66
and quantitative restrictions *see*
   quantitative restrictions
reclassification under different 109
reduction policy 66, 68, 81, 83,
   99–100, 102–7, 114, 116,
   119–20, 124, 126, 128
regional 105
selective approach to 60, 62, 81, 99,
   101–3, 110, 116
single-schedule 53, 57, 83, 84, 98,
   108
Underwood–Simmons Act 1913 59,
   60, 68, 120
Wilson Tariff Act 1894 68
see also exports; imports;
   protectionism; reciprocity
Taussig, Frank 57, 81
Tokyo Round 67, 135, 136, 137, 138,
   143, 165, 166
trade *see* international trade agreements
Trade Act 1974 68, 72
Trade Adjustment Assistance (TAA)
   programme 3
Trade Agreements Act
   1934 83, 107, 116
   1979 70
Trade Agreements Committee 102
trade barriers 20, 51, 82, 115–17, 126–8,
   132, 141
   liberalization of 82
   multilateral approach to 59, 99, 112
   reduction of 120
   see also international trade policy;
     protectionism; tariffs
Truman, Harry S. 102, 119, 124, 131

UK *see* Britain
UN
   Charter on Economic Rights and
     Duties of States 170–71
   Conference on Trade and
     Development (UNCTAD) 165

Conference on Trade and Employment
   see Havana Charter
Declaration of International Economic
   Cooperation 172
Declaration on the Right to
   Development 186–7
ECOSOC (Economic and Social
   Council) 117
Millennium Declaration 183, 184,
   186, 187
NIEO (New International Economic
   Order) 170, 171, 175, 182
Vienna Declaration 187
see also WTO
Underwood–Simmons Act 1913 59, 60,
   68, 120
unemployment compensation 20
   see also employment
unjust enrichment, doctrine of 28–9
Uruguay Round 133–4, 136, 138, 143,
   167–8, 172
USA 10, 11
   American creed 46
   American Revolution 74
   American System 54
   Atlantic Charter 114–15, 118
   Britain, cessation of trade with 52,
     53–4, 73, 114
   Buy American Act 1933 148
   Civil War 49, 54, 55–6, 59, 78
   Clayton Antitrust Act 49, 68, 69
   commercial policy discourse 46–97
   Confederation 52, 85
   Constitution 52–3, 74, 101
   Dingley Act 1897 57, 79, 80
   Executive 53, 57–8, 101, 102
   Executive Order 1947 102
   Export–Import Bank 148
   Federal Trade Commission Act 1914
     71
   Fordney–McCumber Act 1922 60,
     71–2, 82
   Founding Fathers 47, 48, 49, 112
   Fourteen Points speech 81
   Full Employment Bill 1945 120
   Hawley–Smoot Tariff 1930 11, 61,
     62, 63–4, 99, 101, 120
   lend-lease agreement with Britain
     114
   McKinley Act 1890 56, 57, 79

NAM (National Association of
    Manufacturers) 57
National Foreign Trade Council 131
New Deal programme 49–50, 56, 99,
    109, 181
NRA (National Recovery Act) 99,
    105, 109
Ottawa Agreements 64
Payne–Aldrich Tariff 1909 58, 81
Revenue Act 1916 69
Revolution 73–4
Senate 61, 72, 78
SERRV 173–4
Sherman Antitrust Act 68, 70
socio-economic ethos 46–50, 65, 118,
    120, 125, 126, 128, 130
South Carolina secession threat 55
stock market crash 61
Switzerland treaty 77
Tariff Commission 60, 62, 70, 72, 77,
    81, 86, 102, 103
Ten Thousand Villages 173–4
Underwood–Simmons Act 1913 59,
    60, 68, 120
War of Independence 53
Wilson Tariff Act 1894 68
Wilson–Gorman Act 1894 57
see also Congress; fairness;
    international trade policy;
    protectionism

Venezuela, penalty duties 79
Vienna Declaration 187

wage differentials 2, 54, 57, 64
    with foreign wages 60, 62

Washington Consensus 172
Washington, George 76–7, 104
welfare 19, 20, 32, 35, 39, 171
    and distributive justice 3, 4, 29, 31,
        35–9, 37, 48, 184–5
    losses 144–5
    New Welfare Economics 39
    social inequality, acceptance of 48
    and subsidies 134, 139
Wheaton, Harry 78
Wicksteed, P.H. 38
Wilcox, Clare 148, 162–3
Wilson Tariff Act 1894 68
Wilson, Woodrow 58, 59, 68, 81–2, 111
Wilson–Gorman Act 1894 57
World Monetary and Economic
    Conference 9, 84
World War I 54, 59–60, 64–5, 68, 83,
    111, 114
World War II 54, 99, 106, 109–10,
    114–15, 184
WTO (World Trade Organization) 3,
    129, 183, 184–5
    and developing countries 167, 168
    dispute settlement 136, 140, 167, 187
    GATT *see* GATT
    Marrakesh Agreement 186, 187
    Tokyo Round 67, 135, 136, 137, 138,
        143, 165, 166
    Uruguay Round 133–4, 136, 138, 143,
        167–8, 172
    Washington Consensus 172
    see also UN

Zollverein, reciprocal agreements with
    78